Handbook of Microcomputers in Special Education

Contributors

Michael M. Behrmann, Ed.D.
Assistant Professor, Education
George Mason University
Fairfax, VA 22030

Edward Cain, Jr.
Director of Student Services
Commack Union Free School District
Commack, NY 11725

Delores Hagen, Publisher
Closing the Gap
P.O. box 68
Henderson, MN 56044

Elizabeth A. Lahm, M.Ed.
Doctoral Candidate
Department of Education
George Mason University
Fairfax, VA 22030

Sheryl Asen Levy
Doctoral Candidate
Department of Education
George Mason University
Fairfax, VA 22030

Elizabeth MacClellan, Ed.D.
Council for Exceptional Children
1920 Association Drive
Reston, VA 22091

Gail McGregor, Ed.D.
Public School Consultation
207 S. Orange Street
Media, FL 19063

Joel E. Mittler, Ed.D.
Assistant Dean
School of Education
Long Island University
C. W. Post Campus
Greenvale, NY 11548

Scott Stevens, Ph.D.
Assistant Professor, Education
George Mason University
Fairfax, VA 22030

Wayne Thomas, Ed.D.
Assistant Professor, Education
George Mason University
Fairfax, VA 22030

Handbook of Microcomputers in Special Education

Edited by
Michael M. Behrmann, Ed.D.

COLLEGE-HILL PRESS, San Diego, California

College-Hill Press
4284 41st Street
San Diego, California 92105

©1984 by College-Hill Press, Inc.

Library of Congress Cataloging in Publication Data

Main entry under title:

Handbook of microcomputers in special education

    Bibliography: p.
    Includes index.
    1. Exceptional children—Education—Data Processing. I. Behrmann,
Michael M.
LC 3969.H3   1984   371.9'045   84-21433

ISBN 0-933014-35-X

Printed in the United States of America

Handbook of Microcomputers in Special Education

Edited by
Michael M. Behrmann, Ed.D.

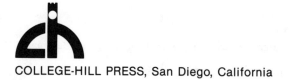

COLLEGE-HILL PRESS, San Diego, California

College-Hill Press
4284 41st Street
San Diego, California 92105

Library of Congress Cataloging in Publication Data

Main entry under title:

Handbook of microcomputers in special education

Bibliography: p.
Includes index.
1. Exceptional children—Education—Data Processing. I. Behrmann, Michael M.
LC 3969.H3   1984   371.9'045   84-21433

ISBN 0-933014-35-X

DEDICATION

I would like to dedicate this book to my wife and my sons who have largely forgotten what I look like and who have given an enormous amount of loving support . . . and to the fish in the bay who I hope will soon know what I look like.

CONTENTS

Networking
Artificial Intelligence
Prosthetics

PREFACE

The *Handbook of Microcomputers in Special Education* is designed to provide a comprehensive overview of computer applications in special education and related fields. Information on how computers work and their uses with exceptional (handicapped and gifted) individuals is given in a way that will allay many persons' fears about using computers. Programming is also explained in terms of the learning needs of exceptional individuals, as are the "best practices" in special educational instructional methods addressing those needs.

While primarily focusing on the school-age population of exceptional individuals, the book also covers computer applications for learning and computers as tools for individuals from birth to old age. It discusses the learning and tools (e.g. word processing) related to most handicapping conditions as well as those of gifted individuals, and it highlights the ways in which computers can best be utilized to meet those needs. As such it is a useful tool for special education teachers, special education administrators, and related services personnel, such as occupational, physical, and speech therapists. Other individuals who might find this textbook useful are rehabilitation specialists and regular educators who may find handicapped children mainstreamed into their classrooms or schools.

The book can be used both as a college or "in-service" textbook and as a resource book for personnel applying computers to the needs of handicapped individuals on a daily basis. The manuscript is divided into three major parts. The first part provides an overview of how computers work and their types of applications in special education. The major focus of this section is understanding computers and comparing the characteristics of computers to the "best teaching practices" and curricula in special education with the learning needs of exceptional children. The second part of the book concentrates on computer applications for various populations of exceptional individuals. It addresses their learning needs and discusses specific learning and tool applications of computers to meet these needs. This section concludes with a chapter on administrative and management needs of teachers and other direct service providers. The third and final section of the book looks toward the future. It addresses the need for preservice and in-service training of teachers and related services personnel as well as methods of evaluating software and hardware. This section concludes with a look toward what future technology may provide to meet the need of exceptional individuals.

In summary, this book takes the reader through three stages: (1) initial understanding of computer technology and how that technology can be a powerful aid for exceptional individuals; (2) familiarity with the learning needs of exceptional individuals and currently available computer technology that can assist service providers in meeting those needs; and (3) insight into what the future might hold for exceptional individuals and methods of assuring that technologic advances are used beneficially.

ACKNOWLEDGMENTS

I would also like to specifically thank Pat King, whose organization and dedication has made this productive year possible. Much thanks also goes to the contributors to this book, all professionals with great interest in computer applications in education.

Finally, I would like to thank Frances Connor, Ignacy Goldberg, Peter Cardullias, and Connie Madsen, mentors and friends, without whom I would not have been able to reach this point in my career.

Part I
Overview of Computers
in Special Education

CHAPTER 1

Computers: How Do They Work and What Can They Do?

"Have you heard the latest? They've developed a mind amplifier!" Most educators would be intrigued at hearing this announcement. Such a device might have great potential for making human thought processes faster and more accurate, with greater potential for storage and manipulation of information. Since education is largely concerned with teaching humans how to take information and process it in ways that solve human problems, it might well be assumed that educators would be in the forefront of the development and use of a mind amplifier. Educators would be well equipped professionally to foresee the device's potential and would enthusiastically seek to incorporate it into their professional activities as well as exploit its possibilities for improving human learning. It might also be expected that educators, being knowledgeable about the complex human interactions that surround the acts of teaching and learning in schools, would be realistic enough to understand that such a device might allow fundamentally sound instruction to be made even better but that the device itself could not improve the quality of instruction without intelligent and wise use.

Unfortunately for the education profession, this scenario has not been realized in several ways, because a real-life mind amplifier, the digital computer, has actually come into the professional lives of many educators during the late 1970s and early 1980s. One way in which the fictional mind amplifier scenario has not developed is that educators, for the most part, have *not* led the movement toward educational computer use. Instead, concerned parents and some interested educators have spearheaded a grass-roots movement to bring computers into the schools with tremendous amounts of stimulation by businesses eager to sell the modern electronic marvel as the key to survival and success for the next generation. The device, developed and nurtured by physical scientists, engineers, and

This chapter was authored by Wayne Thomas.

mathematicians, has been thrust upon educators by forces external to the schools and to the educational profession. Pressures from parents and business persons and the pervasive influence of devices such as digital watches and computer-controlled cameras and automobile engines have forced educators to confront the presence of computers in our lives before many of us were ready to deal with them. Concerns from the public that the next generation must be "computer literate" in order to survive daily life in the coming years have thrust the schools into the computer age regardless of whether or not it is appropriate and whether or not educators are ready.

A second way in which the introductory scenario has not materialized in reality is that many educators have not intuitively understood and accepted the limitations of computers as well as their strengths. As a result of advertising hyperbole some educators have come to believe that computers are mysterious and magical and that, with the proper hand waving and typing of incantations on a keyboard, almost anything is possible. These educators have not understood about mind "amplification" what musicians know well about sound amplification—that well produced and undistorted music can be made to sound truly impressive when amplified but that mediocre or distorted music suffers from amplification because the amplifier exaggerates all that is bad about the music and makes it worse. In education, computer use can make good teaching and good learning skills even better in that computers offer much in opportunities for learning problem solving and other high level cognitive skills. Computers can also deliver well-organized and accurate reinforcement of instruction. But the "amplification" of poor teaching, inaccurate prescriptions for remediation, and uninspiring presentations lead to a much worse learning environment than that which existed without the computer.

In opposition to educators who have become entranced by the superficial appeal of computers and have jumped aboard the computer bandwagon without inquiring as to its eventual destination, there are other educators who shun computers. These people, having been intimidated by the mostly technical computer users of the 1960s and 1970s, have adopted an attitude of avoidance of computers at all costs, no matter how advantageous they could be in a given situation. These people have endured much derision from the computer bandwagon riders and are frequently viewed as obstructing the path of progress. However, their position may be less damaging to education in the long run than the disappointments and even disasters wreaked by the enthusiastically pro-computer contingent.

It should be possible for educators to arrive at a state of mind in which they understand how computers work, what their strengths and weaknesses are, and from which they can professionally assess the positive as well as the negative aspects of using computers in education. It is toward promoting and facilitating this goal that this chapter is geared.

EDUCATORS' QUESTIONS

Educators have responded to their confusion about the use of computers in education by asking (sometimes rather desperately) questions such as:

1. In terms that I can understand, exactly what are computers anyway?
2. In general (and avoiding technical detail), how do computers work?
3. In what ways are computers used in education now? How might they be used in the future?
4. Where did these devices come from so quickly?
5. How will computers influence the ways in which educators think and work as we pursue our profession?

COMPUTER LITERACY

Answers to these questions are not readily available in a form that is useful to educators. Many of us have hoped for enlightenment from the plethora of computer literacy courses that have sprung into existence during the past few years. These courses, frequently taught by noneducators or sometimes by educators who have only slightly more computer experience than their students, have been produced by universities and businesses eager to tap the public's and the profession's desire to be computer literate. However, even the definition of "computer literacy" is still being debated. Many educators have emerged from classes that teach which keys to press on a particular computer's keyboard or that teach programming in the computer language such as BASIC with the vague feeling that education is being "taken" by businesses that are vying to unload one microcomputer or another on parents and teachers alike. This feeling becomes less vague and more definite as educators realize that, although they can manipulate the keyboard and can program simple (and mostly useless) things, they lack almost entirely the confidence to incorporate computer skills into an already existing set of professional competencies.

Educators who know this "So now what do I do?" feeling experience frustration as they realize that they really do not yet know how to incorporate computer skills into their repertoire of existing professional skills. Many either pass along trivial computer skills to students or ignore (if they can) the computers that may be available to them after having been purchased with great fanfare and at substantial cost. In either case, the potential for efficacious computer use in education is thwarted by a failure to link basic computer manipulation skills (e.g., programming in BASIC or LOGO) to the educators' existing professional skills and to provide opportunities for the educators to see how computers can in some situations greatly improve the quality of instruction and, in other situations, make instruction less effective than it was without computers.

COMPUTER PROFICIENCY

Educators need to move beyond "computer awareness" and "computer literacy" to "computer proficiency" at a professionally operational level. Computer proficiency for an educator includes the following:

1. A basic knowledge of the educational functions that can be well accomplished using computers as well as a knowledge of those functions that are difficult or impossible to accomplish by means of a computer.

2. An understanding of and an ability to apply basic "do's" and "don'ts" of machine-human interactions.

3. A lack of fear of computers, a feeling of being "in control" when using them, and the perception that the computer is just another medium for the educational process, which happens to hold rich potential for improving instruction if it can be properly exploited.

4. An ability to match intended instructional outcomes and required levels of cognitive demand of educational activities with what can be accomplished in an instructional presentation or reinforcement using a computer.

In this chapter, several factors are addressed that bear on educator frustration with computers and computer literacy. First, the explanations are nontechnical and rely on the reader's common sense and experience with manually processing information in everyday life. Second, the underlying characteristics of computers that directly influence their use by educators, as opposed to scientists or business persons, are examined. Third, the acquisition of computer skills is treated as the natural extension of competent educators' professional skills, not as a complete professional retooling.

EXACTLY WHAT ARE COMPUTERS ANYWAY?

In general, computers are devices that take information provided in machine-readable form, manipulate it into a more useful form using previously furnished instructions, and provide the results for human use. No new information is created by the computer, but existing information is made more meaningful or useful to humans as a result of computer processing.

The processing of information is not limited to computers; humans process information every day. For example, listing the names of students in a class in alphabetical order makes the information (the list of names) easier for a teacher to use in that a given student's name and other information about him or her can be found more quickly. Alphabetization is an example of sorting, one way information can be processed by humans or by computers. Other ways information can be processed are information selection, listing, storing, translation, merging, or mathematical and logical analysis.

Comparing Humans with Computers

Computers therefore perform many of the same manipulations or processing of available information that humans do. However, computers perform these tasks with different capabilities and with different methods than humans. One example of this is that a computer can process information only by following directions that humans have written down and recorded for the computer to follow blindly. These directions are collectively called a *computer program*. Anything that a computer does happens as a result of its slavishly following the programmed instructions provided by some human. The computer, as yet, has no power of initiating thought, of independent problem solving, of self-determination, or other attributes which we associate with the common organic computer, the human brain. Thus, computers don't really "think" as humans do, but they can be made to appear to do so by clever human programming.

Some say that, within 10 years, there will exist computers capable of at least rudimentary "thought" and "awareness." This may occur, but educators need not expect such qualities from computers we encounter today in educational applications. In fact, many people *overestimate* a computer's ability to deal with the simplest of machine-human interactions, commonly leading to disappointment in the results of the contact and contempt of "that stupid computer." Present-day computers are not even smart enough to qualify as "stupid" because they have no intelligence at all!

A second way in which computers process information differently from humans involves the fact that the computer must have a continuous source of electrical power in order to work. Even the tiniest fluctuations in electrical current, which may not affect any other machine or appliance, can cause a computer to malfunction temporarily by losing information or to suffer permanent damage to its electronic components. Many novice computer users do not realize (and some "old pros" forget!) that all information in a computer which has not been permanently saved by direct command from the human user is subject to being irretrievably lost in an instant of electrical power fluctuation or outage.

A third basic way in which computers and humans process information differently is that computers are much, much faster than humans. Just how much faster computers are depends on the task and the capabilities of the particular computer, but many modern computers can access information in hundreds of billionths of a second and can perform simple computations in hundred-thousandths to millionths of a second. Thus, for sheer speed of information processing, the computer wins hands down when compared to humans.

Computers can also retrieve and process information in greater quantities and with more accuracy than humans can. Computer memories can hold and quickly access from tens of thousands to millions of characters (e.g., letters) of information with complete accuracy, far surpassing human performance. In addition, a computer can maintain much greater precision of computation than humans, routinely providing for more than six decimal places of accuracy.

Humans, on the other hand, are vastly superior to computers in their abilities to receive and process information flexibly. Computers are maddeningly inflexible when information is being entered, so the human must learn to structure information into a form which the computer can handle before successful human-to-computer communication can take place.

Human-to-Computer Communication

This problem has several important ramifications. First, humans who are accustomed to other humans' abilities to understand automatically and interpret correctly the multiple meanings of some phrases as well as the many different ways of expressing a given concept must adjust their thinking when dealing with computers. For example, a person who enters "ten" instead of "10" into a computer should realize that these are not at all equivalent to the computer. If you type in a question such as "What is beauty?," the computer will not respond with a philosophical discussion but instead will display something similar to "SYNTAX ERROR." This is so because its very limited vocabulary of words does not include the words or concepts you had in mind. In addition, for the computer each word has only one specific meaning.

Thus, much of the richness and complexity of human-to-human communication must be abandoned when you communicate with a computer. Instead, the human must learn an artificial language or a set of commands with a small vocabulary and rigid, inviolable rules of syntax. The typical computer program is notoriously inflexible to anything except highly structured and nonvague, nonambiguous responses from the person using it. This is true even with modern hardware devices such as the "mouse," a desk-top pointing device that allows the user to easily point to a picture or a set of words on the screen which indicate what he or she wants the computer to do.

In other words, in any human-to-machine interaction, it is the human who must be flexible enough to accommodate to the machine's inflexibility and limited communication abilities. Also, it is the human who must communicate in a way that is probably quite unnatural for him or her. This is part of the price we pay to tap the advantages of the computer's speed, accuracy, information storage capacity, and precision. We must adapt to the machine's needs because it is either extremely difficult or impossible for the machine to be made to adapt to ours. Although devices exist that allow a computer to recognize limited numbers of spoken words (if "trained" to a particular person's voice), computers that can understand and act upon human requests made in our typical loosely structured and complex conversational language are not in our immediate futures.

A second ramification of computer inflexibility in communication is that all data with which the machine will work must be presented in *machine analyzable* form. Humans can read and use thousands of sheets of typed and pictorial information that may be stored in file cabinets, but a computer cannot, at least not without special processing. We can note that certain types of information are frequently found in different places on the typed sheets but the computer must have standardized units of information as well as standardized placement of each item of information for each case. This factor can be a tremendous disadvantage and deterrent to computer use. The large workload of reentering into a computer hundreds or thousands of pieces of already existing information so that we can "computerize" our work frequently means that it is easier to keep an inefficient manual mode of processing than it is to convert the information for computer processing.

In summary, computers have substantial advantages over humans in several aspects of information processing. However, human advantages in the areas of flexibility, associative thinking, and communicative complexity make computer use a give-and-take situation in many educational applications. Each new way in which computers may be used in education must be examined closely, and the trade-offs that accompany computer use should be evaluated carefully *before* the decision is made to "computerize." Education is a complex set of interactions and events that take place in a complex organism, the human being. We should never forget that the quality of educational experiences *may* be better with computers than without them if proper planning and execution occur, but that these experiences can always be worse with computers if educators do not apply the advantages and disadvantages of computers intelligently and sensitively to the needs of students.

Types of Computers

Computers come in two basic types, analog and digital. Analog computers accept continuous information about physical conditions, such as temperature, and translate them into quantities representing physical changes. These machines are mostly used by physical scientists and engineers for research purposes and are not usually encountered in educational contexts. Digital computers, on the other hand, are capable of manipulating data in the form of discrete numbers or letters and are the type of computer most commonly seen in education, business, and the home. The basic differences in the ways in which these two process information may be illustrated by digital and analog clocks, which are primitive forms of each of these two types of computers. Digital clocks count the passing seconds in discrete units and display them as digits that change. Analog clocks measure the passage of time by means of continuous changes in the placement of the hour and minute hands on the face of the clock. Since most modern computers are of the digital variety, we will refer to them exclusively as we discuss computers from this point on.

Digital computers come in several major categories; commonly these are referred to as micro-, mini-, maxi-, and supercomputers. Although these differ considerably in cost, size, and computational power, there are basic and general similarities in their designs. All computers have five basic parts, each with its own set of functions. These parts are an input device, an output device, memory, data storage devices(s), and a central processing unit (CPU). All of these make up the physical machine, otherwise known as the computer hardware.

The Parts of a Computer

An input device allows us to communicate with the computer. Whether the device is a typewriter-like keyboard, a punched card, a touch-sensitive TV screen, or a mouse, the function of input devices is to allow a human to enter information into the computer. The effective use of an input device usually requires some training of the human user so that he or she can properly structure and enter information and requests for processing information in a way that the inflexible computer will "understand." Unfortunately, information cannot be entered into the computer as yet using ordinary human language, although there do exist some input devices that can interpret a very limited number of words for a few special and highly structured applications. During the past few years, substantial progress has been made in producing input devices that are easy for people to use and that require less human adaptation to the inflexible needs of the computer than in the past. Some of the most exciting potential for computer use in special education lies in the development of input devices that can bring computer use to the severely handicapped.

Output Devices. Output devices display the text or graphical outcome of a computer's processing activities. The most common output devices on modern computers are printers and cathode ray tubes (CRTs). Printers are essentially computer-driven typewriters that may print a character at a time or, on large computers, a line at a time. Printers exist in which letter quality type is provided by the impact of keys on paper, by the printing of a matrix of connected dots on paper (dot matrix printer), by the burning of patterns of dots onto heat sensitive paper, and most recently by ink jets and lasers. Many computers used in education have a CRT (either a television or a television monitor) and a printer of one of the types already noted. CRT output can take the form of computer generated graphics in colors that can be programmed to provide visually appealing and educationally worthwhile displays of information for students.

Memory. A computer's memory is where all information that will be used in a processing operation at a given time must be located. Information stored in memory includes (1) the *operating system* (a manufacturer-supplied set of programs that provides the computer's capabilities to interact among its various parts and to schedule this interaction properly), (2) the computer program that is being used (including associated data), and (3) the programming language (e.g., BASIC, LOGO) in which the program is written. Any of this information may be made immediately available for processing. Storage of information in memory is expensive per character stored compared to disc* storage, and so the size of computer memories is limited in comparison to the need for vast amounts of storage in some applications. Frequently this need to be able to manipulate larger amounts of information than can be held in the computer's memory is met by moving information temporarily not needed from the memory to disc storage and moving needed information from the disc to memory.

There are two basic types of memory, each with several variations. Read only memory (ROM) contains programming instructions that are encoded onto the memory device in a way that cannot be changed by the computer user. Thus, the contents of this type of memory may be read and used, but new information may not be stored there (hence the name "read only memory"). Random access memory (RAM), on the other hand, is available for storage of new information or as the location of information to be read by the computer. The computer user, through his or her computer program, can change the contents of RAM routinely. Computers vary as to what percentage of the total amount of memory is ROM versus RAM. It is not uncommon for the operating system and perhaps a programming

---

*In this book the spelling "disc" is used instead of "disk" (*American Heritage Dictionary of the English Language*, 1982, page 375.

language to be stored in read only memory, since these are typically used but not changed by the average user. In this case, random access memory would hold the user's program and associated data.

Computer memory is stored on chips of silicon called integrated circuit (IC chips). Recently, the development of large-scale integrated circuits (LSI chips) has led to the placement of many thousands of electrical circuits on one small (less than one eighth inch) chip. This has allowed computers to become very small and much less costly than in the past.

An important characteristic of random access memory is that it is volatile. This means that the contents of memory will be lost if there is the slightest fluctuation in the electric power furnished to the computer. Another important trait of computer memory is that its size represents an upper limit on the size of the problem that can be addressed, since any data to be processed must first be located in memory. This means that certain educational problems such as class scheduling or test scoring may require substantially more memory than instructional programs.

Data Storage Devices. Data storage devices allow for the storage of large quantities of information that may not be needed routinely or for which there is no room in memory. Most data storage devices are nonvolatile, meaning that the loss of electric power will not usually result in the loss of data stored on these devices. However, since all processing takes place in memory, any data to be processed must be copied from the storage device to memory when needed. Data are not processed on the data storage devices but only stored until needed. Another function of the data storage device is to act as a temporary location in which the computer can place information that normally resides in memory if memory is in short supply. In some applications, a computer program can move unneeded information from the memory to the storage device, thus making more room in memory for processing, and then replace the information in memory after the extra processing room is no longer needed.

There are several types of storage devices that fall into two major classifications: sequential devices and random access devices. The computer can read data from or write data to a sequential device from the beginning to the end without being able to skip directly to the location of a particular piece of information. An example of this type of device in our everyday lives is the audio cassette tape. In order to play the last song on the tape, the previous songs must be played or skipped over until the location on the tape of the desired song is reached. Cassette tapes and reel tapes are also used on computers in similar ways with the exception that digital data are stored magnetically on the tapes instead of audio information.

Random access devices allow direct access to selected items of data without reading all the preceding data in order to reach the desired item. The most commom of this class of storage devices is the magnetic disc which may be either rigid (fixed) or flexible (floppy). In these devices, the disc spins inside a container while recording heads float just above the spinning disc and read or write information magnetically on the disc under the control of the computer. These devices range in size and cost from the floppy disc at a cost of several dollars and a capacity of up to 1 million characters of data to multilayered rigid discs containing billions of characters of data and costing hundreds to thousands of dollars.

Central Processing Unit. The final part of the computer to be discussed is the central processing unit or CPU. The CPU is made up of a control section and an arithmetic-logic unit, which are linked to the other parts of the computer by means of input-output circuits. The CPU interacts with memory, where both data and programming instructions are stored. The control section of the CPU sequentially examines the programming instructions and sends signals to the other parts of the computer in order to execute these instructions and to control the timing of the operation of the other computer parts properly. The arithmetic-logic unit actually processes the data following the programming instructions as determined by the control section of the CPU. These two parts of the CPU—the control section and the artithmetic-logic unit—work closely together to execute the programming instructions (stored in memory) on the data (stored in memory).

Thus, whether a computer is a micro-, mini-, or maxicomputer (also known as a large mainframe computer), there are some similarities in the operation of these devices in that they all have five basic parts, each of which has specific functions in the overall computer system. There are, however, substantial differences between the types of computers with respect to size, cost, speed, storage capacity, and the ways they may be used. For example, computers range in cost from less than $50 for a small microcomputer with an input device, a memory, and a CPU to millions of dollars for large and powerful computer systems that have many input devices, multiple CPUs, immense memories, vast amounts of storage, and multiple output devices that allow hundreds of persons to be served simultaneously.

Although the boundaries between micro-, mini-, and maxicomputer capabilities have become somewhat blurred by the technologic improvements of recent years, some rough comparisons may be made. These general comparisons may be inaccurate when applied to some specific computers because capabilities vary considerably within these three categories as well as between categories. Table 1-1 provides a summary of these comparisons. Microcomputers generally are placed on a desk top, cost a maximum of $5000 to $6000, require no special electrical or cooling service, and serve one user at a time. Minicomputers may require a portion of a room, may cost up to several hundred thousand dollars, may require special cooling

Table 1-1. Comparison of Micro-, Mini-, and Maxicomputers

	Microcomputers	Minicomputers	Maxicomputers
Size	Desk size	Room corner size	Room size
Cost	Approximately $40 to $6000–$7000	Approximately $7000 to several hundred thousand dollars	Several hundred thousand to millions of dollars
Environment	Normal room	May require air conditioner	Refrigeration or air conditioning, or both
Power	Standard wall power	Special plugs or higher currents	Peculiar power requirements
Speed		Approximately 5–10 times faster than micro-computers	Approximately 20–100 times faster than microcomputers
Storage capacity	Hundreds of thousands of characters	Millions of characters	Hundreds of millions to billions of char-acters
Users	One at a time	Several to tens of simultaneous users	Tens to hundreds of simultaneous users
Internal data movement	One channel for transfer of information	Several infor-mation transfer channels	Many channels
Representative brand names	Apple, IBM, Radio Shack	Hewlett-Packard, Digital Equipment, IBM	IBM, Control Data Corporation, Burroughs

or electrical service, and may serve several to tens of users. Maxicomputers require a room-sized space, may cost millions of dollars, require special electrical and cooling service, and may serve many users.

HOW DO COMPUTERS ACTUALLY WORK?

Information Inside the Computer

For most computers, all information that enters into memory is stored in binary form. This means that all numbers, letters, and symbols are expressed in terms of combinations of ones and zeroes. The reason for this apparently strange feature of computers becomes clearer when we investigate the precise way that abstract quantities, such as the number eleven, could be physically represented by humans as opposed to an electronic device. We use a number system with ten different symbols (0 through 9) in which each symbol has a particular value depending on its position. For instance, in the number 11, the first 1 has a value of ten and the second 1 has a value of one so that the number "11" means "1 ten plus 1 one. " Each position from right to left in our numbers has a value ten times greater than the previous position so that our numbers are made up of ones, tens, hundreds, thousands, and so on. Thus, the number 107 means 1 hundred, 0 tens, and 7 ones. Since ones, tens, hundreds, thousands, and so forth, are all powers of ten, our number system is obviously based on tens and is called a base-10 system.

Example:

Digits	1	0	7
Units	hundreds	tens	ones
Powers	10^2	10^1	10^0

Now, imagine that, instead of ten different symbols, you had only two symbols to work with. Suppose that, instead of fingers, you had only switches to count with and each switch could only be "on" or "off." This is the situation inside a computer. In this case, you would have only 1s (representing "on") and 0s (representing "off") to describe the state of each switch. You would then have a number system based on two instead of ten and your number positions from right to left would change from ones, tens, hundreds, thousands, and so forth, to ones, twos, fours, eights, sixteens, thirty-twos, and so forth. In other words, your base-2 number system would be based on powers of 2 just as our base-10 system is based on powers of 10. In this case, the base-10 number "107" could be represented in the following way:

Digits	0	1	1	0	1	0	1	1
Units	128s	64s	32s	16s	8s	4s	2s	1s
Powers of 2	2^7	2^6	2^5	2^4	2^3	2^2	2^1	2^0

Thus, the base-10 number 107 (1 hundred plus 0 tens plus 7 ones) could also be expressed in base-2 as 01101011 (zero 128s plus one 64 plus one 32 plus zero 16s plus one 8 plus zero 4s plus one 2 plus one 1 = 107). In fact, this is exactly how computers represent both numbers and letters, as combinations of circuits each of which is either "on" (1) or "off" (0).

Each of these binary digits (1 or 0) is called a bit (a contracted form of *bi*nary digi*t*). In most computers, binary digits or bits are grouped eight at a time in a *byte*. The importance of this grouping is that this much computer memory—eight binary digits, each of which is either "on" or "off"—is the amount required to represent a letter such as "A" or most numbers. Thus, a byte of memory (eight bits) equates to one character.

American Standard Code for Information Interchange (ASCII)

In addition to the binary (base-2) number system used by computers to represent and process information, there are other coding systems used to represent information. Two of these are the binary coded decimal (BCD) system and a special form of the BCD code, the American Standard Code for Information Interchange or ASCII (pronounced "as-key")

Binary coded decimal is a compromise between base-2 and base-10 numbers. It works by replacing each decimal digit with its equivalent in four binary digits. For example, each digit in the number 107 would be replaced by four binary digits as follows:

Decimal	Binary coded decimal
1	= 0001 or zero 8s + zero 4s + zero 2s + one 1 = 1
0	= 0000 or zero 8s + zero 4s + zero 2s + zero 1s = 0
7	= 0111 or zero 8s + one 4 + one 2 + one 1 + 7 = 7

Therefore the decimal number 107 is binary coded as 0001 0000 0111. Binary coded decimal is widely used where computer information must be displayed in decimal for ease of human interpretation (as in digital clocks) but where the information is actually represented in binary form.

The ASCII code is a special form of binary coded decimal code in that it uses eight binary digits to express a decimal number. This decimal number is significant because the numbers 0 to 127 have been matched in the ASCII system with corresponding letters, digits from 0 to 9, and special characters such as punctuation marks. For example, the character that is matched to the number 65 is A. When 65, a decimal number, is coded in binary with eight binary digits, it equals 01000001. This binary coded decimal number would then mean "character 65" or "A" to the computer.

The importance of ASCII code is that most computers use it to communicate with printers and other input-output devices. It is also important in communications in sending programs or data from one computer to another.

Information in the Computer's Central Processing Unit (CPU)

As mentioned previously, the CPU has two parts, the control unit and the arithmetic unit. It is the job of the control unit to interpret the instructions provided by the computer program and to direct the sequence of operations to be performed, including the arithmetic (addition, subtraction, multiplication, division) and logic (true-false, and, or, not) operations that are performed by the arithmetic-logic unit.

First, the program and any necessary data must be loaded from an input device or a storage device into memory. The program, originally written by a human programmer in a programming language such as BASIC or Pascal, has already been translated by other special programs supplied by the manufacturer called compilers or interpreters into a series of very specific instructions, which contain information defining which operation is to be performed in each step and an address in memory that tells where data for that operation are stored. These specific instructions and the data upon which the instructions will be performed by the CPU are taken from memory and temporarily stored in circuits called *registers* in binary form. Registers are similar to memory locations in that they usually hold from 8 to 16 binary digits of data or instructions taken from memory. Unlike memory locations, however, registers can be used to manipulate data as well as to store it.

The CPU might fetch instructions from memory that cause a sequence of events to occur if the data processing task to be performed was to add two numbers. First, the CPU would execute instructions to load a register with the contents of a given memory address, then load another register with the contents of another memory address, then add the contents of these two registers, and finally store the result in a given memory location. This multistep sequence of fetching instructions and data from memory and sequentially executing the instructions on the data in a step-by-step fashion generally describes how computers work at the CPU level. Of course, programmers do not have to program on this step-by-step level unless they choose to do so; in a higher level language, such as BASIC, one command generates many specific instructions to the CPU for sequential execution so that most computer users in education can program computers without having to issue the tedious step-by-step programming instructions necessary to accomplish even the simplest of data processing activities (e.g , adding two numbers). The computer itself, though, is really dealing with programming instructions and data on this very laborious level of minuscule steps. Fortunately, the tremendous execution speeds of even small computers makes these many small steps happen extremely quickly relative to the time required by humans to perform the same steps and so it seems to us that computers perform tasks such as addition virtually instantaneously.

Computer Memories

A common memory size for a microcomputer is 65,536 characters or bytes. Why the odd number? This is because each storage location in memory has a numerical address expressed in binary and because the area where addresses are stored contains 16 binary digits. Each of these binary digits can be either a zero or a one. Since there are 16 digits and each can have one of two values, there are two to the sixteenth power or 65,536 different addresses which can be identified. In other words, there are 65,536 storage locations, each capable of storing a character, which can be assigned an address for the computer to use with 16 digits available to store the address. In minicomputers and maxicomputers, there are typically more digits available to identify memory locations and thus, there can be larger memories than in most microcomputers.

Because the address of a given storage location is expressed in binary, the total memory size is always some power of 2. A convenient unit of memory is 2 to the 10th power or 1024 bytes. This is frequently labeled 1 *kilobyte* or 1K, even though a kilobyte really equals 1024 characters, not 1000. Thus, a memory of 65,536 bytes, the maximum for many microcomputers, can be labeled as a 64K memory (65,536 divided by 1024 = 64).

Computers can perform all of their processing operations in binary form. This may require hundreds of thousands of bits, each represented by an electronic switch which is either "on" or "off" (or passing current or not). Consequently, computer memories are made up of many large-scale integrated circuits, each of which may contain thousands of electronic switches representing either a 1 or a 0. A 64K memory contains 65,536 bytes times eight bits per byte or more than 524,000 bits. If memory chips containing 64 kilobits (or 8K) each are used in the computer, the entire memory may be held in just eight integrated circuit chips, each about the size of a thumbnail (although this is constantly becoming smaller with each technologic advance).

Improvements in Hardware and Software

It is the microcomputer, first appearing in January 1975 in the form of the Altair (a computer kit for hobbyists), that burst upon the educational scene in the 1980s and has brought computing away from the exclusive use of scientists and engineers to common use in home and educational applications. Relatively few educators had frequent exposure to the mini- and maxicomputers of the 1960s and 1970s because they were mostly tended and programmed by specialists, and they were also centralized, costly, and relatively difficult to learn to use. As technology has progressed, however, microcomputers have gradually assumed the capabilities of the minicomputers and maxicomputers of just a few years ago because the features of these larger machines have been miniaturized extensively and placed into smaller, much less costly packages. The $300 microcomputer of the late 1970s was much faster, thousands of times more reliable, one ten-thousandth as expensive, and one thirty-thousandth the size of the first large electronic computer built in the late 1940s. These trends have continued to accelerate in the 1980s.

Just as important as the improvements in computers' physical make-up or hardware have been the tremendous improvements in the utility of computer programs (or software) for the average person who is not a computer specialist. There are many examples of software for personal and home use on a microcomputer that are more powerful and much easier to use than older software on mini- and maxicomputers. The micro-computer has ushered in the age of "user-friendly" software (programs that are easy to use and understand by novice computer users), such as personal word processing programs, spreadsheet programs, data management programs, and educational software for which no real analogue exists on most mini- and maxicomputers. For the first time, the power of computers can be brought to professionals, such as attorneys, educators, physicians, who may have received their professional training with a near or total absence of computer background. The "computer literacy" problem facing educators today is really part of a larger problem in most of the professions as practicing professionals who are competent in their fields find themselves confronted head-on by the power and potential promise of computer use in their professional lives.

HOW ARE COMPUTERS USED IN EDUCATION TODAY?

Computers have been used in education for years. However, before the advent of cheap and powerful microcomputers, many educational applications were administrative (e.g., payroll, attendance record keeping, class scheduling) and were performed on a mini- or maxicomputer located in a centralized computer center and staffed by data processing specialists. A number of educators in the 1970s developed extensive amounts of computer assisted instruction (CAI) software using computer terminals that were connected to remotely located computers. This software provided, among other things, drill and practice for students in mathematics computation and in the grammatical and vocabulary knowledge aspects of reading skills. Computer classes for advanced mathematics students and business-vocational students in secondary schools were not uncommon. Large computers were utilized by researchers to score and analyze test data in school settings and to conduct evaluation studies of new and continuing educational curricula and programs. However, the average classroom teacher during the late 1960s and early 1970s was not often touched directly by the computer's influence and was under no serious pressure to make the computer a part of his or her professional activities on a frequent basis. The arrival of the microcomputer and the availability of much greater quantities (but not always better quality) of instructional computer software has changed all that, perhaps permanently.

These days, traditional educational computer applications are still with us but now many of them are implemented on a microcomputer instead of a mini- or maxicomputer. Computer assisted instruction and computer managed instruction remain as two of the most important categories of educational computer use, but now almost every teacher is, willingly or unwillingly, coming to grips with the advantages and disadvantages of these two types of computer use in instruction.

Computer Assisted Instruction (CAI)

In computer assisted instruction, the computer is frequently used as the medium by which traditional drill and practice or tutorial sessions take place. Instead of the teacher or an instructional aide administering or supervising the instructional session, the student works individually with a computer program, which presents material, reinforces key concepts, and asks questions of the student to test his or her knowledge. This instructional situation is often little different from that used in the past except that a computer program is now working with the students on an individual basis rather than a teacher directing a workbook exercise for a class.

Many computer assisted instruction programs are roundly criticized for being unimaginative, for emphasizing skills that involve low cognitive demand, and for accomplishing little more than a textbook might deliver. Unfortunately, these criticisms are often valid. The use of a computer for such activities exclusively may be difficult to justify on a cost-effectiveness basis because even a cheap computer is expensive when compared to texts, workbooks, or other such instructional materials.

Instructional computer software that presents opportunities for students to learn problem solving skills in an interesting format, and which avoids an exclusive focus on lower level cognitive skills, can offer much that typical drill and practice programs or traditional workbook exercises cannot. Software whose graphics are meaningful and interesting, not just flashy and ultimately boring, can enhance student understanding in many areas of instruction in ways that traditional instructional techniques might not be able to accomplish.

Simulations also represent a category of computer assisted instruction that can offer instructional experiences that are more than "business as usual" delivered via computer. A computer program can be furnished with a mathematical description of a system (e.g., the functioning of a city), which the student can then test and experiment with as if the situation were real. The student can learn indirectly by trying various "What if?" approaches and then observing what happens as a result of his or her actions, possibly leading to a richer form of learning than could be attained with other educational media.

It is also possible to use the computer as a means of demonstrating selected concepts or procedures, especially when teaching the physical sciences, biological sciences, or mathematics, which might otherwise require expensive laboratory equipment (e.g., demonstrations of chemical reactions) or which might ordinarily be impossible to demonstrate (e.g., atomic reactions). In this case, the computer is being used for the same purpose as blackboard diagrams, overhead transparencies, or filmstrips with sound. However, even a modest demonstration of an appropriate concept by means of well-designed computer software probably would be more reliable and more instructionally rewarding than with traditional classroom presentation techniques.

In summary, computer assisted instruction (CAI) potentially can provide learning experiences for students that cannot be provided cost effectively using more traditional techniques. As long as the use of CAI is under the guidance of a well-organized and instructionally attentive teacher, students will probably learn basic skills at least as well as under traditional techniques and may learn more powerful problem-solving approaches for later use with similar material. As long as the teacher is knowledgeable enough to either select or write software that is consistent with the diagnosed learning needs of his or her students, the impact of CAI will probably not be negative. Applied creatively and selectively, computer assisted instruction may indeed result in instructional benefits for students over and above those that would have accrued without the use of computers. Unfortunately, this desirable situation is not an automatic outcome of CAI use in the classroom by any teacher, in any subject, at any time, and with any students. In addition, even the successful use of this technology comes at great cost for computer hardware, software, and, most importantly, the training of teachers for its use. Because of this cost, the temptation is present for schools to acquire amounts of hardware, software, and teacher training which are sufficient to cause instructional disruption of the existing curricula and teaching but are insufficient to allow students to receive the positive effects of exposure to instruction via computer.

Computer managed instruction (CMI), a second category of well-established educational computer uses, has also been moved from larger computers to microcomputers since the 1970s. The typical CMI program offers a complete system for keeping records on student attainment of instructional objectives, including diagnostic statements and summaries of each child's performance. Many of these systems are developed by publishers to accompany a textbook series. Some score a child's test as he or she is taking the test, presenting immediate feedback to the student and to the teacher.

There now exist computer programs that are designed to score any standardized or teacher-made test whose specifications have been loaded into the software. Such a generic test scoring system offers much in terms of local scoring of tests under local control and to local specifications at great cost savings. The combination of such general purpose and user-customized scoring systems with data base capabilities for storing and retrieving student records from past testings can provide each school and classroom with testing analyses formerly reserved to system-wide analyses performed on centralized large computers. Test scoring software that allows items to be selected from standardized tests and rescored as a local proficiency test, or which allows criterion-referenced tests to be locally normed and scored as a norm-referenced test, provide the maximum in utility and flexibility for use of testing information by educators.

Many CMI programs deemphasize the testing aspects of instruction and instead focus on allowing the teacher to set up an individualized path through the curriculum for each student. As the student proceeds along this path, the teacher enters records of the student's advances and regressions and makes judgments regarding student progress. Based on teacher judgments, the computer software can then direct students to learning activities more closely matched to their apparent skill levels and can record evidence of the student's progress toward mastery of the skills contained in the software.

Many teachers enthusiastically greeted microcomputer-based CMI programs only to realize that the software is often linked to only one set of curricular materials or that there is not enough storage space in the microcomputer to contain all of the student information that is pertinent for a given instructional decision. However, there are many teachers who believe that this type of system allows for an effective incremental approach to student mastery of many specific skills, with the burdensome requirements for record keeping being mostly handled by the computer.

New Educational Uses for Computers

The advent of microcomputer-based word processing, mathematical calculation, data-base management, and contingency planning software has brought the power of software formerly reserved for large mainframes (or not existing at all) to educational uses. Much work is currently going on at all grade levels in experimenting with teaching students how to write using word processing software. Personal word processing is one of the most exciting outcomes of the availability of personal computers for home and classroom in that students can become more productive writers when the mechanical constraints of creating text are reduced. Students can also be taught to feel more free in exploring their use of language if changes to text can be made easily and quickly. Word processing is also one of the most easily justifiable uses of computers from a cost-effectiveness point of view.

Software that allows for sophisticated calculations, the management of large amounts of data, and the "what if?" contingency analyses of data has been much more popular in business and with advanced students than with educational users in general. These software systems are untapped sources of instructional power, which are powerful, relatively easy to learn to use, and may be introduced into classrooms from home and business sources before they are readily adopted by educators. These types of software have obvious utility in the management and utility of everyday information; the use of improved forms of these may be a "survival skill" of the not-too-distant future, which educators may soon be pressured to teach in the schools.

Computer Languages in Education

Although older programming languages developed for large computers may still be taught in some schools (e.g., *C*ommon *B*usiness *O*riented *L*anguage or COBOL for high school business students), most educational use of microcomputers probably involves the use of the programming languages BASIC (*B*eginner's *A*ll-purpose *S*ymbolic *I*nstruction *C*ode), Pascal, LOGO, or an authoring language, such as Pilot. There are many other languages, which are mostly used outside the field of education, such as FORTRAN, PL/I, APL, C, and FORTH. Educators who take computer literacy courses stand an excellent chance of being exposed to BASIC or LOGO. Like the many other computer languages that have been developed over the years, and which may be still used in noneducational applications, each of these languages has certain strengths as well as lack of capabilities, which were built into the language as it was defined. There is no one computer language that is advantageous in all uses and situations.

BASIC, first developed in 1964, was designed to be easy to learn and to use. It is a relatively general-purpose language, providing for manipulation of text and allowing for fairly sophisticated mathematical computation. Since it is an interactive language, users get immediate feedback from typing a line into the computer. Students can be taught a simple form of BASIC and can write and execute simple programs in an afternoon. Detractors claim that BASIC, although widely encountered, does not allow for the teaching of efficient and structured programming, does not have certain important features such as recursion, and does not facilitate the learning of more sophisticated programming languages. Adherents point to its widespread use, ease of learning, and ability to allow beginning programmers to perform "serious" applications without spending large amounts of time learning a more powerful language.

Pascal is a language whose use encourages structure and logical organization in programming. It is usually taught in secondary school mathematics or science courses and is computationally powerful and relatively easy to learn.

LOGO has received much attention in recent years from educators because it is designed as a tool to facilitate learning about computers, not as a language for applications programming. It is very easy to start programming in LOGO. Many young children have been taught a sense of command over the machine and have discovered powerful problem-solving skills, especially in mathematics, through its use. It encourages the development and refinement of procedures, a set of operations to be performed in a specific sequence, which individually are simple but which can have powerful effects when combined. Proponents claim that it creates an ideal environment for young people to explore complex problem-solving skills and that it facilitates the learning of other sophisticated languages. Detractors say that LOGO exercises can be trivial exercises in graphics unless the teacher possesses a sophisticated understanding of its capabilities. Some critics mention that LOGO is not an applications language and thus it is difficult to do anything "useful" with it in computation or analysis of real-world data.

The authoring language Pilot is different from the programming languages in that it was designed so that teachers could easily provide it with information which would then result in a typical computer assisted instruction program in a given subject. It allows convenient comparisons between words or portions of words (e.g., comparing a correct answer with the student answer) but does not perform complex computations well. A teacher can learn a simple form of Pilot in very short order and can begin to enter text, which will be presented to the student in English sentences in a CAI program, will allow the student to answer, and will compare the answer to teacher-furnished responses.

Where Did Computers Come From?

The history of computing devices of a mechanical nature goes back thousands of years; the need for counting and record keeping is probably at least as old as the earliest human commercial dealings. Although many ingenious devices were developed, none approximated the modern computer until Charles Babbage's "difference engine" and "analytical engine" in the early to mid-1800s. His devices featured the notion that a machine would follow predetermined instructions and that these instructions and any data would be stored in machine-readable form, both important aspects of modern computers. Although his machines were well conceived, they were never completely developed because the technology of the time apparently was not capable of producing gears and other parts to the necessary performance specifications. The realization of Babbage's dream had to wait until the concepts were redeveloped in the 1930s by scientists unaware of Babbage's work.

After World War II, the first modern electronic computer, the Electronic Numerical Integrator and Calculator (ENIAC) was brought into use, beginning the series of events that has led, almost 40 years later, to the proliferation of cheap and relatively powerful microcomputers in education and in the home. During this period, there have been several major technologic transitions and advances in the development of modern computers. At first, computers used vacuum tubes and electronic relays to process and store information and magnetic tapes for the input of data. These were "first generation" computers developed and used primarily in the 1950s.

The use of transistors in computers as an alternative to the control of electronic circuits by vacuum tube marks the beginning of the much smaller, approximately ten times faster, and much more reliable second generation computers, which appeared in the early 1960s. These machines took advantage of transistors' superior ability to respond to incoming electronic pulses by rapidly turning either "on" or "off," thus acting as small, reliable, fast, and power-efficient switches to represent binary 1s and 0s for computer storage of information in binary digits or bits, as discussed previously.

The invention of the integrated circuit in the late 1950s allowed the computers of the mid-1960s to have hundreds to thousands of transistors and other electronic components miniaturized and integrated onto one piece of silicon, a "chip." This meant that these third generation computers could be about 100 times faster than second generation computers because the signals traveled shorter distances and because these electronic "switches" could turn from "on" to "off" faster in representing binary information.

This advance led in the 1970s to the large-scale integrated circuit or LSI technology associated with modern fourth generation computers and made it possible for computer designers to place more and more thousands of smaller and faster electronic components on one chip. This progressing trend of smaller, faster, cheaper, and more reliable electronic devices on a chip brought minicomputers to some educators' use in the early to mid-1970s and has brought microcomputers to almost all educators' attention in the late 1970s and early 1980s.

A concurrent development since the early 1970s has been the tremendous improvements in the ease of use and power of computer software. As more and more persons who had not previously used computers were introduced to them during the 1970s, the need for software that could be used by the nonspecialist in computing was plainly evident. This, even more than hardware advances, has made computers accessible to educators through applications such as personal word processing, personal accounting and spreadsheet programs, and improved software for learning and instruction. Many of these programs were conceived for and written for use on microcomputers and do not have analogues on larger, more powerful computers. In addition, improved microcomputer operating systems, such as the Control Program for Microcomputers (CP/M), are much less cryptic and easier to use than the operating systems on many modern large computers.

The advent of these powerful and cheap devices, which began the modern age of digital watches, calculators, and microcomputers, has, in just a few years, moved computers from the realm of a costly centralized device for specialists to a cheap, powerful, and commonly enountered machine for use by professionals who may have little or no formal training in computer use. It has also led to other, increasingly ubiquitous electronic devices in our equipment of everyday life, such as cars and cameras controlled by "smart" devices. Finally, it has led to a widespread need for educators, parents, and children to become computer literate so that they can understand and manipulate this technology to their mutual advantage. In a certain sense, the computer has become a solution in search of a problem as more and more persons see ways in which it might be used in education and as more and more persons seek the knowledge necessary to implement these educational uses of computers.

How Will Computers Influence Educators?

Educators are already facing the adjustments that computers have brought and will continue to bring to education. The most obvious of these adjustments is to acknowledge the fact that computers will probably not go away and that their presence in education should be confronted and capitalized on. This means that there will continue to be tremendous pressures on educators to become computer literate and computer proficient as new and more powerful hardware and software continue to appear on the scene.

Educators must learn to recognize and capitalize on the advantages of computer use discussed earlier and to recognize and allow for some obvious and some subtle differences in the ways in which computers and humans handle information. For example, humans are accustomed to information having some physical reality, such as being written on a sheet of paper. However, when stored in a computer, information is no longer subject to our physical perception, and we must view it through the filter of the computer. The fact that our important information may exist only as represented by digital circuits may be difficult to get used to. Part of this problem involves the fact that we are not used to relying upon sophisticated technology just to see our information. This is most readily apparent when the computer is "down" for some reason and we are temporarily cut off from access to even the simplest of our information needs.

Educators will also need to remember that error detection is much easier for the informed human than for the programmed computer. The knowledgable human can spot something that "doesn't look right" easily, but programmers who write data editing programs have demonstrated time and time again that it is very difficult to program a computer to recognize relationships and inconsistencies in data that would be obvious to humans. If you try entering nonsense data into your favorite program, you may be appalled at what the computer will accept as allowable unless you have been incredibly conscientious in programming a complete set of editing directions. The most damaging of such errors are the ones whose values are within normal range (and thus are virtually impossible to detect), but whose meaning is totally false.

As computer programs become more powerful, educators should keep in mind that not even sophisticated systems are capable of answering such questions as "How is Johnny doing in learning to read?" that the informed human could readily answer. The ability to distill meaning out of large amounts of data is something that educators cannot expect from computers. This is sometimes easy to forget as computer programs do more and more seemingly incredible things.

Finally, we should not seek to "computerize" existing processess without critically examining the situation to see if an entirely different approach should not be used when a computer is part of the solution to a problem. Many of our time-worn procedures and best strategies result from the needs and demands on manual data processing strategies. We should not be afraid to be more creative in our problem solving when using computers but also prudently wary of untested strategies.

CHAPTER 2

The Computer and Special Education

Computers are rapidly becoming prevalent in educational environments. In the early 1980s educators and parents were often afraid of computers because they did not know how they worked or how to operate them. Thus, there was a tremendous demand for "computer literacy" courses or workshops. Today, this demand apparently has been generally met and the new trends are toward exploring the capabilities of the computer for specific applications and toward achieving an understanding of how to manipulate the computer to accomplish those tasks. This chapter (and the book in general) is designed to assist special educators and personnel in related services who are interested in computers to see how the new technology fits into the field of special education. The computer should be viewed not as a threatening revolutionary device that is going to change the fabric of teaching handicapped children, but as a supplemental instructional medium and a useful tool for both the teacher and student. The computer has the capability to make both teaching and learning more efficient and can reduce the burden of teacher and student.

Computers cannot do everything, and educators must be encouraged to see where they can be utilized appropriately. To achieve this objective, it is perhaps easiest to discuss how computers have the capacity to incorporate many of the best practices of special educational instructional methodology. Additionally, in an attempt to better understand computers, how they work, and how they can be applied to the field, the structure of computer programs will be compared to the structure of good teaching practices.

THE COMPUTER AS AN INSTRUCTIONAL MEDIUM

Special education implies the provision of adapted or different curriculum or instructional methodologies. The use of various instructional media; such as language masters, tape recorders, programmed texts, and

---

This chapter was authored by Michael M. Behrmann.

so forth, is quite common in the field. The primary reason for the widespread application of instructional media is the need to provide efficient individualized education that fits the learning needs of the handicapped child. There are six basic reasons why computers are valuable instructional media for teachers: (1) they can be used in individual or group instruction, (2) they can provide immediate feedback and reinforcement to students, (3) they can collect and analyze student performance data, (4) they are flexible in terms of level of instruction and type of child-computer interactions available, (5) they allow self-paced instruction, and (6) they allow errorless practice.

Individual and Group Instruction

Individualization is probably one of the most visible characteristics of teaching in special education. Abeson and Weintraub (1977) state that individualization means that the educational program must be addressed to the needs of a single child rather than a class or group of children. In regular classrooms, children generally learn regardless of the types of instruction provided by the teacher (assuming they are motivated to learn and the teacher provides reasonably appropriate instruction). The teacher tests and probes at some points, but does not generally utilize an individualized approach to teach and evaluate performance. Handicapped children, however, are usually deviant learners and end up in special placements because they cannot perform in a regular education setting. Handicapped learners also tend to be heterogeneous in their learning styles and needs. That is, the types of learning problems they have and the levels of curriculum at which they are functioning are usually quite diverse across a classroom of children at similar ages. It is this diversity that requires the special education teacher to systematically provide instruction to meet the individual needs of students. To do this effectively, the teacher's instructional time must be efficiently used, grouping children who have similar needs together while identifying where their needs require one-to-one instruction.

Computers have the capacity to assist teachers with many of the tasks designed to provide individualized and small group instruction and to free the teacher to work on children's needs that are inappropriate for technology (e.g., increase social interaction for withdrawn children). Computers may even provide a mechanism that will permit many handicapped children to remain in the regular education placement. Most people perceive computer assisted instruction (CAI) as a one person–one machine interaction, which generally is the manner in which it is used. The computer, however, can present information to both groups or individuals. In a group presentation, the student does not necessarily interact directly with the computer during the presentation of new information. This approach is similar to many traditional instructional media presentations. However, when a computer is used students may later interact individually by answering questions on material previously presented to the group. Another group process incorporates an experiential process with a small group or teams of children making decisions on how to interact with the computer. Program languages such as LOGO can provide a format for a cooperative "discovery" type of learning.

Reinforcement and Student Feedback

The value of reinforcement in learning is widely recognized. It is particularly important for handicapped learners who may be easily frustrated by mistakes or messy work. Computers tend to be intrinsically motivating because they can provide immediate reinforcement, allow the child to work as rapidly or slowly as desired, can be set up in a game format or format that does not become boring, and provide a means of "errorless" learning. Errorless learning and ease of editing allow a child to correct work and produce a "clean" product. Computers can also be programmed to provide the student with personalized reinforcement, such as "That's a good job, Frank," as well as be programmed to call the teacher's attention to good work so that additional social reinforcement can be provided. The teaching environment can make it difficult for teachers to be consistent in the application of appropriate rewards for student performance. Computers are absolutely consistent with their ability to reward performance and can be programmed to provide that reinforcement based upon the tested principles of behavior modification (e.g., using regularly scheduled intervals or random basis). Teachers then are relieved from some of the requirements of providing consistent correction and reinforcement that the computer can provide and can utilize the power of intermittent social reinforcement with the child. It remains important, though, to maintain the human element of praise even when a child is working on a computer.

The real strength of the computer, however, is the ability to interact individually with students and immediately respond to them based on their input. As such, it provides the teacher with an additional medium, which enables the student to engage in an interactive learning environment without requiring one-to-one instruction from the teacher or aide. One of the primary reasons for one-to-one instruction is to provide errorless learning experiences. If errors are ignored, they tend to be reinforced, and this is why monitoring student responses is important (Sloane, Buckholdt, Jenson,

& Crandall, 1979). Computers can be programmed to provide that monitoring and, if desirable, branch to remedial instruction or allow the child to respond again. They can also be programmed to call the teacher if the child is unable to get the correct response within the set mastery criterion. Immediate feedback is one way of providing appropriate reinforcement to the child in that he or she sees the mistake and is able to correct it in a nonthreatening situation. That is, the mistake is not made public, and possible embarrassment is avoided. It should be noted here that even though the computer allows the child to correct a mistake and produce a perfect product, the computer can be programmed to collect data on all correct and incorrect responses the child made, allowing teachers to monitor on-going performance.

Data Collection and Analysis

One of the requirements of an individual educational program (IEP) under P.L. 94-142 is the inclusion of a plan for evaluating progress toward annual goals and short-term objectives. Good teachers collect and analyze data according to student needs and pragmatic considerations for data collection and analysis. Generally, teachers evaluate students through tests and by analyzing and grading work samples. When student performance indicates a problem, a closer examination of the work is indicated. It is unrealistic to expect teachers to do a "finegrained analysis" of all of the work that each child in the class does. Therefore, teachers often tend to analyze work in a child's major problem area(s). Otherwise, the data tend to pile up, and the process of evaluation is overwhelming.

Evaluation of student performance data with the computer can be done utilizing standardized tests or work samples or through observable measures, such as those developed under behavioral and precision teaching models (White & Haring, 1980). Utilizing the latter, data can be collected on such things as rate, accuracy, duration, fluency (rate of correct responses), latency, and frequency. Work sample measures assist in evaluating performance (e.g., the frequency of correct responses can be measured) and also provide teachers with the data upon which to base an evaluation of the type and pattern of errors an individual makes. This type of evaluation is called an error analysis.

One of the truly valuable characteristics of computers is their ability to collect and analyze student performance data. As noted previously, even when students change their responses, the computer can collect that information for later teacher evaluation. The computer will be able to calculate such things as accuracy and fluency and graphically depict them for the teacher. Additionally, the computer is capable of analyzing errors and error patterns. It is conceivable that patterns of grammatical mistakes or mathematical errors will be detectable by the computer through work sample analysis. This makes the computer unique as an instructional medium, since enormous amounts of data can be collected, analyzed, and formatted for easy teacher evaluation. This capability will eventually enable teachers to perform the fine-grained analysis of student performance on all student work done on the computer.

Computer assisted data analysis is not limited to evaluating student performance data collected by the computer. There are a number of data analysis packages that allow direct input of both data collected in traditional ways and data on behaviors that are not compatible with direct collection on the computer. Thus, such things as out of seat behavior, tardiness, or even cursive handwriting mistakes can be entered in the computer for analysis and graphic representation. Finally, it should be noted that eventually, computerized student demographic and performance data may be available for inclusion into computer assisted management packages for administrative planning and reporting (see Chapter 12, section on Integrated Software).

Individualizing Levels of Instruction

The concept of individualizing instruction relies on more than providing instruction in a small group or in a one-to-one relationship, providing reinforcement and feedback, or collecting and analyzing student performance data. It is also critical that the teacher provide appropriate content combined with an instructional methodology that fits the learning needs of the handicapped student. Computers are unable to make these judgments, and teachers need to understand that this technology is just another (albeit powerful) tool to assist children in learning. Computers can be programmed to reflect good individualized teaching practices and high quality curricular content, but teachers have the ultimate responsibility to determine if, when, and where their application is appropriate to meet the learning needs of handicapped students. Chapter 10 provides some guidelines for making these decisions.

The definition of the IEP includes an assessment of current level of performance of the child. This concept implies that the educator must know the levels of knowledge and skills a child brings to the learning environment as well as the type of instructional environment that is necessary for the child to succeed. First, in a given content area, teachers must determine if the child needs to be presented with new knowledge. Computers have the ability to present new knowledge through a tutorial process. Second, teachers must decide if the child needs to master knowledge or skills already acquired. Computers can utilize drill and practice programs to assist the child in attainment of those skills and knowledge. Finally, the teacher must evaluate whether the child is ready to generalize previously mastered knowledge and skills to new situations. Computers can provide these opportunities through simulations or problem solving programs.

The computer can also provide basic knowledge, and it can help develop student skills as well. It is able to probe for responses that illustrate mastery of the knowledge or skill. The computer can be programmed to provide remedial instruction if it does not get a correct response by providing hints or cues for the children or by giving additional examples that illustrate the knowledge or skill. The concept of making decisions on what to teach next (e.g., remediation) is called "branching" in a software program. The computer probes for a student response, determines if the response is correct or incorrect, and then makes a decision whether to move to the next level of instruction, go to remediation, end the session, or call for the teacher to provide the additional help needed. In essence, the computer is making an instructional decision based on the student interaction, just as a good teacher would. The presentation of basic knowledge and skills by the computer combined with the ability to evaluate and remediate follows the concept of tutorial programs in which the computer is actually working as a tutor. Tutors and tutorial situations are used in teaching special education students all the time.

Flexibility

The next area to consider within the computer's ability to individualize is flexibility. One of the things teachers need to do when working with handicapped children in order to meet their individual learning needs is to be flexible in the way in which they provide information to children and in the way in which information is accepted from children. The computer can be programmed for this type of flexibility. The two modes the computer has of providing and receiving information are called "output" and "input."

Output

Output refers to the information the computer is giving to the student who is interacting with it. Computers have the capability of providing information to users in a variety of ways: graphics, text, voice, and so forth. The content of the programmed software can be designed to adjust to different cognitive or reading levels, thus better meeting learning needs of the individuals. Outputs can also be used alone or in combinations (e.g., text and voice). Just as good special education teachers often select the best mode of instruction (auditory, visual, tactile) for handicapped learners and give additional cues or clues to highlight important information, computers can be programmed to do the same. Computer outputs can utilize auditory or visual modes of presentation and in some cases can provide tactile information (e.g., operating an electrical vibrator). In the area of adjusting for cognitive or reading levels, text generated on the screen must be acceptable for the reading level of that child. Computer programs can be designed to adjust the reading level of the material being presented to the student. This is particularly important when the area of instruction is not in "reading" and inability to read directions or material that provides other information hinders learning. Generally, however, this problem currently is not well addressed in software and it is not unusual to have a primary software program that has directions requiring a high reading level. Utilizing auditory or visual modalities can also be ways to adjust for cognitive or reading level discrepancies in handicapped children. State of the art software such as that used on the Apple Macintosh computers use icons (pictures representing functions) rather than menus of words. Another method of adapting for reading level is to utilize an auditory channel and have "voice synthesizer" available to read the direction to the child.

Modality of presenting instruction relates to more than just adjusting to students' cognitive or reading levels. It is a critical component in adapting to the learning style and needs of the handicapped learner. The computer has a variety of flexible modes in which to present information. For visual learners graphic presentation using a variety of colors highlighting important items, using white on black or other instructional methodologies, can be incorporated into learning. Graphics and textual presentations can be simple for easily distractible students or can be quite complex, with highlighted cues where necessary. Computers can also access other peripheral visual devices, such as video disc, video tapes, and filmstrips. Utilizing the visual modality allows teachers to present information in a more concrete manner as well as to present material that is difficult to describe, such as motion. For example, teaching sign language to a hearing impaired child requires the presentation of a model. Video tape or video disc can use a visual model to teach that concept individually, allowing the teacher to work on refining the hand movements of the child after the initial concept is attained.

For auditory learning, computers have the capability to utilize voice synthesis as well as to control tape recorders, record players, and so forth. Voice synthesis technology is still relatively unsophisticated. The capability of voice synthesizers to translate any text to speech is limited because they use phonetic rules, and written text is not spelled phonetically. As a result, artificial voice often results in a difficult to understand, "robot" type speech. The speech does become more understandable with practice, similar to the way in which an experienced teacher eventually learns to understand the speech of a child who has cerebral palsy. There are a number of developments in technology that should eventually overcome problems associated with artificial speech. Digitized laser audio and bubble memory are very promising (see Chapter 12). Currently, there are software packages that have libraries of words phonetically spelled and better text to speech voice synthesizers are also being marketed now due to the demand by computer programmers. There also are speech synthesis devices that contain human digitized voice on programmable memory chips. At present, the problem with these devices is the limited amounts of speech available, which reduces the potential uses of these chips.

Computers also have the ability to interact with traditional types of auditory teaching devices, such as the tape recorder. The computer can turn the tape recorder on and off. The major limitation with this is the linear design of tapes. Teachers have to know the exact sequence of instruction so that the computer turns the tape on and off appropriately. Tapes produce better speech but reduce the computer's flexibility in terms of branching for remediation, which requires random access to speech.

In some cases, the computer is able to provide tactile outputs as well. An example of this would be through the use of an automatic Braille device through which textual matter can be converted to Braille. It also should be possible to utilize robotics to provide tactile feedback to learners (e.g., a robot arm might be able to manipulate a child's hand through fine or gross motor tasks).

In summary, the computer can utilize various output modes of instruction and can even combine the various modes of output. It can utilize graphics, video, text, auditory, and tactile outputs, depending upon the needs of the child. If a child needs a multisensory approach, the computer has the capability of presenting information through multiple channels.

Input

Input is the manner in which a student provides information to the computer. Handicapped students often are impaired either physically or cognitively in the manner in which they are able to express themselves. They may have difficulty with writing or verbalization (expressive language), or they may have physical or sensory impairments that hinder their ability to communicate. Computers allow for flexibility in the way a child can communicate or interact in a learning environment.

The most common input device is the keyboard. The keyboard uses the alphanumeric system (numbers and alphabet) to allow students to type in information. The keyboard can be adapted so that only one key or set of keys is used for inputs. An example of this might be dividing the keyboard in half so that pressing any key on the left side provides a "yes" response and any key on the right is a "no" response. In some cases, particularly with physically handicapped children or children who would be too distracted by the keyboard, other types of input are desirable. Another type of input would be electronic pads or electronic communication boards. These are often called adapted keyboards, since they often can provide the computer with the same input information as a keyboard, only they are adapted to meet the physical needs of handicapped users. The technology of communication boards used by the physically handicapped and the communication disabled is becoming more sophisticated. One phenomenon in the field is that many of the communication devices that have been developed and are affordable for nonspeaking populations now have outputs that can be directly linked to the computer as inputs. The computer reads them as if they were the keyboard.

By utilizing software or hardware that "emulates" or looks like keyboard inputs, it is possible to use adapted switches for input into the computer. The concept of adapted switches is something that is currently being used in research with very young handicapped and cognitively low functioning children (Behrmann & Lahm, 1984).

Computers can use sensors as well as switches or keyboards for input devices. These sensors can detect touch, movement, light, temperature, sound, and so forth. Sensors are currently being used with computers to control temperatures in buildings, to turn on lights automatically, or to detect intruders for burglar alarms. There are a number of applications for which sensors are being used to control computers for handicapped children. A wheelchair can be operated by head movements utilizing two sonar devices that sense the position of the head of the individual in the chair; in this case, head movements actually control the movement of the motorized chair. Computers can also be activated by voice so the computer recognizes a voice command and discriminates between different words or vocalizations. The ability to sense touch or pressure is another type of sensory input to the computer. Pressure-sensitive pads can discriminate X-Y coordinates. This type of device allows children to touch a picture or word, and the computer can respond accordingly. A touch screen monitor allows bypassing of the keyboard entirely, circumventing keyboard distractions and allowing direct interaction with the computer's output stimulus (e.g., graphics). When it is necessary to be sure that a child understands that interacting with a keyboard or switch results in a reaction on the monitor, a touch monitor removes another level of abstract thinking. It allows a direct interaction with the stimulus.

The flexibility of input devices, such as those described, makes it possible for children to better accommodate to their handicaps. The computer can provide a means of maximizing the capabilities of the individual to input information in an efficient manner. For example, if a child knows how to spell a word or group of words but typing or selecting the appropriate letters through an adapted keyboard is a long and laborious task, the computer can be programmed to enable that child to select the word(s) with one or two inputs through a communication program.

The final area related to input flexibility of computers that should be addressed is the ability of computers to recognize variations of an input. One of the major limitations of many computer programs is rigidity in terms of the type of input they can recognize. Computers can look for more than one response (i.e., variations on the specific input). For example, the computer program may ask, "How old are you?" If the computer is programmed to look for a numerical answer, it will accept "29," it will not accept "twenty-nine." It can, however, be programmed to accept both answers or to probe for more specific information, just as a teacher might do when trying to elicit a specific answer.

Pacing and Practice

Handicapped learners have basically been identified as deviant, i.e., they do not learn at the same rate or in the same way as most other children. Therefore, one of the most predominant characteristics of teaching special students has been the necessity to pace instruction to individual learner needs to allow as much practice as the student needs to master a skill. Practice, particularly errorless practice, is important because many handicapped children do not attain skill levels as quickly as other children. Other handicapped children, because of a physical disability, do not have the opportunity to practice certain skills. Lack of practice in language development can be seen in hearing impaired children partially because they do not have the opportunity to practice language skills in a natural way. Physically handicapped children also may not be able to practice certain fine motor skills because of their handicap.

Combining practice with appropriately paced instruction is also important. Utility of computers in individually pacing instruction is based on two characteristics of good teaching. The first is the ability of the computer to provide immediate performance feedback to students and the second is the computer's ability to collect performance data and utilize that information to make predetermined instructional decisions. These decisions can be used to provide more practice, to provide remediation (tutorial), to move to the next level of instruction, or to summon the teacher.

Computers, by the very nature of the type of interaction they have with students, provide self-paced instruction. They prompt a student for a response and then will wait until the student gives that response. Computers are infinitely patient (unlike many teachers) and will allow students whatever time is necessary to respond unless they are programmed to do otherwise. Children are able to process information, check themselves and respond in an unpressured situation.

The concept of pacing instruction using computers relates not only to slowing down instruction, but also to incorporating the ability to speed up instruction. Students do not have to wait for a teacher to finish with another child before being asked to respond to another item. This is a particularly important characteristic for gifted and talented children and for children who are motivated to work independently. In addition, the capacity of the computer to allow unlimited practice, adjust to the rate of the student, and provide immediate feedback on errors will allow the building of fluency, that is, improvements in both speed and accuracy, which are common problems for many handicapped children.

The concept of self-paced, self-correcting instructional materials is not new. The literature in education generally concedes that immediate feedback on correct or incorrect responses is highly beneficial to the learning process (Mercer, Mercer, & Bott, 1984). Efficiently providing feedback quickly to all students in a class has always been a problem for teachers. In the 1960s, programmed textbooks were popular. Students were presented material in textbooks, responded to questions, and then were able to check their answers on the following page. This did begin to address the issue of providing immediate feedback and, when students did not succumb to looking up answers before responding, it provided a way to evaluate student performance and provide quick feedback. What this process did not address, however, was the second important component of self-paced instruction—the ability to evaluate performance immediately and automatically provide remediation or drill and practice when necessary.

Computers have the capacity to be programmed to make instructional decisions based on student responses. Teachers can predetermine the mastery level at which they believe a student should perform. The computer can then use that information to decide whether to move to the next level of instruction, provide more opportunity to practice a skill, move to remediation, or alert the teacher that the student is experiencing difficulty in mastering the skill. Thus, it is the ability of the computer to utilize student response data to make instructional decisions that differentiates computer assisted instruction from other instructional media as a means to facilitate good individualized, self-paced instruction.

COMPUTER PROGRAMMING AND INSTRUCTIONAL METHODOLOGY

One of the most common comments from teachers regarding the use and application of computers is, "It's all Greek to me. I can't understand how they work or what they can do and don't have the time to learn to program one." As can be seen in the previous section, computers can work in special education much as good teachers do. They can ease the instructional burdens of teachers and improve learning in children. Now that good instructional computer programs have been developed, so long as the teacher has the skills he or she should have in selecting instructional materials to meet the needs of their handicapped learners, knowing how the computer works and how to program one is not mandatory or even strongly suggested. However, exceptional children do have a way of "falling between the cracks" and sometimes the instructional materials available "don't quite fit the needs of the child." In these cases, teacher-made materials are often the answer. So, with computers, some knowledge of how they work and how programs are constructed is desirable.

Criterion Referenced Testing and Task Analysis

Special educators are lucky, because two of the most important skills in which they have extensive training provide an excellent framework from which to view programming concepts. These are criterion referenced testing and task analysis.

Criterion referenced testing can be defined as measuring performance against an instructional objective. In a tutorial session in which a teacher probes a child for a specific response, the child can respond only one of two ways, correctly or incorrectly. While the child can "be close" if a specific instructional criterion is set, the answer must be one or the other. A computer uses this method to determine if the child's input is correct or incorrect, measuring that response against predetermined correct "criteria." The computer, according to its programmed instructions, makes a decision. In programming this is considered an "if. . .then" statement. For example, if the student gives the correct answer, then ask the next question. If the student gives the wrong answer, then ask the question again. Sophisticated programs have the capability of asking the question a predetermined number of times and if the student does not meet criterion, the program provides remediation. As mentioned previously, there does not have to be only one correct response, but the response must fall into the selection of correct responses. The inputs of "twenty-nine" and "29" can be correct and all other inputs incorrect; that is, they do not meet the criteria for a correct response. When it is not processing the last input, the computer is always waiting to evaluate whether the next input is correct or incorrect before it processes that information and acts according to the program instructions.

When children are unable to meet a criterion of acceptable performance that is set by their teachers, the most common "best practices" approach to determining what to teach in order to have the student attain that skill is a *task analytic approach*. According to Williams and Gotts (1977) a task analysis can usually be done in seven steps: (1) delineate the behavioral objective; (2) review any relevant instructional resources; (3) derive and sequence the component skills of the objective; (4) eliminate unnecessary component skills; (5) eliminate redundant components; (6) determine prerequisite skills; and (7) monitor student performance and revise sequences accordingly.

The process of developing an instructional software package follows a similar procedure. As with any instruction, the delineation of goals and objectives for the software is the first critical step. Next, the logical thing to do is review available software to determine what is available and what is needed. If software is available, the developer must determine whether spending the time and money to develop a better package is feasible.

Once the decision is made to develop the instructional software, the developer must derive and sequence the components of the software program. This third step is done in two stages. First, the developer must determine the components that must be incorporated and make a programming plan. This plan usually is in the form of a *flowchart*. Planning the flowchart is generally where expertise from professional educators is most important. The next part of this step is sequencing the components. Computer programs are read by the computer in a linear sequence. That is why program lines are numbered 10, 20, 30, and so forth. They are usually given in increments of 10 because this system allows the programmer the flexibility to change the program by adding line 11 or 12 without having to renumber the entire sequence.

Step four of the task analysis model attempts to eliminate unnecessary components. While the actual programming does not have to be done by the teacher, it is a good idea to work with a programmer during development. This allows the teacher to determine whether the software program is performing to expectation, and allows the programmer to make suggested deletions or additions more easily.

The fifth step of a task analysis eliminates redundant components. Computers achieve this task by utilizing "subroutines" or "procedures." In BASIC, when a programmer has already developed a routine that performs a function or component that will be used over, he or she does not have to reprogram all of the lines. Rather, a GOSUB statement is used to send the program to the first line of that component. For example, at line 1000, if the input was yes, then the programmer might write GOSUB 2500. The computer would then start working from line 2500 to the end of the subroutine (marked "return") and then return to the next line following line 1000. The programming language LOGO uses a similar concept called procedures. An example would be to program a box and a triangle. To build a house, instead of programming a box with a triangle on top, the program would tell the computer to place the "triangle procedure" on top of the "box procedure."

The sixth step of the task analysis is to determine the prerequisite skills of the student user. As with any instruction, this is a critical component to successful learning. Depending on the sophistication of the software design, the software may "pretest" the child to evaluate prerequisite skills or provide documentation to allow teachers to determine the appropriateness of the software application for a given student. The importance of allowing teachers to evaluate the appropriateness of software and determine whether students have the prerequisite skills to successfully use it cannot be overstated.

The final step of a task analysis is to monitor performance and revise the sequence accordingly. In the program development process, this is often called "alpha" and "beta" testing. In alpha testing, the completed program is tested by the teacher to make sure there are no "bugs," and the program does what it was designed to do. In beta testing, the completed program is put to the acid test and used with students. The concept of monitoring student performance is also a characteristic of good instructional software. The program, utilizing preprogrammed criterion decision rules, can make instructional decisions based on student performance. Thus, the program can revise the instructional sequence and branch to remediation or more drill and practice, or even jump to more challenging levels when a student is doing well.

Flowcharting

The content of this chapter has been directed toward elucidating how the training of special educators relates to the learning needs of handicapped children and showing how the "best teaching practices" to meet those needs can be found with the characteristics of computers and good instructional software programs. The increasing sophistication of software and hardware may soon make it possible for teachers to easily program instructional software without knowing a rather complex programming language. There are already a number of simple authoring languages, such as Planit, Tutor, and Pilot, which have very few command statements to learn. An even simpler format is utilizing authoring systems, which use built-in logic, requiring the teacher only to fill in the type of presentation, questions and answers, type and schedule for feedback, and remediation sequences for incorrect responses. Authoring systems include such programs as Ticcit, Genis Courseware Development System, Blocks, and GraForth II (Taber, 1983).

Whether teachers choose to learn a higher level programming language, use an authoring language or system, or work with a sophisticated programmer, the most important component of developing quality instructional software is planning. Teachers trained in special education should be able to draw on their knowledge and experience in curriculum and instructional design and combine these with the concepts discussed in this chapter to develop such software. To make the process efficient, this planning should be systematic, and, as a good IEP does, it should show what the instructional objectives are and how the teacher plans to achieve those objectives. While the concept of flowcharting is not the only way to do such planning, it provides a structured format that will enhance communication with programmers, with whom most teachers probably will be working.

The concept of flowcharting is relatively simple. Figure 2–1 lists the five components usually found in a flowchart: The Start or Stop component signifies the beginning or end of a program; the processing instruction indicates that an action is being performed by the computer; the input component signifies what the user must "put in" to the computer; the output component signifies what the computer "puts out;" the decision component indicates that a choice must be made about correct and incorrect responses; and the flowlines connecting the components show what happens next.

A simple flowchart of the Task Analytic process is shown in Figure 2–2. When following the process, keep in mind that all movement proceeds in the direction of the flowlines. In this flowchart the first symbol marks the start of the process. The second, a processing component, shows the teacher delineating the behavioral objective. A process component follows as relevant resources are gathered. An output product charting both the objectives and the available resources is presented for review. In the next processing component, the objectives are matched with available resources. A decision is then made: if appropriate resources are available, the process stops; if not, the process of deriving the components of the task analysis occurs. The next process is to sequence the components of the task. Then an output results in a list of sequenced components. The next step, the process of reviewing the components, leads to a decision question: Are the components properly sequenced? If the answer is no, the flow returns to sequencing the components; if yes, the next decision point occurs: Are there

Figure 2-1

Start or Stop

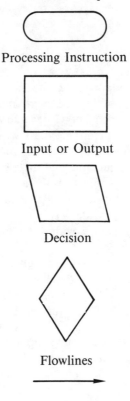

Processing Instruction

Input or Output

Decision

Flowlines

unnecessary components? A yes response brings the flow back to deriving the components of the objective. A no response leads to yet another decision: Are there redundant components? If so, we are led back to deriving the components; if not, we are led to the next process, determining the prerequisite skills to the objective. Again, a decision question arises: Does the student have the prerequisite skills? If the student does not, the flow returns to deriving the components. If the student does have the prerequisite skills, the next process is to monitor student performance. We now face a new decision point: Did the student achieve the objective? If the response is no, the flow once more returns to deriving components of the objective. If the response is yes, the task analysis is successfully completed and we exit (or stop).

Figure 2–2. Flowchart: Task Analytic Process.

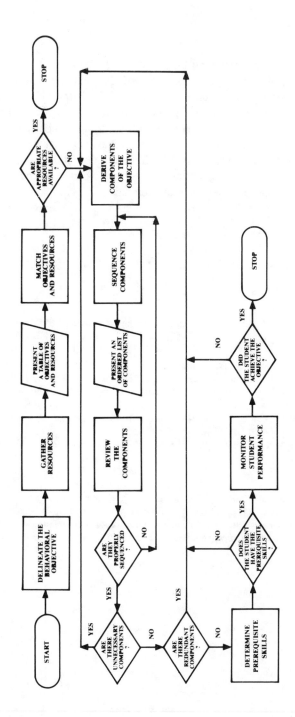

CONCLUSION

As computers become more common in the schools, fear of operating them or of applying them to the needs of handicapped children should begin to decrease. There are many ways in which the characteristics of computers match how handicapped children need to learn and the ways in which special education teachers are trained to meet those needs. Special education and related services personnel have extensive training and experience and, as discussed in this chapter, these skills and knowledge can be utilized in applying technology. Synthesis of new knowledge and skills is always easier when they are related to previous learning, and it is those skills that teachers bring to the computerized environment that will mandate the development of high quality instructional software.

REFERENCES

Abeson, A., & Weintraub, F. (1977). Understanding the individual education program. In S. Torres (Ed.). *A primer on individualized education programs for handicapped children*. Reston, VA: Foundation for Exceptional Children.

Behrmann, M., & Lahm, L. (1984). Critical learning: Multiply handicapped babies get on-line. In M. Behrmann & L. Lahm (Eds.), *Proceedings of the national conference on the use of microcomputers in special education* (pp. 181-193). Reston, VA: Council for Exceptional Children.

Mercer, C., Mercer, A., & Bott, D. (1984). *Self-correcting learning materials for the classroom*. Columbus, OH: Charles Merrill.

Sloane, H., Buckholdt, D., Jenson, W., & Crandall, J. (1979). *Structured teaching*. Champaign, IL: Research Press.

Taber, F. (1983). *Microcomputers in special education*. Reston, VA: Council for Exceptional Children.

White, O., & Haring, N. (1980). *Exceptional teaching*. Columbus, OH: Charles Merrill.

Williams, W., & Gotts, E. (1977). Selected considerations on developing curriculum for severely handicapped students. In E. Sontag, (Ed.), *Educational programming for the severely and profoundly handicapped*. Reston, VA: Council for Exceptional Children.

CHAPTER 3

Types of Computer
Applications

Current microcomputer applications in special education fall into three broad categories: computer assisted management (CAM) is used by school officials to track and manage personnel and student demographics, to handle statistics for inventory and resource allocation, and to generate reports for state and federal requirements. With computer managed instruction (CMI), teachers utilize the computer for data collection, data analysis regarding student achievement, and assistance in writing reports and instructional education programs (IEPs). The third category, computer assisted instruction (CAI), is used in the classroom for direct student instruction. The concept of CAI incorporates the use of computers both as an instructional medium and as a student tool for working in the learning environment (e.g., word processing).

COMPUTER ASSISTED MANAGEMENT

School districts are already using computers for a multitude of tasks: to keep records for state, federal, and local requirements, to schedule classes, to report grades and attendance, to bill for transportation or therapies, and to prepare budgets, among other things. These applications fall into a category called "information management." The computer can also be used to predict needs regarding related services, enrollment, teachers, and materials (Wilson, 1982). In these types of applications the computer is being used as a "decision support" system, with the computer providing educational decision-makers with a set of tools to utilize information in a more data-based, efficient manner.

Table 3–1 lists some of the applications of computers in special education administration.

The educational use of computers in these areas is similar to computer applications in business, and as it does for them, it probably will increase efficiency in office staff, personnel, and building procedures. The increase

---

This chapter was authored by Michael M. Behrmann.

Table 3-1. Specific Applications of Computers in Special Education Administration

Student Tracking

    Counts of students screened, assessed, placed, and reviewed
    Status of student due process and compliance with P. L. 94-192
    Child counts cross-referenced by class, teacher, school, and handicap
    Lists of incomplete information on student records
    Maintaining health history and special medication

Finance and Budget

    Reimbursement computation according to state and federal formulas
    Audit trails for program placement and review
    Financial planning programs for "what if" analysis and budget
      planning

Reporting

    Generation of standard local, state, and federal reports
    Reports on student achievement and evaluation status
    Detailed records and summaries of diagnostic testing
    Interactive creation of IEP goals and objectives from curriculum files
    Generation of quarterly student reports

Communication

    Personalized mailings to parents regarding IEP and review meetings
    Recommending appropriate activities for students
    Electronic mail to staff and other professionals

Resource Management

    Locating learning materials
    Describing diagnostic materials
    Interactive access to related service information– e.g., transportation

---

of efficiency may well save administration costs, allowing more money to be used for direct instruction of children.

Information Access

One of the most powerful technology benefits for administrators is access to more and better information. The computer is a valuable link with other professionals in the field. Electronic networking through computers is a source of information gathering and synthesis that is becoming more and more important. Access to nationwide expertise and resources as well as to local information will provide a better and more efficient means of administering special education programs.

Bibliographic Information

Access to various data bases is an area that is expanding with the increased number of stand-alone computers with telecommunications capabilities. Data bases such as ERIC, which used to be available almost exclusively through libraries, are now available at the home or office. Bibliographic Retrieval Services (BRS) is the primary vehicle to access a variety of data bases. BRS can access a number of sources of information on the handicapped including CEC's ERIC Clearinghouse on Handicapped and Gifted Children. Other data bases on the handicapped include the Handicapped Exchange (HEX) and Vital Information (VI), a national clearinghouse on software that includes information on software for the handicapped.

Communication

There are also a number of different services available for instant nationwide communications, with The Source and Compuserve among the most well known. These information networks, however, are aimed at general audiences, and are neither sophisticated enough nor have the critical mass of special education subscribers to be of value to most professionals. Special educators have a telecommunications service—SpecialNet—which is dedicated primarily to their interests. To use it, individuals must have access to either a terminal, a microcomputer, or a word processor with telephone communication capability (modem). By calling a local or "800" telephone number, a subscriber is connected directly to the GTE Telenet Service nationwide system of computers through which information is transmitted. The Telenet system is able to relay messages in electronic postcards or "packets" through the most economical routes. Once at their destination, these "packets" are reassembled to form the original message. It is possible that different parts of the message traveled to the final destination via completely different paths.

Formed in 1982, SpecialNet boasts over 2000 accounts in 50 states, Canada, Guam, Puerto Rico, and Australia. Many accounts have several users, and they represent state and local education agencies, resource centers, colleges and universities, handicapped education projects, and the federal Education Department. Thus, the number of actual users, who may also be information sources for others, makes this a powerful national information network.

An information network's uses are varied, ranging from data collection and information management to sharing resources and solutions to educational or administrative problems. There are two major categories for communicating. "Electronic mail" is a system of sending private or group messages instantly from one place to another via computer. "Electronic bulletin boards" display mail for semipublic or public information.

Personal Communication. With electronic mail, the computer bypasses delays and personnel costs that normally occur in drafting, editing, and sending a letter through the United States Mail or express mail services. The system can use word processing software so that messages can be edited easily on the computer terminal or messages can be typed directly on-line. Longer messages can be precomposed on a word processor or microcomputer to save money, and "uploaded" into the system. Users are charged for the amount of "connect" time on the system. Therefore, precomposing long messages before connecting to the system provides the most economical way of sending information from point A to point B. Depending upon the time of day and amount of time "on-line," electronic mail costs are comparable or lower than the cost of other methods of communicating quickly over long distances. If desired, a "return receipt" can be requested for any message sent, which will show the exact minute it was received and read. Electronic communication formerly was highly technical, required special telephone lines, and was more or less limited to engineers or computer experts. Now, using simple commands and "user friendly" software, mail and even professional articles are transmitted by the growing number of special educators who have computer terminals.

Creative Uses of Electronic Mail. From coast to coast, special educators using SpecialNet are finding multiple uses for the electronic mail system. State education agency officials in Alaska, Kansas, West Virginia, and Missouri, for example, conduct business efficiently with their local school districts using a preset user list. These lists are easily changed or can remain permanent. Subscribers of the newsletter *Education Daily* can elect the option of receiving it electronically. Pennsylvania's school districts, intermediate units, and colleges and universities use the mail system to report state and federal data about handicapped students and conduct research surveys. Pennsylvania has also developed a special education management information system on handicapped individuals of ages from birth to 21 years.

Posted Communication. The second major use of an electronic communication system is the posting of public or semipublic information on national, statewide, or local "bulletin boards." Here electronic mail is displayed by subject area or special purpose. Hundreds of local user groups have started their own bulletin boards, usually centered on sharing information related to a specific type of computer, e.g., an Apple User Group. To start a bulletin board, all that is required is a computer, a modem that can answer the telephone, and a communication package and program that allows callers to access and post information on the bulletin board.

There are more than 25 different national bulletin boards on SpecialNet. They are managed, for the most part, by education experts but include professionals from the fields of technology and law. The National Association of State Directors of Special Education (NASDSE), for which SpecialNet was developed, manages several boards. On the "Federal" board, NASDSE posts messages about the activities of the Congress, including items on special education legislation and the budget. The "RFP" board has a broad range of entries, including rehabilitation, arts, transportation, and migrant education. A local school administrator might want to check boards routinely or post notices devoted to computer applications, mechanical and electronic aids for physically handicapped, early childhood, deafness, upcoming conferences, or job openings.

Perhaps the board that draws its information from the widest range of SpecialNet users is "Exchange." Here, special educators request answers to problems and post information that may be of use to others in the field. Hard-to-answer questions are always forwarded to appropriate professionals in the field and SpecialNet ensures a response to each inquiry.

The following are examples of the way in which the "Exchange" board is used: A local district in Montana that was looking for a specific kind of adaptive equipment had a reply from an occupational therapist from Kentucky. A request from a local special education director in Illinois for computer literacy materials for psychologists brought six responses from around the country. In another case, eleven school districts volunteered to field test a curriculum developed in Philadelphia for deaf-blind children. Similarly, an educator asked for suggestions for materials for regular classroom programs for a gifted quadriplegic cerebral palsy student who was starting kindergarten. The board has also been used to find replication sites for research and program implementation, as well as provide information on teacher education program development.

COMPUTER MANAGED INSTRUCTION

The second type of computer application in special education brings the impact of high technology directly to the classroom teacher. It is called computer managed instruction (CMI). Burke (1982) has defined CMI as the systematic control of instruction by the computer. It is characterized by testing, diagnosing, learning prescription, and thorough record keeping. It is the products of the CMI program that form the basis of monitoring and developing individualized education programs. This is an important application in special education because P.L. 94-142 holds teachers "accountable" for having a method of evaluating student progress toward the goals and objectives described in the IEP. Computer managed instruction can be a stand-alone system operated and utilized by a single teacher or a small group of teachers; alternatively, the data it collects and analyzes can be the schoolwide data base that is used in computer assisted management (CAM).

Currently, there are two major utilizations of CMI for special educators. The first is computerized IEP programs. Systems of generating IEPs can be based on district-wide program of studies school- or a teacher-based curriculum. Teachers are able to diagnose children's problems, select goals and objectives from a data bank, or write their own and generate written IEPs for their children with a minimum of effort. Some programs may even have the ability to monitor achievement of those goals and objectives as well as generate regular reports to parents. Others have the ability to cross-reference objectives with several curricula in guides or in teaching activities. IEP computer-based programs can, however, limit the education of handicapped children if they are not flexible or do not allow the individualization of goals and objectives to meet children's needs rather than school system or computer software needs and capabilities.

The second use for CMI that is of particular importance to teachers and administrators is the development of software programs that collect and analyze student performance data. One example of this type of software is a program called AimStar. This software program, written for a microcomputer, allows teachers to collect data on children's performance utilizing the principles of precision teaching. Teachers can enter individual student performance data into the computer at the end of the day, or a skilled programmer can construct data files readable by AimStar that are collected directly via the computer. The teacher determines the instructional strategy, chooses the kind of data to be recorded (e.g., accuracy, interval data, latency), and determines the specific objectives and the rate at which a student is expected to achieve mastery (for example, the student taught a list of words via flashcards will be correct 95% of the time by June 31). Finally, the computer can conduct an analysis based upon data decision rules developed by White and Haring (1980). A program readout indicates whether the child is proceeding at the expected rate, performing at an accelerated rate, or not performing at the rate expected. For poor achievers, the computer will suggest changing the instructional strategy.

The type of record keeping and data analysis done by such a computer managed instruction program addresses two of the major problems that teacher trainers often observe in the field. Many teachers tend either to collect no data at all (because it is too complicated or time consuming) or collect reams of data and never use the data to make instructional decisions (because there is too much information to process easily). The type of program just discussed requires little or no teacher time beyond the initial collection of data. It takes 5 or 10 minutes at the end of the day to enter performance data. It is important to note that data entered at 3PM or later by the teacher often uses the same equipment children used during the day for computer assisted instruction. Thus, the cost-effectiveness of computers is significantly increased.

Computer managed instruction has the capability to positively influence the education of handicapped children. As mentioned earlier, it provides a means for teachers to record, analyze, understand, and act upon a large quantity of information. The key to truly benefiting from computer managed information and not letting it "stack up," like students' graded papers, depends upon the teacher's view of how data can be utilized. If teachers believe that systematic record keeping can lead to implementing more effective instructional programs for children and are willing to rely on data, rather than solely on intuition and experience, then computer managed instruction can make that process more efficient. However, the data must be collected and *used* or the computer will turn into a very expensive filing cabinet.

COMPUTER ASSISTED INSTRUCTION

The third area of computer application, computer assisted instruction (CAI), also directly affects teachers. CAI can be viewed from two distinctly different perspectives. The first is to look at computers as an instructional medium. The primary objective of utilizing them as such is to impart knowledge or skills, or both, to learners. The second perspective is to view computers as a tool for children to use to facilitate the learning process. As a tool, the primary objective of the computer is to assist the learner in the manipulation of information or materials in a curricular domain in which the computer is not being used for direct instruction.

Computers as Instructional Media

In order to understand the possible roles of computers in instruction it is necessary first to describe and define an instructional hierarchy in which computers can be utilized and second to define the types of computer software that are available and identify where they can fit into the instructional hierarchy.

Successful instruction of handicapped learners is based on the teacher's successfully attending to four basic steps or processes: assessment of instructional need; determination of what to teach; identification of the instructional level, and evaluation of ongoing progress (Given, 1984). Table 3-2 provides a version of Given's instructional hierarchy adapted to determining instructional applications for computers.

Assessment

The concept of assessment is basic to meeting the individual needs of handicapped learners. Information gleaned through formal and informal testing and observation provide the basis for the development and implementation of the IEP. That is, teachers need to have accurate information on what a child can do (current performance), what he or she has learned (past performance), strengths and weaknesses, and ways the child learns best. In addition to performance in various curriculum domains, assessment should answer questions related to the child's learning style. Questions germane to assessment related to CAI would be the following: Is the child an independent worker? Does he or she learn best using auditory, visual, or tactile processes or combinations of these processes? What kinds of reinforcement work with the child? What is the child's reading level? Is the child highly distractible? What is the child's attention span? What kind of learning environments does the child function best in?

What To Teach Next

The second level of the instructional hierarchy determines what to teach. It focuses on establishing priorities of what should be taught to the child. Decisions made here articulate the objectives for levels 3 and 4, identifying type of instruction and evaluating progress. There is only a limited amount of instructional time available, and it is important to provide instruction that will be most beneficial to the child. Using the information from initial assessments and the recommended program of studies, teachers must determine the subject areas to be addressed. Depending on the nature and severity of the child's disability and placement (e.g., resource room, special class, and so forth), instruction may encompass one subject, such as mathematics, or all subject areas. Once the subject area(s) are identified, the components of the subject(s) must be identified. Specific curricular decisions are involved at this level. Many school districts have specified programs of study for both regular and special education. Identifying at what level a student is performing within the appropriate program is critical here, particularly identification of areas in which the student has deficiencies that need remediation. With students who have serious

Table 3-2. Computer Assisted Instructional Hierarchy*

1. Assessment of Instructional Need
   a. Interview
   b. Testing
   c. Observation

2. Determination of What to Teach (What Do I Teach?)
   a. Subject Area(s)
   b. Components
   c. Scope and Sequence
   d. Decide when CAI is beneficial compared with other modes of instruction

3. Identification of Instructional Level (Where Do I Begin Instruction?)
   a. *Tutorial Software*: Acquiring New Skill or Knowledge (specific instruction is needed)
      (1) Computer introduces skill ("This is _____.")
         (a) Specific instruction is given
         (b) Mnemonic cues are used to aid storage and recall
         (c) Student repeats and copies skill
         (d) Student relates skill to his or her life
      (2) Student recognizes item ("Find another_____.")
         (a) Student matches item with like item
      (3) Student identifies item ("Show me _____.")
         (a) Without matching student picks out item from samples
         (b) Student selects item from several samples; aided recall
      (4) Student produces item
         (a) Student uses total recall to perform task, such as read the word, write the letter, compute the problem, etc.
   b. *Drill and Practice Software*: Developing Proficiency of Skill
      (1) Student consistently produces skill accurately
      (2) Student consistently produces skill accurately at an acceptable rate/pace
   c. *Simulation Software*: Generalizing New Skill (problem-solving with mastered skill)
      (1) Student uses skill in games and novel situations
      (2) Student adapts and applies skill to new situations

4. Evaluation of Ongoing Progress/Feedback
   a. Error Tracking (keeping track of correct and incorrect responses)
   b. Charting (recording progress for student motivation)
   c. Changing instruction if progress is not being made
   d. Providing feedback to students

*Adapted from Given, B. (1984). *The instructional hierarchy*. (unpublished paper). Fairfax, VA: George Mason University.

deficiencies, particularly older students, it may be necessary to make decisions as to what components of instruction will be most functional to the student when he or she leaves school, rather than what comes next in the curriculum.

Once the subject area and components are identified, the teacher must determine the scope and sequence of instruction. Here, the concept of task sequencing (structuring the sequence of tasks to be taught) and task analysis (breaking the instructional task into teachable components) are important. It is at this level of the instructional decision-making process that determination of potential application of computer assisted instruction occurs. Surveying relevant instructional materials is an important step in task analysis (Williams & Gotts, 1977). Teachers need to look at their instructional objectives to determine whether application of computer based instruction can be beneficial. If the objective is better suited to group instruction or if social interaction is desirable, use of a computer may not be desirable. If the objective is amenable to computer use, the teacher must determine whether there are appropriate computer software programs available to meet the instructional objective(s). Teachers should also consider the possibility of incorporating computers as only one part of the instructional scope and sequence. Computers should be viewed as a supplemental mode of instruction in most cases, and it is important to evaluate their potential benefits within the perspective of the entire instructional hierarchy. (See Chapter 10 for a more detailed description of how to evaluate the potential benefits of a computer software program.) Finally, and also included within the scope of a task analysis, the teacher should determine how best to motivate and reinforce the student to achieve the instructional objective. Computers are particularly motivating to students because of the personal interaction available and systematic and consistent reinforcement in good software. Students are also able to make mistakes and correct them without having peers or teachers see them. Additionally, good instructional software can provide appropriate competitive and challenging activities, as are found in many programs that utilize a game format.

Level of Instruction

Level three of the instructional hierarchy is where the three major types of instructional software are found. The three major components of identifying the instructional level of the learner are: (1) acquiring new skill or knowledge; (2) developing proficiency with the skill or knowledge; and (3) generalizing the new skill or knowledge. The corresponding types of instructional software are: (1) tutorials; (2) drill and practice; and (3) simulations.

Tutorial Software. The first step in learning is the acquisition of a new skill or knowledge. This is often done through a process called "tutoring." In a systematic hierarchical structure (note that not all learning occurs systematically), the student must first be presented with or introduced to the concept. Specific instruction can be given by the tutor (or computer) and the student should be provided with mechanisms to recall the concept, repeat or copy it, and relate it to previous learning. Next the student should be able to recognize the concept or object (matching) and then differentiate it from other, similar concepts or objects. Finally, the student should be able to produce the skill or knowledge using only recall (no clues provided).

Hofmeister (1984) notes that one of the characteristics attributed to good teaching in special education is that of insightful, empathic, and effective tutoring. *Tutorial* software can assist the student in the acquisition and basic mastery of new skills and knowledge. Characteristics of good tutorial software should include the following:

1. A pretest to determine relevant prerequisite knowledge or skill as well as the level of knowledge or skill related to the particular instructional objective of the tutorial. This information relates specifically to Levels 1 and 2 of the instructional hierarchy—assessment and determination of what to teach. With good software, both the teacher and the computer can engage in assessment of performance (prerequisite skill levels) and determination of where to begin teaching.

2. A method of providing immediate feedback to students on correct or incorrect responses. As noted in Chapter 2, student feedback is a critical element to effective learning. The concepts of contingent reinforcement and motivation are also important here.

3. A means of providing correct answers and cues to help learners discover the right answer or the right problem-solving process. This approach can assist the learner to move through a structured problem-solving process that should assist the student to develop an internal structure for remembering the skill or concept (Mercer, Mercer, & Bott, 1984).

4. A method of "branching" to a more detailed (task analyzed), fine-grained remedial presentation or to similar items that allow practice when errors are made by the student.

5. A record-keeping process. This tutorial software characteristic relates to level four of the instructional hierarchy (evaluation of ongoing programs). The tutorial program should not only be able to identify the number and percentage of errors that a student makes but also have a means to identify the types of errors made (error analysis). This information will provide the teacher with data upon which to develop other methods of instruction to meet individual learner needs. It will also allow teachers to differentiate between idiosyncratic errors and patterns of errors that a child makes.

Hofmeister (1984) suggests that a more sophisticated level of tutorial type program is an "artificial intelligence-based system" in which a tutorial program can simulate the actions of a human expert tutor. In this approach, the data collected on student performance are cumulatively used by the computer to make instructional decisions when to branch to remediation or move to a higher level of instruction. The computer utilizes preprogrammed formulas such as those developed by White and Haring (1980) in their precision teaching data decision rules. Instructional decisions can then be made based on probability statistics, both for the individual student or for data collected on other pupils tested previously. In the long run, instructional decisions could be made much more intelligently and instructional strategies could be changed more quickly, resulting in more efficient instruction to handicapped students.

Drill and Practice. Providing handicapped students with the opportunity to master skills and knowledge at a high level of proficiency is common special education practice. With many of our handicapped students, the concept of overlearning is critical to the maintenance and generalization of skills and knowledge. Drill and practice software thus has an important role in the instructional hierarchy for handicapped children. Drill and practice programs are most appropriately used for subject matter that needs to be mastered to facilitate effective performance of higher level skills after the concepts related to these skills have been taught (Hofmeister, 1984). Once these skills have been mastered, they may be expected to be used in the next level of the instructional hierarchy— generalizing to a new situation.

There has been much criticism of drill and practice educational programs because much of the software is poorly designed. These programs are relatively abundant because they are easy to program. They do not require the sophisticated type of programming that is necessary in developing a tutorial program. As can be seen in the instructional hierarchy, drill and practice is only one small part of the learning process. Much of this software is marketed as a method of teaching new concepts or skills which it fails to do. Additionally, many drill and practice programs fail to provide adequate data collection that will yield helpful information for teachers. As with tutorials, drill and practice programs should provide error tracking and error analysis information for teachers.

Simulation. The highest level of the instructional hierarchy is providing opportunities that allow students to apply knowledge or skills previously mastered in new or novel situations or use them to solve problems. Simulation software may incorporate some of the characteristics of tutorial programs, but central to their design, they reflect real-life situations or environments (i.e., they simulate a specific true event). There are consequences to student inputs or responses and characteristically there are no correct or incorrect answers. Like the tutorial, student inputs are analyzed and the program branches to the appropriate situation. Unlike the tutorial, student inputs are utilized as only one variable in the total program sequence. The student suffers the consequences of decisions or enjoys the successes of the end result. Simulations are commonly utilized in situations in which training would be extremely costly or mistakes could be disastrous. Airline pilots, for example, are initially trained using simulation software since an accident in an airplane could be both expensive and hazardous.

A potentially dramatic use of simulation could utilize a video disc simulation for mobility training of severely handicapped individuals. A video presentation could be developed of mass transportation through a local community, filming the various buses or subways that could be used. Each route, with all stops and the various destinations, could be filmed (even so far as entering buildings, such as supermarkets, places of employment, and so forth). The classroom based software simulation could then offer the handicapped student with a safe and realistic opportunity to determine which bus to take, where to get off, what to do if the wrong options were selected, and so forth. This mode of presentation provides the ability to teach a population that characteristically has difficulty in generalizing with a much more real life training environment and in a manner that may be less hazardous and intensive to achieve the instructional objectives. (See Chapter 12 for a more detailed description of video disc technology.)

Evaluation of Ongoing Progress

As can be inferred from the incorporation of good data collection and analysis in the three types of software programs discussed previously, ongoing evaluation is critical to the teaching process. Computers offer educators a means of collecting and analyzing greater quantities of data than were previously feasible using traditional teaching techniques and data collection procedures. Computers also make it possible to provide a finer grained analysis of data. More discrete error analysis is possible to discern patterns of errors in such areas as evaluation of writing samples, correct or incorrect responses, latency of responses, rate, and so forth. It is also possible to build visual displays of data into instructional software and utilize the computer to make data based decisions for branching to other levels of instruction.

Instructional technology in special education has developed a significant reliance on data collection and analysis of student progress. The passage of P.L. 94-142 has made teachers accountable for providing a method of evaluating student progress toward IEP goals and objectives. The advent of the computer should help teachers carry out this mandatory and necessary level of the instructional process more efficiently.

THE COMPUTER AS A TOOL IN LEARNING

Its ability to be used as a tool as well as an instructional medium is what really differentiates the computer from other instructional media (filmstrips, teaching machines, and so forth). This medium can be utilized to teach children skills and knowledge, but they also need to be taught the fundamentals of operating and managing the equipment as a tool for learning or as a tool for accommodating to a handicapping condition. Hofmeister (1984) suggests that only about 7% of the handicapped population will utilize the microcomputer as an assistive device to interact with their environment. (This type of utilization will be discussed in detail in Chapter 6.) However, tool uses include such applications as word processing and programming. A broad spectrum of handicapped children can be thus expected to make use of the computer as a tool in learning. As a tool, the computer allows easy access to and manipulation of information that previously was a burden to deal with. By removing that burden and frustration, handicapped individuals have a better chance of keeping up with their peers. For example, the learning disabled student with fine motor problems who previously was frustrated by writing and research can now use word processing and electronic encyclopedias. The ease of information production and manipulation allow the objective of the learning task—writing—to be met. A similar example is in the area of programming. With the edit features of most programming languages (for example, BASIC and LOGO), the burden of producing written code is lessened. Additionally, programming a computer often leads to advanced abstract cognitive development, particularly in the area of mathematics and logic.

Computers are already pervasive in our society. Calculators, once viewed as advanced technology, are now incorporated into watches and pens. Banking and shopping can be done from home via computers. Society is truly beginning to utilize computers as tools to increase capability to learn as well as make life less burdensome. It is difficult to see where this new frontier will lead, for the kindergarten child of today will graduate in the year 2001, and will probably view the computer as his or her parents viewed the paper and pencil.

REFERENCES

Given, B. (1984). *The instructional hierarchy* (unpublished paper). Fairfax, VA: George Mason University.

Hofmeister, A. (1982). Microcomputers in perspective. *Exceptional Children, 49*(2), 115-122.

Hofmeister, A. (1984). The special educator in the information age. In M. Behrmann & E. Lahm, *Proceedings of the National Conference on the Use of Microcomputers in Special Education*. Reston, VA: Council for Exceptional Children.

Mercer, C., Mercer, A., & Bott, D. (1984). *Self-correcting learning materials for the classroom*. Columbus, OH: Charles Merrill.

White, O., & Haring, N. (1980). *Exceptional teaching*. Columbus, OH: Charles Merrill.

Williams, W., & Gotts, E. (1977). Selected considerations on developing curriculum for severely handicapped students. In E. Sontag (Ed.), *Educational programming for the severely and profoundly handicapped*. Reston, VA: Council for Exceptional Children.

Wilson, K. (1982). Computer systems for special educators. In J. Dominguez & A. Waldstein (Eds.), *Educational applications of electronic technology*. Seattle, WA: WESTAR, pp. 1–22.

Part II
Current Applications
in Special Education

CHAPTER 4

Using Computers to Educate Gifted Children

For over 25 years, computers have played a part in the education of gifted children. In 1957, the Soviet Union launched Sputnik, an act that thrust the world into the Space Age. With the realization that their status as a world superpower was in danger, the government of the United States began an all-out campaign to enhance the nation's scientists and mathematicians. At that time, computers were expensive and cumbersome; consequently, access to the machines for instructional purposes was limited to select groups of gifted and talented students. As the size and expense of computers have come down, however, the number of students using them has increased tremendously. Computers now play an important role in the education of all children, not only the gifted.

Although educators have come to realize the possibilities for using computers in the regular classroom, they sometimes forget that there are certain kinds of computer-related learning experiences that are especially appropriate for the gifted. This chapter focuses on those experiences. Before discussing the ways in which computers can enhance the education of gifted children, the chapter provides a brief explanation of the term "gifted" and some of the major goals of programs for gifted children.

WHO ARE THE GIFTED?

Historically, educators have tended to think of gifted children as those who are very intelligent, i.e., those who attain high scores on intelligence tests. Over the past 30 years, however, educators have come to realize that giftedness is a much broader concept; it encompasses not only intellectual ability but also creative ability and social ability. Children can be gifted in many areas: academic fields, such as mathematics, science, or languages; vocational fields, such as carpentry or mechanics; and artistic fields, such

---

This chapter was authored by Elizabeth McClellan.

as music, drama, and art. The concept of giftedness may also include notions related to achievement, motivation, physical dexterity, aesthetic sensitivity, success, and interest.

Since giftedness is such a complicated concept, saying that a particular child is gifted provides little information about the nature and extent of the student's specific abilities. Gifted children are by definition exceptional. They are endowed with capabilities that allow them to perform at higher levels than their peers. If students are to develop their abilities, they must receive educational services that are designed specifically for that purpose. In designing these services, educators must realize that not all gifted children are alike; individual differences among these children indicate that the educational services appropriate for one gifted child may not be appropriate for other gifted children.

Because many gifted children have become avid computer users, it is easy to assume that all gifted children will enjoy learning to use the computer. Although most educators agree that all students need to become computer literate, they cannot expect all students to become computer buffs. The same is true for the gifted. Not all gifted students want or need to become computer experts. Computers can, however, become a vital part of every gifted student's learning environment.

COMPUTER APPLICATIONS FOR GIFTED CHILDREN

Computers serve two ultimate purposes. They make life easier by performing tedious or time-consuming tasks, and they expand the limits of human potential by performing tasks that are beyond the capabilities of humans. A computer operates in essentially the same fashion as the human brain; it receives information, processes the information, and provides output. The raison d'être of the computer is its ability to handle tremendous amounts of information at superhuman speeds. One of the goals of computer education is to help students understand and appreciate this machine-brain analogy. The analogy is particularly important in the education of gifted children in that they can benefit from understanding how computers can maximize their human potential for processing information.

The uses of computers dovetail very nicely with the goals of education for the gifted. One such goal is to teach children how to make decisions. Gifted children are considered to be the leaders of tomorrow. In this age of high technology, students must learn to use computers to make far-reaching decisions. Computers help students reach this goal in a number of ways. Educational computer games and simulations allow students to experience the decision-making process. In simulation programs in particular, they learn to explore alternate solutions to problems and to see the consequences of their decisions. By learning how to write programs, students begin to see that computer logic is very similar to human logic. Being aware of this similarity can help students apply the steps of programming logic to other types of decision making.

A second goal of education for the gifted is to help students become independent learners. Gifted children have interests and abilities that often render traditional curricula and learning experiences inappropriate. In many instances, teachers have neither the time nor the expertise to respond to students' individual needs; thus, students must learn to take the responsibility for their own learning. Computers can be very useful in this regard. With computer assisted instruction, students can work independently; subject matter and level of difficulty can be tailored to each student's level. Using appropriate software, students can learn to control their learning environments by setting their own pace and by working at their own level. By participating in computer networks, students can contact resources that exist outside the realm of the traditional school environment. Using telecommunications, students can access huge data banks of information; they can also communicate with people who share their interests. This access to outside resources increases students' opportunities for independent learning.

A third goal of programs for gifted learners is to help them develop higher level thinking skills. Certain kinds of software, especially simulations, require students to use higher level cognitive processes. Programming a computer requires that the programmer give the computer explicit, logical directions; this process teaches students the habits of clear, rigorous thought. By using simulations or by learning to write programs, students begin to think about thinking, i.e., to become aware of the processes involved in thinking. Computers are a vehicle for teaching students thinking skills that they can use in environments and situations that are not related to computers.

THE COMPUTER AS AN INSTRUMENT OF LEARNING

In general, computers are used in the education of gifted children in three ways: in computer assisted instruction (CAI), in developing thinking skills, and as tools for facilitating the accomplishment of specific tasks.

CAI is the use of software to teach concepts or processes in an interactive learning environment; it is different from programming. In CAI the program provides the content to be learned and the structure within which the content is to be presented. In programming, the programmer provides the content and determines the structure.

Computers are also used to teach students to use higher level thinking skills. Many traditional learning activities call for the student to do no more than recall or comprehend information. These activities present little challenge to intellectually gifted students. Many computer related learning activities, on the other hand, provide fertile ground for students to use higher cognitive processes, problem-solving strategies, and creative thinking.

Programs for gifted children often focus on individual students' needs and interests by encouraging the students to work on independent research projects or to develop products in their areas of interest. Computers can make these activities much easier. For students conducting research, computers can provide access to virtually limitless sources of information. For students developing products, computers can expand the range of possibilities for the content and format of the product. Computer capabilities for word processing, for example, greatly enhance students' writing. Graphics programs and music keyboards facilitate the development of creative products.

COMPUTER ASSISTED INSTRUCTION

The role of computer assisted instruction in the education of gifted children is to develop decision-making skills and to foster independent learning. In CAI, the computer presents information, asks questions, and verifies responses in much the same way a teacher does. Unlike traditional means of instruction, however, CAI allows students to work at their own level and pace. This mode of instruction can be very beneficial to gifted students in that these students often have interests and abilities that go beyond the regular curriculum. If gifted students seek to become knowledgeable in fields outside the realm of the curriculum, schools may have difficulty responding to their needs, interests, and expertise. CAI is a way of encouraging students' interests and diversity.

There are four main modes of computer assisted instruction: drill and practice, tutorials, games, and simulations. In general, drill and practice and tutorials help students of low ability more than they help the gifted (Mandinach & Fisher, 1983) in that they depend on the lower level thinking skills of recall and comprehension. Games and simulations, on the other hand, often require the use of the higher level cognitive skills of analysis, synthesis, and evaluation.

Drill and Practice. Drill and practice programs provide students with practice using material they have already encountered. Because these programs cover various levels of many subject areas, they can be used for both remediation and acceleration. Gifted children do not always excel in all subjects; they may need help mastering areas in which they are not as proficient as their peers. In most classrooms, drill and practice routines reinforce recently acquired knowledge and skills. In foreign language classes, for example, students practice verb conjugations and noun declensions. Programs such as Spanish or French Hangman help reinforce and increase students' vocabularies. In music, programs such as Minnesota Educational Computing Consortium Music Theory help students practice various aspects of harmony and theory. For gifted students, the primary role of drill and practice programs is, however, to help students who want to go beyond the lockstep curriculum by acquiring new skills. This means, for example, that a drill and practice program might be used by a fourth grader who is interested in communications and wants to learn Morse code. As another example, a drill and practice program could be used to teach a college-bound student how to type, thus eliminating the necessity for spending a semester in a classroom learning the same skill.

Tutorials. Tutorials provide new information. Typically, a program presents a body of information and then questions the student on the information. Like drill and practice programs, tutorials can be a form of enrichment for gifted students who want to explore areas of content that may not be in the regular curriculum, at least not at a time when a gifted child might want to learn the subject. "Chemistry of Living Things," for example, is an interactive tutorial designed to teach students the rudiments of biochemistry. The program is designed for students in grades 5 to 8. Since the program requires no previous training in chemistry, it might be appropriate for bright younger students. Tutorials are also a means of accelerating content. If, for example, a gifted student can and wants to learn Algebra I in a shorter period of time than his or her classmates, tutorials are a means for doing so.

Games. When educators speak of educational computer games, usually they are not referring to arcade-type games. Educational games are those that provide intellectual challenge, stimulate curiosity, and serve as a source of motivation. Good computer games include variable-difficulty levels, multiple-level goals, hidden information, and randomness.

There are two categories of games that may be appropriate for gifted children: adventure games and mind-teasers. Adventure games put the player in situations in which he or she has to use problem solving skills and creative strategies to overcome obstacles. The player must provide explicit directions to the computer. Games such as "Zork" or "The Wizard and the Princess" are highly motivational means of providing practice in developing alternate strategies for solving problems. Adventure games can also help students develop prediction skills. Students learn very quickly to evaluate all possible outcomes before making a move.

Mind-teasers are often the computerized version of conventional games. "BAGELS," for example, is similar to "Master Mind." In this game, the computer randomly generates three numbers, and the player tries to guess the numbers in order of sequence, in as few moves as possible. Computerized chess and backgammon are also popular.

Computer games are an excellent source of motivation, but they seldom have high content value. Since most students will willingly spend hours on an educational game, their use must be monitored by a teacher.

Simulations. Simulations are among the most powerful learning tools for gifted children. They are based on the discovery approach to learning, i.e., learning by doing. Simulations provide situations that are analogous to real situations, but they control limiting factors that exist in the real situation, such as danger, expense, time, and space. "Three Mile Island" is an example of a simulation that allows the player to take charge of a nuclear reactor that is threatened by a meltdown. As with most simulations, this program requires decision making by the players. Since simulations can be repeated, students can see the effects of using different strategies in solving the problems presented by the program.

"Civil War" is a simulation game that gives students an opportunity to make decisions about the allocation of resources during certain battles of the war. Once a student makes the decisions, he or she sees the outcome of his or her choice. The student also learns how the resources had actually been allocated and what the outcome of the real battle had been.

"Rendezvous" is an interactive simulation that recreates a space shuttle flight. The program is divided into stages: launch, orbital rendezvous, and approach and docking with an orbiting space station. The program is made realistic by the use of high resolution, three-dimensional graphics, animation, real physics, and real time.

DEVELOPING THINKING SKILLS

One of the major goals of programs for the gifted is to help students develop higher level cognitive skills, problem-solving skills, and creative ability. Through the use of programs designed for this specific purpose, and through learning to write their own programs, students can develop modes and strategies of thinking that will affect the way they think in situations that are not related to the computer.

Gifted children are believed to be particularly adept at learning to use the cognitive skills of analysis, synthesis, and evaluation. Analysis refers to the ability to break a skill or conceptual structure into its components. Synthesis is the building of complex skills or conceptual structures from simple parts. Evaluation calls for the comparison of skills and structures and the making of judgments about them (Bell, 1981). Some games and simulations (e.g., Mensa Master and Limits) are aimed at helping students develop these skills.

To learn how to be proficient at problem solving, students are taught to (1) pose the problem, (2) precisely define the problem, (3) gather information pertinent to the problem, (4) develop a solution strategy, (5) find the solution, and (6) check the solution (Bell, 1981). Computer programming is an excellent vehicle for teaching problem solving because these six steps are essentially the same steps that programmers use in writing programs.

Creativity involves another kind of thinking, divergent thinking. Guilford (1950) breaks the concept into four parts: fluency, flexibility, originality, and elaboration. Fluency refers to the ability to think of many responses or ideas. Flexibility means being able to change directions in thinking. Originality is the production of new ideas. Elaboration means adding to or embellishing ideas. As is the case with the development of cognitive skills and problem-solving skills, students can explore their creative potential by using software that is designed specifically for that purpose or by creating their own unique and interesting programs. "Creativity Life" is an example of a program that encourages students to write poetry, compose music, or draw pictures. Other programs show students how to develop strategies for creative writing; such programs direct students through the process of writing, virtually forcing them to think divergently.

Teaching children to write computer programs can also help develop their thinking skills. Students are taught that a computer is very similar to the human mind. Like the mind, a computer has both a long-term memory and a short-term memory. The steps that a computer goes through in running a program are much the same as the steps a person goes through in solving a problem of logic. When students learn to see the analogies between the computer and the brain, they begin to see how they can apply computer logic to other kinds of problems.

In programming, there are two kinds of problems to be solved. The first centers on the steps involved in writing a program. Students learn to break a problem into its components and to tell the machine how to deal with each of the components. The second kind of problem involves "debugging" the program, i.e., solving the problems that are related to the logic and sequencing used in creating the program. Both kinds of problem solving require the use of thinking skills associated with analysis, synthesis, and evaluation.

In learning to program a computer, students learn one of several programming languages, or words and procedures that tell the computer what to do. One popular computer language is LOGO. Unlike most languages, LOGO was designed specifically to teach young children how to program a computer. It was developed in 1968 as a part of a National Science Foundation project. The language is based on the learning theories of Jean Piaget. According to Piaget, learning takes place as children interact with their environments. Because learning is active and self-directed, children are the builders of their own intellectual structures. Piaget makes a distinction between the "concrete" reasoning of young children and the "formal" thinking of adolescents and adults. The basic premise of students learning to use LOGO is that the computer can shift the boundary between concrete and formal thinking so that the knowledge that is typically available only through formal processes can now be approached through concrete processes, i.e., LOGO gives concrete form to abstract ideas (Papert, 1980).

LOGO is a procedure-oriented language. It provides students with concrete ways to think about problems systematically. Students divide problems into smaller problems by writing small procedures for each problem. One of the most fascinating aspects of LOGO is turtle graphics. Students learn to form geometric patterns by issuing a few simple commands to a cybernetic turtle that lives on the computer screen. Students give the turtle commands to move forward, backward, right, or left. As the turtle moves, it leaves a trail on the screen; thus, the user can immediately see the effect of his or her commands (Papert, 1980). Turtle graphics and the mathematical computation capabilities of LOGO make the language appropriate for use in art and mathematics and physics. In addition to graphics, complete versions of LOGO contain Instant LOGO which can be used with preschoolers. List processing and text manipulation make it possible to create poetry or interactive texts, such as graphics (Cheshire, 1984).

The second major computer language being taught in schools is BASIC, which stands for Beginners All-Purpose Symbolic Instruction Code. BASIC was invented in 1963 by John Kemeny and Thomas Kirtz to teach students how to use a computer. At the time it was invented, microcomputers were still a concept in the minds of electrical engineers and computer scientists. Since the creation of the microprocessor, BASIC has become the primary language of most microcomputers. It is the language taught most frequently in schools, despite the subsequent creation of more efficient languages, such as Pascal.

One of the current methods of teaching students to write programs in BASIC is to show them how to create graphic designs on the screen. As in LOGO, teaching graphics is a good way to help students see the flow of computer logic. Creating graphics is very motivating for students, especially when they learn to animate the pictures. With animated graphics, students can create their own simulations and adventure games.

Students learning BASIC begin with a few commands that allow them to plot a design on the screen. The design is incorporated in sets of instructions. By changing the specifications of the instructions, students can change design. BASIC is structured so that one part of a program can branch to another part. For students learning graphics, this means that they can write the program so that a certain picture is presented on the screen for a specified time, and then another picture or bit of text will appear. Branching can lead to the development of very elaborate or even unwieldly programs. It is important for students to learn how to plan their programs so that they flow logically and efficiently.

THE COMPUTER AS A TOOL

A tool is a device that makes work easier. A computer is a tool in that it can perform tasks that humans cannot do, and it can function at speeds that are beyond the capabilities of humans. Of particular use to gifted children are the computer's capabilities for processing data, word processing, creating designs in art and music, facilitating the creation of programs through the use of authoring languages, and linking students with outside sources of information.

Processing Data. One of the goals of educational programs for gifted children is to foster independent learning. To achieve this goal, students are encouraged to conduct their own research. An example of such a program is found at the Talcott Mountain Center in Connecticut. At this center, gifted students conduct experiments on wind speed and direction by tracking helium-filled weather balloons. Students use the computer to analyze the data from their experiments (Barstow, 1979). At the Paducah Tilghman High School in Paducah, Kentucky, high school students can participate in a program called "Chemics." This course is a combination of first year physics, second year chemistry, and beginning computer science. Students study computer science so that they can run data from the experiments they perform (Johnston, 1981).

Word Processing. Word processing has changed the way composition is taught. Before the age of the microchip, writing and rewriting were often troublesome, especially for students who have poor handwriting or those who demand perfection in their work. Now students can enter, store, edit, and print text in many different formats. Sentences can be altered or paragraphs moved with the push of a button. Word processing packages greatly facilitate students' efforts to make editorial changes, thereby reducing their reluctance to rewrite compositions. Special spelling programs can go through a text checking for and correcting misspelled words. Other programs provide an analysis of writing styles by calculating features such as the number of times a certain word is used or even the frequency with which students use active voice and passive voice.

Creating Art and Music. Students can create works of art on the computer in several ways. Some software packages, such as Delta Drawing, allow students to use the keyboard to draw pictures on the screen. "Doodle Drawer" uses a joystick as a paintbrush. Some programs, such as "Paint," allow the user to control not only colors but also textures and brush strokes. In addition to programs, students can use graphics tablets to create designs. Students place light pens at various points on a tablet, and the corresponding design appears on the screen. In this fashion, students can create pictures and designs.

Students can also create music on the computer. Some programs, such as "The Magic Melody Box," make it easy to create four-voice harmonized songs. With this program, students select from twelve rhythm patterns and then draw a melody line in a box displayed on the screen. A more sophisticated program is the "Advanced Music System" is which students are required to enter notes and specify their parameters (octave, duration, dynamic level, articulation). Students write music for up to four independent voices. With this particular program, sounds are reproduced through television speakers.

Electronic keyboards make writing music easy for students who play the piano. Like graphics tablets, keyboards are peripherals that can be interfaced with a microcomputer. As a user plays the keyboard, the notes and their parameters are temporarily stored in memory. If the composer wants to change the composition, he or she may do so. The piece can then be saved on a disc for later use or further alteration.

Authoring Systems. Authoring systems and languages allow users to create computer programs even if they know every little about conventional program languages. Typically, authoring programs allow the user to create drill and practice or tutorial programs. "The Learning Box" is an example of a program that helps teachers design software that is specific to the needs of their students. Authoring systems can also be used by gifted students who want to create interactive software without going through the usual stages of programming. As is the case with many tutorials, software created with authoring systems presents a narrative, asks a question, waits for a response, and provides a reinforcing statement. Author I, for example, is a system that allows the user to develop programs that include features such as graphics, branching, and score keeping.

Networking. Networking is a popular term that refers to the process of sharing information. In its most simple form, a network is like a grapevine; one person shares some information with a second person, who passes it on to a third. The age of technology has greatly expanded human capabilities for sharing information. In education, computers have allowed students, teachers, and administrators to obtain and share information with sources outside the school.

Because gifted children often have interests that lie beyond the scope of most traditional school curricula and resources, they can benefit tremendously from networking. In some instances, gifted children form their own networks; in other cases, they can hook into networks established by other individuals, organizations, or businesses. Runion (1982) describes, for example, a program in which gifted students formed a resource file of local people, organizations, and documents that could be used by students interested in researching certain topics. The students started by identifying key topics, such as academic areas, careers, and creativity. They then divided the topics into subtopics according to different kinds of resources, such as documents, people, and organizations. The information was entered into a computer, where it is easily retrieved and updated.

The real power in networking lies in the capability of microcomputers to communicate with other computers. To do this, a microcomputer is attached to a modem. A modem is an electronic device that converts the computer's binary code to auditory signals and sends the signals to other computers via telephone. Once a microcomputer is connected to a modem, it can function like a terminal of the computer to which it is connected. In this manner, students can access the information stored in a mainframe computer even if the mainframe is thousands of miles away. By using telecommunications, students can contact large data banks, information services, or electronic bulletin boards. If, for example, a student is interested in researching a particular area of medicine, he or she can dial Dialog, which would link him or her to 150 on-line data bases. Using a modem, the student could conduct a search for certain kinds of articles as well as order printed documents. Another data bank that might be of particular interest to gifted students is The National Scholarship Research Service. This data base provides information to students seeking information on private sector scholarships, fellowships, grants, and loans.

In addition to data bases, students can also contact one of the general information systems, such as CompuServe or The Source. These services offer a wide range of current information, including news, weather, sports, financial markets, and airline schedules. CompuServe offers the World Book Encyclopedia online as well as information pertaining to child care and health. The Source offers electronic mail, a system where users can send messages to each other via computer.

Electronic mail is usually associated with electronic bulletin boards. Such bulletin boards exist in certain fields (e.g., SpecialNet in special education). Electronic bulletin boards function essentially in the same way as traditional corkboards. A user can post a message asking for information on a topic of interest or send a message to other members of the network. An electronic bulletin board differs from a corkboard in that the user can specify the audience. He or she can contact all of the users on the system or limit contact to people who are members of a specific interest group. Electronic mail and bulletin boards help put students and teachers in contact with resources outside their immediate environments. This access to information is crucial for students who are conducting research on unusual or complicated topics.

CONCLUSIONS

As with much of the field of computer applications in education, there is little empirical research on the benefits of computers for gifted children. Learning to use a computer can be both a means and an end unto itself for gifted children. Computer learning experiences are a way for students to learn to make decisions and to solve problems. Computers can enhance the development of independent learning. Computers can help students develop higher level thinking skills. In this age of high technology, it is important for students to see the computer as a tool. It is a tool for facilitating time-consuming and tedious tasks, and it is a means of opening doors to vast resources. By using tools, students can greatly increase their potential for developing their special capabilities.

Appendix A provides a list of software and other resources of interest in teaching gifted children.

REFERENCES

Barstow, D. (1979). The Talcott Mountain science center. *onComputing*, *3*, 34–36.

Bell, F. (1981). Classroom computing: Beyond the 3 R's. *Creative Computing*, *5*, 68–70.

Cheshire, F. (1984). Introduction to LOGO. Workshop presented at the CEC/CASE Conference on Technology in Special Education, Reno, NV.

Guilford, J. P. (1950). Creativity. *American Psychologist*, *5*, 444–454.

Guilford, J. P. (1967). *The nature of human intelligence*. New York: McGraw-Hill.

Johnston, S. (1981). The Paducah Tilghman High School "Chemics" program. In J. Nazzaro (Ed.), *Computer connections for gifted children and youth*. Reston, VA: The Council for Exceptional Children.

Mandinach, E., & Fisher, C. (1983). Review of research on the cognitive effects of computer assisted learning. Report for the National Institute of Education. Berkeley, CA: Lawrence Hall of Science.

Papert, S. (1980). *Mindstorms*. New York: Basic Books.

Runion, T. (1982). *Stewardship: Training the gifted as community mentors*. Reston, VA: The Council for Exceptional Children.

CHAPTER 5

Using Computers with Mildly and Moderately Handicapped Children

The mildly and moderately handicapped population constitutes the largest proportion of individuals receiving special education and related services. Blaschke (1984) reported that currently there are over 60,000 microcomputers in special education, with 45,000 of them used for instructional purposes. It is estimated that by 1985–86 there will be approximately 150,000 microcomputers used in special education, with 30,000 used for administration. It is therefore logical to conclude that instructional strategies for mildly and moderately handicapped individuals will be significantly impacted by trends in technology application.

Application of computer technology in regular education has far to go in terms of applying appropriate content and strategies, as well as in monitoring student performance. Even when appropriate computer based materials are available for these children, it does not necessarily follow that they will be appropriate for mildly and moderately handicapped individuals. Historically, special educators have either had to develop their own materials to meet the needs of students or attempted to adapt materials designed for nonhandicapped populations. It is hoped that, as with other instructional materials for handicapped children, commercial publishers will start to develop the type of computer software that is flexible enough to meet the varied needs of handicapped children. A beneficial side effect of such materials should be that they will be useful for the nonhandicapped child as well. In short, well-designed software that can meet the needs of handicapped children can be used in regular education, whereas those designed to meet the needs of the average student are often not appropriate for handicapped children. Thus, special educators have the opportunity to influence this developing field.

This chapter will attempt to describe some of the current applications of technology for mildly and moderately handicapped individuals. In addition, a case study is used to illustrate many of these applications. This

---

This chapter was authored by Delores Hagen and Michael M. Behrmann.

particular case study provides not only an illustration but also the viewpoint of one of the authors, who is a parent of a child growing up during the early 1970s. Although the child described in this case is deaf, many of his learning needs are similar to those of mildly and moderately handicapped individuals.

Marc Hagen, A Case in Point

I can remember my first experience in watching a teacher motivate my deaf son. She wanted to convey "Good job," "That's super," "You made the right choice." Marc was 1½ years old at the time. Since the activity being taught prevented his watching her lips (his only clue to communications intended for him at the time), she tapped his arm and placed two M&M candy bits in his mouth.

This introduction to "sugar communion," as my husband called it, was enlightening but also frightening. My son's response was favorable. Indeed, he understood the sweet reward system and smiled brightly as he reached for the next sized colored ring to add to the rocking shaft of the toy. I sat pondering: If candy was "Yes," what in the world did she use for "No"? When I asked, I received a rather curt reply. "Candy works," she answered, "we don't reward incorrect behavior with anything. Only correct answers get rewards." Suddenly, I had visions of a 300 pound teenage boy with bad teeth, the price my son would have to pay for learning.

That experience was over 13 years ago. My son is now 15 years old. The "sugar communion" began and ended that day. He is a bright, healthy, lean, 160 lb teenager without a cavity in his mouth. It wasn't always easy to motivate Marc, but we chose alternatives to food rewards, especially sweet ones.

Marc is profoundly deaf. He does not fall into one of the "high incidence" handicapped classifications, but his learning problems are very similar to those of children with learning disabilities. His communication problems are different but require many of the same kinds of teaching techniques used to overcome other learning disabilities. Motivating him to learn language (standard English) was a challenge that continues today.

Motivating any child to learn can be a tricky business. In Marc's case, some of the teaching techniques used over the years seemed to dismiss his overall development, ignoring everything but his specific disability. This appears to stem from the special education professional's delivering "one-on-one services" to meet the individual education plan goals and objectives—meeting the needs of that one child. It does sound good, but unfortunately, in practice it sometimes isn't. The very delivery of that service can single out a child as being "different" when the most important thing is "belonging," being "one of the gang." For Marc, it often seemed that the system was designed to serve the needs of the teacher rather than his. The various specialists hovering around him, waiting to isolate him in their special rooms, to do their special teaching, in removing him from the normal flow of school life acted for their convenience, certainly not his. Each time he was pulled out of mainstream, he carried another label that said "different," and each time he was faced with the challenge of overcoming the peer pressure induced by the system.

The most successful motivating force we ever found for Marc has been the microcomputer. Granted, there were many years between the M&Ms and the computer, but we found ways then also. I can't say that all of them were as successful as the microcomputer has been, but at least they were nondestructive to the body. Convincing teachers to address Marc as a whole person, to acknowledge his normal intelligence, and to understand his disability as part of him, not something to attack with vengeance while ignoring the rest of him was not always easy. After all, his teachers were delivering the best "learning environment" they had been taught to deliver, within a system over which they have little control. Asking them to change did not always meet with agreement, nor did we insist that the educational system change just for us. We were always able to obtain cooperation and understanding from the teachers and bent a few rules, at least enough to keep Marc's desire for learning intact. This situation lasted until he was 13. Then the bottom fell out, and a lot of changes had to take place.

Marc was 13 years old. He had always been a doer; but in a new situation, just entering junior high school, having normal teenage desires to "belong," he reached his limit of implied inferiority. The communication difficulties, unintentional labeling by special teachers, and the peer pressure resulted in his losing all desire for learning. His answer to continued expressions of "do it again," "say it again," and "you're different, you come with me" was to reject school altogether. He sat at the breakfast table one day and said through the tears, "No, Mom, no more. I won't go!"

Obviously, something had to be done. How do you tell a trusting child that he must go back to face what he considers a private hell? All at school were doing their best to teach, yet their efforts were killing the one thing absolutely necessary for learning—the desire to learn.

We found the answer to Marc's lack of desire to learn in a microcomputer. The school had several Apples and the decision to put one to work in special education met with cooperation from all concerned. There was little software available except games, so we used authoring systems to create the lessons. These systems allowed us to develop courseware without programming knowledge. As soon as Marc was introduced to the machine, things began to change.

The procedure was relatively simple. Vocabulary words that Marc did not understand were put into the microcomputer with an authoring system called MicroQuest. This is a drill and practice program created by TIES (Total Information Education Systems, St. Paul, MN). The format allows questions to be entered with a multiple-choice answer selection. Marc was able to access these new vocabulary words on the computer before they were introduced in class. Because they were on disc in a random order, he could review the disc as many times as necessary, both at school and at home, until he became familiar with the terms and comfortable with their meanings.

It did not take long to decide that if Marc were going to use the microcomputer for drill and practice, traditional keyboard skills would be necessary. I certainly didn't want him to become a "hunt and peck" typist, and after some explanation to the staff of what a typing tutor was, we put a typing tutor objective into his IEP.

The change to include a typing tutor for Marc was not difficult to make. Everyone concerned with Marc's education understood how helpful typing skills could be for him. As a result, a 20 minute practice period each day became part of his microcomputer time.

DEFINITIONS AND LEARNING NEEDS

The learning needs of Marc are much like those of learning disabled and other mildly handicapped individuals. Children with a variety of mild and moderate handicaps are reaping the benefits of computer technology with help from skilled educators. Although special hardware and software modifications have often been made for students with specific disabilities, such as the sensorily impaired, mildly and moderately impaired students as a large group can also benefit from computer technology to meet their learning needs.

Definitions

The populations of individuals usually associated with mild and moderate handicaps include the traditional classifications of mental retardation, learning disabilities, and emotional disturbances. Section 121a.5 of the Rules and Regulations of P.L. 94-142 provides the following definitions for these categories:

'Mentally Retarded' means significantly subaverage general intellectual functioning existing concurrently with deficits in adaptive behavior and manifested during the developmental period, which adversely affects a child's educational performance.

'Specific learning disability' means a disorder in one or more of the basic psychological processes involved in understanding or in using language, spoken or written, which may manifest itself in an imperfect ability to listen, think, speak, read, write, spell or to do mathematical calculations. The term includes such conditions as perceptual handicaps, brain injury, minimal brain dysfunction, dyslexia, and developmental aphasia. The term does not include children who have learning problems which are primarily a result of visual, hearing, or motor handicaps, or mental retardation, or of cultural, or economic disadvantage.

'Seriously emotionally disturbed' is defined as follows:

(i) The term means a condition exhibiting one or more of the following characteristics over a long period of time and to a marked degree, which adversely affects educational performance:

(A) An inability to learn which cannot be explained by intellectual, sensory, or health factors;

(B) An inability to build or maintain satisfactory interpersonal relationships with peers and teachers;

(C) Inappropriate types of behavior or feelings under normal circumstances;

(D) A general pervasive mood of unhappiness of depression; or

(E) A tendency to develop physical symptoms or fears associated with personal or school problems.

(ii) The term includes children who are schizophrenic.

The term does not include children who are socially maladjusted, unless it is determined that they are seriously emotionally disturbed.

Special educators will admit that these categories are far from clear-cut, but the labeling of children in this way has provided a basis for communication between professionals regarding broad learning characteristics for classes of disabilities. The categories also are the means for directing federal, state, and local funds to target populations.

Educators, however, both know and expect that no matter the label, each individual will exhibit some behaviors or characteristics typically found in definitions of other categories. Thus, it is not unusual to find a mildly mentally retarded child with neurologic problems similar to those of a learning disabled child, or, as in Marc's case, a hearing impaired child with problems similar to those of a learning disabled child.

It is the Individualized Educational Program (IEP) that enables special educators to begin to address the overlap of learning needs between children placed in different categories. The IEP provides a mechanism to ensure that specific special educational and related services will be available to meet the learning needs of each child. In truly individualized plans, the goals and objectives resulting in placement and services included in the IEP are not associated with a specific disability.

For the purpose of broadly defining the population of mild and moderate handicaps this text will use definitions given by Hardman, Drew, and Egan (1984):

"Individuals with mild learning and behavior disorders exhibit academic and/or social-interpersonal performance deficits that generally become evident in a school-related setting and make it necessary for the individuals to receive additional support services beyond those typically offered in a regular education setting. However, it is assumed that a mildly disordered student would remain in the regular education setting for the majority of the school day. The severity of the performance deficit for this population ranges from one to two standard deviations below the interindividual and/or intraindividual mean on the measure(s) being recorded" (pp. 82–83).

"An individual with moderate learning or behavior disorders exhibits intellectual, academic, and/or social-interpersonal performance deficits that range between two and three standard deviations below the interindividual mean on the measure(s) being recorded. These performance deficits are not limited to any given setting but are typically evident in the broad spectrum of environmental settings. . . . Individuals with functional disorders at this level will require substantially altered patterns of service and treatment and may need modified environmental accommodations" (p. 85).

As has been indicated, there are some differences between the mildly handicapped individual and the moderately handicapped one. Primarily the difference is in the pervasiveness of the disability across settings, rather than in types of interventions or learning needs. The mildly handicapped individual is basically seen as deviant only in an academic or school settings, whereas the moderately handicapped individual may also be perceived to be deviant in social or work settings. The remainder of this section will address many of the needs associated with children having such mild and moderate disabilities.

Learning Needs

The population discussed in this chapter is a heterogeneous one, with each individual exhibiting in it a combination of unique learning needs. In general, the learning needs of mildly and moderately handicapped individuals can be classified in the following areas: (1) behavioral, (2) intellectual, (3) language, (4) academic, and (5) vocational.

Many mildly and moderately handicapped children have some sort of behavioral problem. The problem may be physiologic or environmental, a primary problem (i.e., the primary disability may be an emotional disturbance), or a secondary one as a result of frustration and failure. In any case, the child's behavior generally has an adverse effect on learning. Typical behaviors exhibited by this population that may directly affect academic work include distractibility, hyperactivity, low frustration tolerance, or perseveration. Additionally, children may exhibit a variety of inappropriate social behaviors that interfere with learning, such as aggressive behavior, inhibited behavior, or bizarre or self-abusive behaviors. Behavioral problems often make it difficult for teachers to motivate children to work. They may also interfere with an individual's ability to work cooperatively with teachers and peers or to work independently.

Intellectual difficulties may be associated with retardation or neurologic difficulties, or they may be related to behavior. Since various disabilities such as emotional disturbances may have adverse effects on intelligence tests, resulting in "pseudoretarded" populations (Blake, 1981), the primary emphasis of education should be on remediation or accommodation for dysfunctions in the intellectual processes (those operations performed as one learns) rather than worrying about the cause of an intellectual problem. Problem areas associated with intellectual processes include difficulties in memory, perception, conceptualization, and thinking. As a result of these problems, children with mild and moderate disabilities often work much more slowly than others. A computer does not care whether the child is disturbed or works slowly, and it can wait patiently until the child is ready to respond. Typically, interventions to address the above-mentioned problems are oriented toward teaching children to pick up on visual or auditory cues or developing techniques for problem solving. In many cases, teachers use overlearning through drill and practice to ensure learning.

Language difficulties are the third common problem area. Many mildly handicapped individuals have receptive or expressive language problems, or both. These problems can be manifested in either oral or written language. In written language, reading and writing are important tools for most other academic areas of learning, such as social studies or history. Intensive intervention to develop these written language skills is important in order to limit the impact of a language deficit. Oral language difficulties present a different set of problems. Receptive and expressive oral language provides the basis for developing many cognitive skills as well as good written language skills. Poor oral language skills can inhibit the ability of an individual to understand others, and can adversely affect academic and social development. This can lead to secondary handicaps, including behavioral disorders.

Academic skills, the fourth area, are affected by behavior, intellect, and language. Academic skills include the traditional three R's as well as other academic curriculum areas. They are particularly important, however, because they are the basis for identifying a child as handicapped. In the assessment of children for special education placement, most handicapped children will perform at least one year behind expectation in at least one academic area. A child may have a severe perceptual problem that is characteristic of a mild handicap, but if he or she is able to accommodate for that problem and perform academically at grade level without special educational services, he or she will probably not be identified as handicapped. Therefore, a remedial educational program in at least one academic area is nearly always required. Often such services will be given in the regular classroom or in a resource room setting. With the moderately handicapped, problems may be severe enough to require a self-contained placement.

Vocational training is an area that has recently received much more attention at state and federal levels. Although mildly handicapped individuals may be able to accommodate for their disability and function in many jobs, the moderately handicapped may be limited to semi-skilled or unskilled jobs. Because of past employment limitations that this population has experienced, education must give these individuals as many skills and good work habits as is possible. With technology changing the work environment, these skills and habits will be more and more important. When employment skills for this group are honed and refined to meet the demands of the 1980s and 1990s, poor interpersonal skills and behavior may be circumvented by work at home or isolated work setting.

IMPLICATIONS OF TECHNOLOGY FOR MILD AND MODERATELY HANDICAPPED INDIVIDUALS

The need for instructional applications for computers has been documented by Blaschke (1984), who reviewed several studies of perceived needs of special education teachers and administrators. The areas of particular need included reading, word attack skills, mathematics, and social behavior. Other areas of interest include tutorial programs to introduce concepts, problem-solving software, and drill and practice materials. He also reports that manufacturers are beginning to respond to this need, with three firms (Developmental Learning Materials [DLM], Hartley Courseware, and Random House) having released over 100 programs that can be adapted for special education students.

Computers have a number of advantages in meeting the learning needs of mildly and moderately handicapped individuals. They are increasingly found in academic areas, such as diagnosis and remediation of spelling (Hasselbring, 1982; Hasselbring & Crossland, 1981) and reading (Mason, 1980). Popular educational software has often taken the form of educational computer games (Chaffin, Maxwell, & Thompson, 1982) that challenge and motivate students to participate in an individualized learning environment, often for much longer periods of time than teachers could ever imagine they would maintain interest. The game format utilized in such software pays particular attention to the motivational features of video arcade games, providing instant feedback, a challenge to improve performance, a fast pace with a large number of user responses required, and an unlimited ceiling on performance. Such formats utilize the capabilities of the computers to produce special effects through sound and graphics. In addition to the motivational aspects of a game format, computers offer a number of additional advantages to meeting the learning needs of handicapped children. Schiffman, Tobin, and Buchanan (1982) have discussed a number of advantages of computers for learning disabled students. Table 5-1 provides a similiar list for all mildly and moderately handicapped students.

What almost every teacher or parent learns when a microcomputer is used as a tutor for a handicapped child is that the computer provides *motivation!* There is something about this nonemotional, learner-paced machine that really makes a difference. One aspect of the effectiveness of the microcomputer appears to be based on the fact that there is no human element visible to the child. Much of the one-on-one teacher or parent drill and practice that goes on to defeat the handicapping condition, and much of the human tutorial intervention that is delivered to remove the effects of the handicap, often leaves out one very important element, the opportunity for the child to be *independent.*

The concept of independent or "discovery learning" is not new. "We learn by doing" is a saying as old as Methuselah. However, the need to have a measure of independence and discovery in the learning environment of mild and moderately handicapped children has often been overshadowed by teams of specialists attempting to provide a structure that maintains

Table 5-1. Advantages of Microcomputers for Mildly and Moderately Handicapped Children

1. Computers can be "user friendly" and personalized.
2. Computers are nonjudgmental.
3. Computers give the child undivided attention.
4. Computers are patient and let the child work at his or her own pace.
5. Reinforcement is immediate and continuous.
6. Drill and practice can be varied or in a challenging game format.
7. Computers are particularly suited to independent and discovery learning.
8. Computers are able to assist in developing problem solving skills, particularly through programming.

accountability. In their attempts to help these children overcome their handicaps, the disability takes on the characteristic of an enemy to be driven away as an evil spirit. The "help" is there, certainly, but sometimes at the risk of destroying the self-worth of the child and ignoring the value of independent discovery learning.

For certain children in special education, there has been little or no independent learning environment available because there has been no alternative to human intervention. Human intervention has primarily been motivated by the need to constantly monitor performance in order to provide "errorless learning" and to maintain enough information to analyze mistakes students make in order to adjust interventions. Now that microcomputers as tutor is a reality and the drawbacks of human intervention are avoidable, the next step is to get computers into use with handicapped students as tools of learning.

For many children, the microcomputer, when used properly, is a very motivating and stimulating learning tool. The question then becomes, "What is proper use?" Based on practical experiences thus far, a number of uses have proved to be successful. Discussions follow on using the computer for drill and practice, tutorials, and simulations for educational use and as a tool for problem solving and life-skill development. All of the uses are proper if combined with appropriate teaching to meet the individual needs of the child. Improper use comes when poorly planned applications are implemented, when educators lack the essential knowledge of the beneficial uses of computers, or when knowledge of operation and maintenance of equipment is lacking.

Drill and Practice

One of the historically successful uses for the computer is drill and practice. What is there about drill and practice on the microcomputer that actually stimulates learning?

1. The computer allows independence. The microcomputer and software designed as drill and practice of knowledge and skills can offer the opportunity for the mildly handicapped child to drill independently without heavy reliance on a teacher. For some children, making errors on a machine is less embarrassing than doing so in front of a teacher or other classmates. The computer can also monitor and analyze performance for later teacher analysis.

2. The microcomputer is nonemotional. It will present questions and wait for answers impartially. The microcomputer is capable of distinguishing between right and wrong answers or inputs and that is all. If the software is designed properly, there will be positive reinforcement for correct answers and encouragement to try again when incorrect responses are given.

3. The microcomputer, using appropriate software, can deliver material at the child's pace. Taking cues from the learner's responses, the machine proceeds only when the child responds correctly and is ready to go forward. If it takes one child longer to read the information or to understand the question than another child, the same software can accommodate the learning differences of the children.

4. Drill and practice on the microcomputer is motivating. "I do it over and over again, but it's different every time," said one nine year old. He was fascinated by the random selection of questions presented by the computer. His teacher said, "We couldn't get these kids to do similar worksheets over and over yet when the lesson is on the computer, we can't tear them away." The factors responsible are many, and may differ from student to student, but the overwhelming evidence from teachers using computers over time is that, indeed, the computer is more motivating than pencil and paper drill.

While the advantages of drill and practice on the microcomputer are many, including allowing teachers to utilize their time more effectively, educators must beware of the danger that drill and practice will become the only use of the microcomputer in the classroom.

Tutorial

Tutorial uses of the microcomputer have some of the same advantages to the teacher as drill and practice. They provide a motivating, useful way to deliver new concept materials, provide independent learning opportunities, and allow for more effective use of teacher time. They also offer valuable learning opportunities to the child, especially for those individuals who respond well to a mechanized learning environment.

Tutorials are interactive dialogues between the computer lesson and student. They vary in their format. Some present concept materials, and then query to ascertain a child's understanding. The software may branch to another position of the lesson if initial material is understood, or encourage the child through a review component if more information is needed to achieve understanding. A tutorial program can include graphics, color, even management systems to record the student's progress for later review by the teacher.

Tutorial software for special education has been slow in developing because of the complexity in designing a branching system that can flexibly meet the needs of a variety of students. In current practical application, it is tutorials with built-in authoring systems that allow teachers to meet many of the individual needs of mildly or moderately disabled students.

For example, Pilot, a public domain course authoring language developed by Dr. John Starkweather, a physician at the University of California, was designed as one of the first tools for teachers who wanted to develop courseware that could be interactive. It is a relatively simple language to learn, with eight core commands. The enhanced version for Apple computers, E-Z Pilot, by Earl Keyser (White Bear Lake, MN), offers tremendous power to the teacher.

Marc

As Marc's sophistication with computers grew, so did the courseware we used. A much more complete authoring system called E-Z Pilot was added. Lessons were prepared with interactive, dialogue-type concept materials as part of the tutorials. E-Z Pilot supports branching, sound, and graphics, so that very professional courseware could be prepared without programming knowledge.

We used these authoring systems to develop support materials for two mainstream classes: science and social studies. Marc used his normal study hall for "computer tutor" time and the changes were immediate.

Instead of begging not to go to school, Marc couldn't wait to get there. His smile returned. His grades began to climb. But far more important than any of the outward signs of change were the changes taking place inside; the desire for learning had returned. As Marc said in a story he wrote, "The computer doesn't laugh at me, it just teaches me."

Using E-Z Pilot, we were able to develop courseware to support mainstream curriculum for Marc. Standard seventh grade textbooks were used as the guidelines, but the vocabulary was rewritten to about third grade level. The power of E-Z Pilot was thus used to introduce new vocabulary and to check for comprehension on material whose content was grade appropriate. With the addition of a small, inexpensive graphics tablet (Koala Pad) and Microillustrator software, sophisticated graphics were added to the courseware where appropriate. The color capability of the computer and five different character sets (type styles) were used to emphasize certain words or phrases. The result was courseware that met the exact needs of a low language student. This tutorial package was used over and over again until each objective being taught was mastered.

The concept of course authoring systems is not unique to special education. In fact, there are relatively few systems that are geared to the learning and instructional needs of the field. One of the major drawbacks to many general purpose authoring languages is their inability to utilize a multisensory approach. Basically they just deal with textual material. Two systems that have had some success with handicapped populations are BLOCKS, developed for deaf students at the California School for the Deaf (Slovick, 1982) and ASSIST, developed as an outgrowth of a research project at RMC Research Corporation for the U.S. Department of Education. The former utilizes a combination of graphics and text to develop courseware; the latter is reported to have favorable results in teaching mathematics, reading, and language skills to learning disabled middle school children in California. One result of the percieved need for more authoring languages to meet the unique needs of disabled students has been the response of the Office of Special Education in the U.S. Department of Education in supporting development of such authoring languages through their Microcomputer Software for Individually Managed Instruction projects. One is currently being developed at the Applied Physics Laboratory at The Johns Hopkins University, another is being developed at Kent State University in Ohio, and the third at the Denver Research Institute of the University of Denver.

Authoring languages can also be combined with other compensatory technology for mildly and moderately handicapped students. For students who might be assisted by the additional cue of oral language (e.g., those individuals with dyslexia), a speech synthesizer, such as the Echo II by Street Electronics, Carpenteria, CA, can be incorporated to read aloud text written on the screen. The speech synthesizer can be turned on and off by the student, allowing assistance to be given only when needed.

If typing on a keyboard is a problem because of motor or perceptual problems, such as those found in dysgraphic individuals, access to the computer through any number of alternative keyboard or computer peripheral devices or emulators is available. For instance, the Scott Voice Based Learning System (VBLS) for Apple computers provides a means of training the computer to recognize words spoken into a microphone instead of a keyboard entry. The system's Voice Entry Terminal can be used with other tutorial software or course authoring systems, or it can use the authoring software provided with the system. For example, a lesson could be developed to learn the parts of speech. The user, under teacher supervision, could train the system to recognize a voice input for the various parts of speech. A branching tutorial program could then be used that requests vocal inputs instead of keyboard entries. The VBLS authoring system has two additional important features. It can maintain a student performance record that can be displayed for the teacher or student, or both, and it has the capacity, using an optional interface card, of controlling peripheral audiovisual devices, such as an audiocassette recorder or filmstrip projector. Finally, it should be noted that this system is not restricted to certain languages or content. The system can be trained in languages such as Spanish or Korean, and the content and structure of the tutorial is limited only by the creativity of the teacher or developer of courseware.

Today it is possible for educators, parents and other to purchase "off the shelf" products, such as an authoring system, graphics tablet, and speech synthesizer, and build a multisensory learning environment that meets the precise needs of the child. Adjustments can be made in types of input and output for the computer as well as in the content of material, which in turn meets the different academic or learning needs of various learners. There is no need for computer programming knowledge—the individual only requires "computer user" skills. Relatively sophisticated courseware can be produced with very little additional training.

Simulations

Educational simulations allow mildly and moderately handicapped individuals to engage in another type of discovery learning. Since simulations are programs that are designed to emulate real-life situations and utilize principles of discovery learning, most simulations developed for the general educational population can be used by mildly and moderately handicapped children. Exceptions to this would be simulations that have too many rules or are extremely distracting, or games that require a reading level that is above the capability of the child. Blaschke (1984) notes that educational simulations designed for handicapped students should be appearing on the market during the next year.

Simulation software programs do not typically provide reinforcement for correct answers, since there are no truly correct or incorrect responses. Additionally, the computer "hides the consequence or answer" until the child makes a response, preventing the child from second-guessing the computer or "looking up the answer." Natural consequences of decisions are the most commonly used means of providing reinforcement. For example, if a child makes a wrong turn in an adventure game he or she may fall into a bottomless pit. In a simulation that is teaching a skill such as shopping in a store, the child may have to decide what items to purchase with a limited amount of money. If too many "luxury" items are purchased, the natural consequence might be a missed meal on one day, or a punishment from a parent. These types of software programs allow children to develop problem solving skills. Since the simulation may be played over and over, the player is able to try different choices and see the logical results of those choices, and is thus involved in a discovery learning process.

MICROCOMPUTERS AS TOOLS

The educational uses of microcomputers in the classroom and for special children go far beyond the traditional CAI (computer assisted instruction), simulations, and tutorials commonly used in education today. The reasons are obvious. Today's microcomputer technology has provided tools for learning and functioning in our society as well as learning tools (instructional medium). Technologic advances can bring speech to the nonvocal, Braille or speech to the blind, universal telephone use to the deaf, and decrease the reading, writing, and problem solving blockades for the mildly and moderately handicapped. These are "tool" uses of technology. In meeting the special needs of individuals, they also meet the normal information needs of these populations.

Tackling Learning Impairments

A mildly or moderately handicapped child or individual who cannot read (for whatever reason) can provide one example of the usefulness of microcomputer technology as a learning tool. The addition of a speech synthesizer to a microcomputer system will "speak" otherwise inaccessible written information to that person. That makes the microcomputer a tool. That tool meets the special needs of the user by accommodating for the inability to read by providing auditory information in addition to written output on the screen. Now the user can have the same information as his or her peers. The combined multisensory auditory and visual display can also assist in the improvement of reading skills. Even though a disabling condition may rule out reading as a means of obtaining information, the microcomputer as a tool can provide it. A special need has been met, but it is the normal needs this individual can then pursue that demonstrates the real power of the microcomputer. Everyone needs information, and nearly everyone can have it if microcomputer can be used as tools.

For the population of individuals with mild and moderate handicaps, there are two major tool applications of microcomputers that are currently being explored extensively. The first is utilizing programming languages as a means of developing problem solving skills, and the second is using word processors as a means of developing reading and writing skills.

Problem Solving Through Programming. Although there is a relative paucity of empirical evidence to support programming as a tool for learning, it has been postulated by many that learning to program and think in the manner in which a computer processes information does benefit mildly and moderately handicapped individuals (Halpern, 1984; Schiffman et al., 1982). Skills developed in this process include the problem solving ability of breaking tasks down into small, sequential steps. This is much the same as the analogy of comparing the process of task analysis to software program design and programming described in Chapter 2. Additionally, searching for "bugs" that cause the program to stop can sharpen children's problem solving and logical analysis skills (Kearsly & Hunter, 1983).

The programming language that has received the most attention as a problem solving and educational tool is LOGO, developed by Seymour Papert of Massachusetts Institute of Technology. LOGO is designed to let children explore problems by themselves and is meant to improve their thinking abilities rather than train them as programmers (Kearsly & Hunter, 1983). It has been used by children of all ages and all ranges of ability including those who are learning disabled, emotionally disturbed, retarded, physically handicapped, and autistic. LOGO has been used for teaching such diverse curricular areas as mathematics, physics, electronics, writing, and spelling (Weir, Russell, & Valente, 1982).

The primary feature of LOGO is that it provides a learner-driven activity that capitalizes on previous learning. For instance, the LOGO turtle moving on the screen allows children to utilize the spatial concepts they have learned from moving around their own environment to move the turtle on the computer screen. It is not unusual to see a child involved in a problem solving activity moving around the room, stepping out the pattern he or she wants the turtle to imitate on the screen. Thus, concepts like left and right, forward and backward, angles and distance are all related to previous learning. Children can capitalize on and refine their spatial concepts and coordinate various types of tactile, kinesthetic, visual, and motor information into the control of the turtle.

Teachers can adjust the level of difficulty by providing activities that are commensurate with the child's abilities. Simpler versions of the language can adapt for physical or cognitive abilities, and more complex activities can be assigned to children with higher functioning. Other educational objectives can also be made to work with a programming language such as LOGO. Social relationships and cooperative problem solving are commonly used by forming teams of children to work on problems. Thus, children are able to assist each other and can try different approaches to solving a single problem.

Using a programming language such as LOGO will not provide all the answers to problem solving in education, but it is one more tool in the teacher's "bag of tricks." It may reveal hidden strengths in children (e.g., a strong ability to utilize the spatial mode of learning) and can provide teachers with additional insights into the learning styles of the children with whom they work. Weir and colleagues (1982) suggest that the impact of LOGO is threefold for children who are failing in school: (1) it provides the possibility of experiencing success and demonstrating expertise; (2) it allows further development of the preferred spatial mode; and (3) it is a diagnostic tool that suggests to teachers new ways of creating more appropriate curriculum by harnessing spatial skills.

Producing Written Language. Many children with mild and moderate disabilities have difficulty with written language. The struggle with pencil and paper tasks is very real for this population. Their work is often characterized by graphic imperfections (erasures, pencil pressure marks, size and spacing irregularities, and so forth), misspellings (including phonetic spelling, letter or syllable omissions, and so forth), grammatical errors, semantic errors, and errors related to frustration associated with self-monitoring (Weiner, 1980). With the advent of microcomputers in the educational system this pencil and paper blockade can be lessened or eliminated. Word processors can help learning handicapped children by improving their ability to communicate, through a written product, their thoughts or ideas.

The concept of utilizing word processing as a learning tool is gaining wide acceptance. "The word processor is not a substitute for the teacher, but rather a complement to the teacher" (Gula, 1982, pp. 31-32). Some benefits of using word processing are listed in Table 5-2.

Using software called typing tutors, students can learn to manipulate the keyboard. There are typing tutors for all major brands of micro-computers, although some are more comprehensive than others. By and large, it should be possible to find one that meets the needs of different students. Some are designed as games, others as pure drill and practice. The game formats are useful for very young children and even junior high and high school students who need a motivational shot in the arm. The

Table 5-2. Benefits of Word Processing

1. There is no penalty for revising.
2. It is easy for students to experiment with writing.
3. Interest in the writing task is maintained.
4. Editing is simple: spelling, punctuation, and grammar can be changed or checked.
5. Writing and editing are less time consuming.
6. Frustration is minimized.
7. It is easy to produce perfect copy.
8. Computerized spelling checkers are available.

more sophisticated ones are extremely effective both in teaching typing skills to older students and for brush-up by the rusty adult typist.

In addition, word processing can be introduced at the same time. From both personal experience and the experience of some 500 teachers dealing with language development, the publishers of *Closing the Gap* have found word processing to be one of the most effective language development tools ever introduced. Even if a child can't write with pencil and paper he or she can probably push a key or switch to generate a specific letter. If errors in verb tense, spelling, or punctuation are made, they can be corrected without retyping the entire text because the text can easily be reorganized or edited by simple keyboard commands.

For mildly and moderately handicapped learners, it is the power to correct, manipulate, and reorganize written language without recopying that makes word processing so important. The ability to create a first draft and correct mistakes in words or phrases is heaven for anyone without handicaps and a special blessing for language handicapped children. Think of the struggle these children have just to create a first copy. As soon as they pick up the pencil the problems begin.

Marc

Before the introduction of word processing Marc hated writing anything. He always made mistakes. He would choose a wrong verb tense or make syntax errors, spelling errors, and so forth. Before he developed even one paragraph all desire to continue was gone. His only option was to erase and after six or seven corrections the paper was a mess. His papers always reflected the struggle, not the accomplishment—and that was if he finished it to begin with; most often he gave up long before completion.

Marc's introduction to word processing was accidental. He had been watching me work each morning writing a book. One day he simply tapped me on the shoulder and said, "Mom, can I do that?" I thought for a moment, got up from the computer and said, "Sure you can," and hurriedly wrote down five simple commands that represent the beginning power of Screenwriter, the particular word processing software I was using.

Marc said he had a 500 word science report to do. When I asked him when it was due he replied, "Today." Obviously it would have to be a crash course in word processing. He sat down to the computer and I showed him how to delete a letter, a word, and a line, how to insert, how to move the cursor up and down the screen, and how to save his work on disc.

From that point on he was on his own. He sat there, and before my eyes a seventh grade science report was born. It had all the language errors common to his written attempts, but I let him go on and on. When he said, "Done," with a big smile on his face, I said, "Okay, let's print it."

The first draft came off the printer and we proofread it together. I circled the errors, made some suggestions in the order of presentation, and then showed him how to bring his report back to the screen from disc storage. He was amazed when he saw his work before him and immediately began to make the corrections.

Actually, it was at this point that the real learning took place. There was a question as to whether Marc had ever been asked to correct his errors in written language before. His errors had been pointed out because he had notebooks full of written language assignments covered with red circles and handwritten notes made by teachers, but nowhere did Marc actually recopy his work to produce errorless, correct written language. That is understandable, too, for few would have the heart to ask a language handicapped child to recopy again and again to the point of errorless copy.

Marc made all the corrections and again printed out the report. It was a moment always to remember, for there in front of us was the first perfect paper Marc had ever generated. It reflected the accomplishment, not the struggle. He was so very proud, and so was I. Together we had found a tool to help him with written language and one that instilled a new kind of motivation. This tool allowed Marc to generate written language in a way that made him feel good about his work and himself.

Other Valuable Tool Uses. Another tool that has proved to be useful is telecommunication or "visual communication" over telephone lines. For this use a modem or acoustical coupler must be connected to the microcomputer and terminal software that allows the computer to interact with another computer. The practical applications are endless for millions of persons in this country (and millions more around the world) who use computers. This tool permits access to educational and consumer electronic data services that provide everything from the daily newspaper to shopping at home. It even provides many work-at-home opportunities for those who are unable to travel to the workplace. If a disabled individual is unable to get to the library or cannot easily communicate his or her desires, telecommunication stands ready to give them a new method to access and interact with this information.

Marc

In Marc's case, a telephone call between Marc and a hearing friend of his was to be the first time Marc was ever able to use the telephone for personal communication—something most people take for granted but an option that is limited for deaf people. The call came in and Marc watched the words fly across the screen. "Hi Marc. How are you? Did you actually go to the dance with Wendy on Saturday?" Marc's first reaction was "Wow, I have to learn to type that fast." The next was to watch "language with a purpose" take place. Suddenly, the language on the screen had a personal meaning. Marc began to answer the questions put to him by emulating the language presented. His answer read, "Yes, Shawn, I went to the dance with Wendy. We had fun." As the conversation progressed Marc took an interest in actual written language. His interaction with his friend on the other end demanded written language and it also provided a model for that language to develop.

What we have learned over the years with telecommunication use for Marc and other deaf and learning handicapped children is that its use provides an unequaled language development tool. Data collected over a period of two years show a sharp increase in written language skill development. But what is even more interesting is the samples of spontaneous oral language taken within the same time frames as the samples of written language. Marc's oral skills developed on the same curve as the written language, only about six months later.

Increases in language development as a result of meaningful language interactions via telecommunications seem to be developing with other children using telecommunication as a tool. Interviews with parents of both deaf and learning handicapped children using telecommunication show their experience to be much the same. This, unfortunately, is unscientific research, being merely parent observation. To date there appears to be a lack of any clinical or institutional data to support these conclusions because little applied research or practical application is under way with telecommunication in the educational environment. Written language development appears to be a natural byproduct of visual communication, or what we call "language with a purpose." Educators interested in the premise should pursue research related to this technology and attempt to determine if these hypotheses are valid.

Vocational Applications. Futurists predict that it will not be long before there are employment opportunities for as many people homebound by choice as those homebound by necessity. The information age brings with it the need and potential for people to handle information. This means that some individuals with microcomputer skills will be able to choose their work environment—which includes the disabled who have the proper equipment and training. This is not theory or dream, for the products that will allow it exist today. Disabled individuals can have an equal chance to share in those employment opportunities if they can operate a microcomputer in a competitive work environment. Even today nearly every occupation has employment opportunities in which microcomputers are used in information management. Handicapped individuals who can use a microcomputer skillfully surely can compete for these jobs.

In Sweden, for example, a completely computer-controlled furniture manufacturing facility currently employs developmentally disabled individuals. One person places the raw material on a conveyor belt, and pushes a button. At the other end another individual removes the finished product, places it on another conveyor belt, and pushes another button. A third individual receives the boxed item, attaches a computer-generated inventory control sticker, and sends the box to inventory. The inbetween stages of cut, assemble, box, and so forth, are handled by computer-controlled machines. Persons who can use the computers that are the results of "information age" technology are able to compete for jobs in the marketplace. The moderately handicapped individual who is well trained and reliable and has the ability to maintain performance in such a repetitive type of employment may even be a better candidate for such a job. In Saskatoon, Saskatchewan, a disabled worker sets type for a printing plant using a microcomputer terminal in his home. The advances in technology allow him to work at his own pace and to utilize the capacity of the computer to check such things as spelling, punctuation, and arithmetic. When the data entry is complete, he transmits it directly to the printing facility by telephone using a telecommunications device.

In both cases, technology and the use of computers have provided employment opportunities for disabled individuals that did not exist before. Every form of business and industry soon will look to microcomputer technology as a means of handling all kinds of information. That is the way information will be stored and manipulated throughout the world. Humans have adopted microcomputer technology as a tool to reduce burdensome tasks and accommodate for human error. It just happens to be a tool that disabled individuals can be trained to operate and use to their benefit in accommodating for their disabilities.

CONCLUSION

Today's microcomputer technology offers the same conveniences and applications to the disabled population as it does to anyone else. The educational, vocational and recreational applications are for everyone. For once the disabled can feel they are included with the rest of the population. The computer revolution was not conceived or designed for the handicapped, but it just happens to be overwhelmingly more useful to this group. Mass production has broken the price barriers that would have existed had these products been designed for handicapped only. In truth, a gap has been closed and a common tool for all has come forth. Now let's use it!

REFERENCES

Blaschke, C. (April 12, 1984). Technology trends in special education. Paper presented to the CAESD Conference, Los Angeles, CA.

Blake, K. (1981). Educating exceptional pupils: An introduction to contemporary practices. Reading, MA: Addison-Wesley.

Chaffin, J., Maxwell, B., & Thompson, B. (1982). ARC-ED curriculum: The application of video game formats to educational software. Exceptional Children, 49(2), 173-178.

Gula, R. (1982). Beyond the typewriter. Classroom Computer News, 2(5), 31-32.

Halpern, N. (1984). Artificial intelligence and the education of the learning disabled. Journal of Learning Disabilities, 17(2), 118-120.

Hardman, M., Drew, C., and Egan, M. (1984). Human exceptionality: Society, school, and family. Boston: Allyn and Bacon.

Hasselbring, T. (1982). Remediating spelling problems of learning-handicapped students through the use of microcomputers. Educational Technology, 22(4), 31-32.

Hasselbring, T., & Crossland, C. (1981). Using microcomputers for diagnosing spelling problems in learning-handicapped children. Educational Technology, 21(4), 37-39.

Kearsly, G., & Hunter, B. (1983). Electronic education: Computer-assisted instruction could change not only how we teach our children, but where. *High Technology*, April, 38–44.

Mason, G. (1980). Computerized Reading Instruction: A Review. *Eductional Technology*, October, 18–22.

Schiffman, G., Tobin, D., & Buchanan, B. (1982). Microcomputer instruction for the learning disabled. *Journal of Learning Disabilities, 15*(9), 557–559.

Slovick, L. (1982). CAI at CSDF: Microcomputer-based Authoring Systems. *American Annals of the Deaf, 127*(5).

Weiner, E. (1980). Diagnostic evaluation of writing skills. *Journal of Learning Disabilities, 13*(1), 48–53.

Weir, S., Russell, S., & Valente, J., (1982). LOGO: An approach to educating disabled children. *Byte*, September, 342, 347, 358, 360.

CHAPTER 6

Using Computers with Children With Sensory and Physical Impairments

The population of disabled individuals to whom this chapter is addressed are those with physical impairments. These physical impairments can be primarily sensory, (i.e., a visual or hearing impairment), motor impairment, (e.g., spina bifida), neurological impairment, (e.g., cerebral palsy), chronic illness, (e.g., asthma), or a combination of handicapping conditions. Overall these individuals learn like normal students and can be educated in a regular educational setting (Dykes, 1983). The development of new computer-based technology to assist these individuals to accommodate to their handicaps has even further assisted their integration into the mainstream of regular education. In these instances the computer is basically utilized as a tool, enabling the student to maximize the physical abilities he or she has or providing a mechanism to circumvent the handicap.

There are, however, a significant number of individuals whose impairments are so severe or are combined in such a way as to interfere with normal learning. The combinations or severity of the impairments may have effects on cognitive growth, language and communication, and social or emotional development. The following section will discuss how sensory and physical impairments can affect the learning process.

DEFINITIONS AND LEARNING NEEDS

Visual Impairments

There are two major classifications of visual impairments, blind and partially sighted. Legally, the definition of blindness refers to the inability to correct vision in one eye to 20/250 (i.e., the individual sees at 20 feet what the normally sighted can see at 250 feet), and partially sighted refers to the inability to correct vision to 20/70. However, these definitions have little meaning to how a person learns, since most legally blind individuals

This chapter was authored by Michael M. Behrmann and Elizabeth Lahm.

are able to read using large print materials (Willis, 1976). For educational purposes, however, a functional approach provides a better method of defining visual impairments. This approach distinguishes between the ability of the individual to read print or the necessity of providing an oral or mechanical mode (Braille or electronic) of presenting information. In addition to impairments of vision, visual perception problems may also be present. These types of visual impairments are often associated with neurologic impairments, such as those associated with cerebral palsy (CP).

In terms of the function of vision in learning, vision is the sense that coordinates most of an individual's sensory impressions of the events and objects that surround him or her. It provides a mechanism that assists in the process of categorizing those events and objects. While lack of visual acuity does not prevent the utilization of other senses to learn, experiencing some aspects of life will be impossible; a person cannot, for example, feel colors or hear the moon. Additionally, perceptual problems involving figure-ground, reversals, part-whole relationships, and so forth, may impair an individual's ability to learn effectively. Individuals may rotate words and see them upside down or backwards. Others may see only part of an image or not be able to pick out the relevant parts of a picture (Dykes, 1983). Thus, language concepts may be impaired by inabililty to discriminate relevant material (from written or pictorial material) or inability to produce written language.

Spatial concepts and concomitant mobility problems are also associated with visual impairments. Knowing where one's body or body parts are located in space is a common difficulty of blind and neurologically impaired individuals. Thus, concepts of understanding the surrounding environment and how to function or move within it present educational challenges.

Lack of visual acuity or severe visual perceptual problems may also affect the ability to learn by imitation. As noted in the Chapter 7, the concepts of modeling and vicarious learning are important to the learning process. If this type of incidental learning is impaired, it may be necessary to deliberately teach many additional tasks, such as how to smile appropriately, establish eye contact, and so forth. These learning problems can also lead to the development of inappropriate secondary behaviors, sometimes called "blindisms," including such things as rocking and poking the eyes, which may inhibit the "normalization" of the individual.

Hearing or Auditory Impairments

As with visual impairments, hearing impairments may be physiologically based but may also have functional bases that are more relevant to education. Physiologically, hearing impairment is defined by decibels (units relating to the intensity or loudness of sounds) of hearing loss. Deafness connotes a loss of auditory sensitivity to the point that auditory communication is difficult or impossible without amplification (Reynolds & Birch, 1982). A hearing impairment refers to a malfunction of the auditory mechanism, which in turn affects the ability of the individual to function in daily living, particularly in the area of communication (receptive or expressive, or both). It is important to note here that a hearing impairment can be the result of the malfunction of parts of inner, middle, or outer ear or damage to the neurologic processes involved in hearing. Many children with CP have hearing impairments that are neurologically based. In terms of an educationally functional definition, there are five major factors to consider. The first is whether the primary channel for learning and communication is through visual means or whether the auditory capabilities of the child can be used extensively. The second is the severity of hearing loss. The third is the age of onset. Age of onset is perhaps the most critical factor, since the amount of language that a child has acquired before deafness will be a significant factor in the ability to develop speech and language skills. A child who has a hearing loss before developing spoken language is said to be prelingually deaf, whereas an individual who learns to speak before onset of the hearing loss is postlingually deaf (Kneedler, Hallahan, & Kauffman, 1984). The fourth and fifth considerations are not traditionally associated with hearing impairments, but have significant educational implications, particularly with neurologically impaired children. They are auditory memory deficits and auditory decoding problems. Individuals with this type of impairment may not have a visible or medically determinable hearing loss, but their inability to recall auditory messages or the inability to perceive sounds, parts of words, or parts of sentences may have significant adverse affects on learning.

The loss or impairment of hearing is probably one of the most severe disabling conditions because it affects the development of language. The importance of language in the learning process is significant, and any handicap in this area often leads to secondary disabilities. This sensory impairment can result in perceptual, speech, communication, cognitive, and social or emotional developmental delays, which in turn have a significant effect on the educational and vocational training needed by this population (Boothroyd, 1982). Additionally, the impairment of receptive and expressive language tends to isolate this population from the rest of the world, where spoken language is a basic skill, and few hearing individuals are able to communicate well with hearing impaired individuals with poor speech.

Generally, in terms of technology to address the needs of this population, much work has been done to help hearing impaired individuals communicate with the rest of the world. They are able to access much more information and use technology to more efficiently communicate with both hearing people and other hearing impaired individuals, both through direct communication and over the telephone lines. In the area of accommodating to the handicapping condition, technology has enabled the hearing impaired to enjoy television (through captioning), and work is even being done on a prosthetic ear. Many of these new and developing technologies are being applied to educational settings where special software and hardware should make appropriate educational material more available to meet the learning needs of this population.

Motor Impairments

As stated earlier in this chapter, individuals with motor impairments generally have the same learning characteristics as nondisabled individuals. The population discussed here include children with "crippling conditions" and those who have chronic health impairments that limit their ability to interact physically with their environment in a so-called normal manner. The types of physical impairments include spina bifida, cerebral palsy, traumatic spinal cord injuries resulting in paralysis, amputations, and arthritis, among others. Motor impairments may also be a result of such disorders as Legg Perthes disease, which affects bone growth and subsequent motor functioning (Bigge, 1982), poliomyelitis, hemophilia, cystic fibrosis, muscular dystrophy, and multiple sclerosis, the latter two being degenerative and generally fatal. Reynolds and Birch (1982) characterize children with motor impairments alone as an "artificial grouping, educationally speaking." In general, technology for these children is aimed at prosthetic devices (i.e., tools) to enable them to accommodate to their motor handicaps.

Motor impairments can inhibit an individual's ability to learn by interfering with "normal" interactions with the environment. Computer-based technology is now providing the means to maximize the physical capabilities of physically impaired individuals so that they may interact with their environment by using the computer as an extension of their bodies. The three major areas in which technology can assist learning by enhancing environmental interactions are communication, environmental control, and environmental manipulation (Behrmann & Lahm, 1984). Motor impairments, particularly in individuals with CP, often prevent verbal communication, which is important in social, cognitive, and language development, as well as the ability to use the fine motor control needed for written communication. Motor impairments can also inhibit individuals from independently interacting with their environment. In young children, this can hinder learning experiences, and in older individuals it causes frustration and dependence. Environmental control devices allow individuals to extend their physical capabilities. An extension of environmental control is environmental manipulation. Many necessary activities of daily living are not amenable to electrical on-off control, and it is necessary to manipulate or move things through the environment. Robots can fulfill the need to manipulate many of these items. While the area of robotics for the handicapped currently is limited, there are now a number of relatively inexpensive robots available, and new ones with greater capacity to lift objects and utilize advanced sensory technology are sure to come. Additionally, robots can be expected to incorporate voice input technology and be able to fulfill multiple functions, including communication and environmental control tasks.

Multiple Impairments

Within the population of individuals with sensory impairments, there are a significant number of individuals with multiple handicaps or whose impairments are so severe that learning and functioning in many areas are adversely affected. It is estimated that there are nearly 60,000 multiply handicapped children in schools and institutions across the country (Dearman & Plisko, 1981). These conditions may affect such educational areas as communication and language development, intellectual and academic development, self-help skills, recreation, and leisure skills. In an individual with multiple disabilities, mental retardation is probably the most common handicapping condition. As much as 60% of the CP population, which is probably the largest group of motor impaired children, has some degree of retardation. Hearing impairments are also found in 10% to 15% of the institutionalized retarded population (Kirk & Gallagher, 1983).

Multiple impairments, particularly those affecting cognitive abilities in conjunction with sensory impairments, require intensive and systematic intervention strategies to implement an effective educational program. The technologic applications needed to assist multiply handicapped individuals in the learning process may need to incorporate both the methods and technologies (tool and instructional) discussed in the remainder of this chapter with those discussed in previous chapters.

IMPLICATIONS OF TECHNOLOGY FOR SENSORY AND PHYSICALLY IMPAIRED

The sensory and physically impaired populations, with their variety of disabilities, at first appeared to be an illogical group of candidates for whom to design microcomputers. The standard computer comes with a keyboard that certainly seems to be of limited use to blind and upper extremity disabled individuals. The standard output is the CRT or video screen. Visually impaired persons are obviously not best suited for that form of output. The hearing impaired have the most realistic opportunity for working with the standard system because it does not generally rely on auditory information.

Designers of computer systems know that there are a number of alternative ways to interact (inputs and outputs), which can be built into every system. Although the standard computer system uses the keyboard and video screen as the primary alternatives, these choices are not final or necessarily the "right" ones. Recently the Apple Macintosh has developed a "mouse" as the input device, which, for the most part, allows the user to bypass the keyboard. This is usually a box with a rotating ball on the bottom side. The user holds the box and manipulates it around any flat surface, such as the table top. An additional consideration is the numerous reports in the news questioning the effects of sitting at video terminals all day. Thus, even for nonhandicapped populations, the standard microcomputer system might not be best, and new alternatives to video screens are called for.

A number of reasonable alternatives have already been developed for both input and output devices. "Reasonable" in this sense can be interpreted as of relatively low cost and available commercially "off the shelf." Other input and output devices have also been developed, but some are not considered reasonable alternatives. As with most developing technology, with time they too may become economically feasible.

Input Devices

A microcomputer is a logical machine that processes sequential information. The user must feed that information into the system. The standard or most common device for entering information is the keyboard. Physically handicapped individuals have significant disabilities by definition, and if these disabilities affect the upper extremities the keyboard may not be a useful device. One very simple, nontechnical compensatory device to access the keyboard is the headstick. The neck muscle group is the one relied upon for use of this device; control of the neck muscles is more common in quadriplegics than is control of the upper extremities. Although it is inexpensive and available, unless the headstick is the user's only alternative, it is probably not the most appropriate device for input of information into a computer system because of the slow rate at which information is entered. Three groups of more sophisticated technical input devices are (1) simple switches, (2) video pointing devices, and (3) voice recognition devices.

Switches. Simple inexpensive switches, which have been used in special education classrooms to control battery-operated toys, can also be used as input devices for microcomputers if software programs are written to read them. This requires custom software, an expensive alternative, or specialized hardware for decoding switch inputs into keyboard inputs. The advantage of utilizing these switches lies in their flexibility. Virtually any small muscle with voluntary control can be used to activate a switch if the movement or performance requirements are completely analyzed and the switch is constructed adequately. Utilizing small muscle groups can result in better performance than using the large muscle groups, such as those of the neck. Data can be entered into a computer more efficiently, thus taking better advantage of the capabilities of a microcomputer.

Tracy and Bevans (1984) suggest 10 rules for selecting switches. Switches should (1) be safe (e.g., no electrical shock flowback to the user), (2) require minimum effort while maintaining maximum comfort for the user, (3) be reliable, (4) be minimally noticeable to others, (5) be easy for the user to find even after moving, (6) be easy to disassemble for cleaning and maintenance, (7) be constructed of standard components for increased availability and ease of replacement, (8) be simple, (9) be sturdy, and (10) be easily duplicated. Depending on the user's motor abilities, one switch or many switches can be incorporated into a system. Each of these switches may have single or multiple functions. Generally speaking, the greater the number of switches the fewer functions each will have and the more efficient the system will be (e.g., one switch moves the cursor horizontally and the second moves it vertically). The most efficient number of switches for a given individual should be identified, but a survey of available software that already accepts switch input is recommended before deciding on a configuration of switches. This is primarily because customizing software to utilize the switches can be expensive. The majority of switch input software adaptations are limited to one or two switches. Consequently, a configuration that is physically and cognitively efficient for a user may not be available for use in any existing software.

Pointing Devices. The second group of input devices, generally referred to as video pointing devices, includes joysticks, light pens, and trackballs but also devices such as the mouse, digitizing tablets, touch tablets, and touch screens. These devices allow the user to use linear movement to move the cursor quickly around the screen. The location of the cursor on the screen is read by X-Y coordinates, which have meaning for a particular software controlled function (e.g., erase text). The selection of a function is indicated by a single input, making it a much faster method than keyboard entry of commands. This ease or simplification of the input process has significant implications for handicapped users. While some of these devices require a good amount of motor coordination, others only require a single touch to the screen or a touch pad. The mouse and joystick require the user to manipulate a remote object in the appropriate direction and proportion to the screen in order to place the cursor at a prespecified location. A finger or any blunt instrument can be used to indicate a choice when using the touch tablet, or a special electrical stylus can be used with the digitizing tablet.

Voice Recognition. Another type of input device that has been developed for microcomputers is voice recognition. Human voice or other sound sequences can be interpreted by the microcomputer and be used as the input information. This requires the user to "train" the system to understand the voice command. The system is really measuring the frequencies of the sound pattern and storing them in memory. It uses that stored information as a dictionary with which to compare future commands. When it hears a command that matches one in its dictionary it performs the function or task for which it has been preprogrammed. For example, the user may give the command "Run" to the system. Upon hearing it, the system analyzes the command to see if it is recognizable. If so, a prespecified program will be started. Again the keyboard is completely bypassed. One disadvantage to this technology at present is the exactness of the sound that is required in order to find a match. Although tolerances can usually be set, the user must be quite consistent in speaking a word (or providing a nonverbal sound) in order for it to be recognized. This also results in a single user system, because the computer will be trained to recognize only one individual's voice.

Output Devices

As with the input devices normally used with computer systems, many of the output devices are not appropriate for physically and sensory impaired individuals. Adaptations and alternatives to these devices are available. The outputs will be considered in five categories: (1) video screen, (2) print, (3) voice, (4) telecommunications, and (5) physical action.

Video Screen. The video screen normally displays its output in dot matrix format. This means that each letter, character, and picture is made up of a series of dots. There are no continuous lines, although the higher quality video screens or CRTs (high resolution) are perceived as continuous lines. A simple adaptation for screen output is to enlarge the print by magnifying the screen or using software control to proportionally enlarge the letters. Dot matrix characters are initially difficult to read, and magnification also increases the space between the dots, resulting in additional loss of clarity. The task of reading the print becomes even more difficult, especially for the visually impaired. Alternatives that enlarge the print by means other than blowing up the image already there provide better quality video output and a viable output mode for the partially sighted.

Print. The second group of devices is concerned with the print output or hard copy. Special applications software programs are available that enlarge the print, similar to the screen adaptations. These are useful for the teacher of the visually impaired in preparing classroom materials. Another alternative is output in Braille. This tactile medium can be read by numerous blind individuals.

Voice. Voice output is an alternative to the standard video screen and paper printout. It is available is two types, analog or digital, each with advantages and disadvantages. Analog speech is less expensive than digitized and utilizes voice chips that store phonemic rules and exceptions. It uses these to translate text into speech. It has the advantage of great flexibility, as it will attempt to say any word. The quality of the speech is its major disadvantage. It sounds "robot-like" and is often hard to understand, especially for new audiences. Digital speech, on the other hand, is more human-like but is stored word for word. In order to have access to a large vocabulary, a lot of computer memory must be available. Accessing a sequence of words to form a sentence can be a slow process as each word must be individually found in the dictionary. In short, although digital speech sounds more human-like, it is more expensive. Analog or text-to-speech synthesizers are cheaper but at present could never be considered for articulation models for speech therapy.

Telecommunications. Sound can be used in ways other than for speech generation. Morse code can be generated using in-house computer tones without special equipment. In some applications a simple tone system may be all that is needed (for example, in sending emergency signals). A more sophisticated use of auditory signals is for telecommunications. The output of the computer is sound transmitted through the telephone wires via modems (which modulate and demodulate sound transmissions) for the purpose of communicating with another computer. This practice is becoming more and more commonplace as the number of data bases and bulletin boards increases, but the implication for handicapped users is that it may be their most efficient means of communicating with other handicapped users or the nonhandicapped world. Combinations of auditory signals should also not be overlooked as alternatives to the video and printed formats of standard output in telecommunications (e.g., a talking terminal).

Physical Action. The final area of output alternatives results in a physical motion or action on the environment. Some common examples of these types are controlling electrical devices via the computer or directing a robot to perform a routine. The outputs here do not have to be visual or auditory but are primarily motor. This area of output is relatively new in nonindustrial applications of computer systems but holds a lot of potential for the physically and sensory impaired populations.

Developing Alternatives

While a number of input and output alternatives can be considered reasonable in terms of cost and availability, some that have great potential for handicapped individuals have not made it to the general market yet. Some exciting alternatives in the motor group lie in biomedical research, where microcomputers and microprocessors are being utilized to give motor movement to previously disabled limbs. Biofeedback also can be used as another source of input signals for severely handicapped users (Goldenberg, 1979; Lavine, 1980). Biofeedback retrieves information from muscle groups that is normally not available or useable. The electrophysiologic technology is utilized to sense various body changes and enhance that information by converting it to appropriate machine readable signals or numbers. The individual with very minimal control can elicit responses using small muscle groups or use partial responses of muscle groups so as to not trigger reflexes. An innovative input method that is being researched measures the reflection of light from the eye's retina to determine the direction of eye pointing (Lavine, 1980). For the number of individuals who currently can use eye pointing as the only method of communication, the increased accuracy of this new application will certainly reduce the frustration of misinterpretation and the time now being consumed for each selection made. For more information on what the future may hold, see Chapter 12.

APPLICATIONS FOR THE PHYSICALLY AND SENSORY IMPAIRED

By combining adaptive inputs with adaptive outputs, the handicapped user has a great number of options available to meet individual needs. Figure 6–1 illustrates these options. Any input category can be utilized and information transmitted via any of the output categories. Descriptions of

Figure 6–1. Microcomputer input and output options.

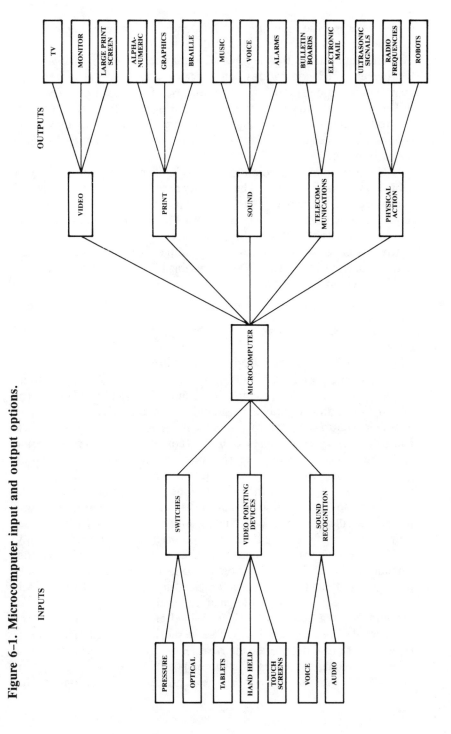

some of the specific input and output devices currently available will be included as each disability group is discussed.

The applications that are available for the physically, visually, and hearing impaired populations can be categorized into two groups: (1) instructional, and (2) tool uses. The purpose of applications software in the instructional category is to teach a skill or provide practice for that skill to assist the learner in its mastery and generalization. This application is commonly called computer assisted instruction (CAI) or computer based instruction (CBI).

There are numerous commercially available programs in a variety of subject areas and user levels. The majority have been prepared for general audiences. The alternative inputs and outputs reviewed earlier are generally not available for use with these programs. The customization of software to meet the needs of handicapped users is an expensive and time-consuming process. If programmers were aware of simple changes they could make in developmental stages to make them usable by special consumers, wider audiences could be reached.

Instruction

The key elements of instructional software are discussed more completely in Chapter 10, but the major characteristics of good software are worth repeating. First, to provide maximum flexibility and extend the user audience, all key parameters should be alterable. That is, the teacher or student should have control over such items as speed, number of trials, and criterion correct responses. Some less common parameters that could easily be made adjustable are size of print, amount of information presented on one screen, the input mode (switch, keyboard, light pen, touch tablet, and so forth), and the output mode (video, print, voice, Braille, motor, and so forth). These parameters are most important in making a program available for physically and sensory handicapped. In many cases only a few lines of code need to be changed to offer significant flexibility.

The second major programming consideration in instructional software is the ability of the program to assess the user's abilities and progress and branch to appropriate places in the program to meet their individual needs. Software designed to teach a skill to handicapped individuals often needs to be finer grained and more flexible than the educational software generally available. In short, the instructional software programmer must incorporate many varieties of teaching techniques, fine tune the teaching sequences as much as possible, and make the options available to the user. However, these programs, if appropriate for handicapped users, should also provide the flexibility needed for a general audience.

Tools

Microcomputers can be used as tools to accomplish a variety of tasks for handicapped users. This category of tool uses can be further divided into three groups: (1) information management, (2) communication, and (3) environmental manipulation. Many of these applications are not unique to the physically and sensory impaired but require the alternative inputs and outputs to accomplish them. In the information management area, some common examples are word processing, data base management, and telecommunications. Although these are also frequently used by the general population, they often provide the only means for completing a task for the handicapped user. An example is the individual with upper extremity involvement who cannot manipulate any writing instruments but who can, by using a head switch, use word processing software to produce written communications.

Communication devices are not new tools that have been made available with microcomputers. The microcomputer does, however, offer more capability and flexibility, and for many provides a more efficient mode of augmentative communication. The memory capacity of these machines provides users with larger vocabularies and faster access. Additionally, they are generally easier to reprogram with revised vocabularies.

Environmental manipulation provides a group of tool applications that have the potential of extending the abilities of many handicapped individuals to levels of independence previously unavailable. Computer-controlled robots extend the limits of the user's accessible environment and can substitute or supplement his or her sensory capabilities.

Visually Impaired

Goldenberg (1979) voices a frustration at the lack of equal coverage of handicaps in technologic advancements. He states that early references to computer assistance for the handicapped and conferences on the subject rarely addressed all handicapped populations but were more heavily focused on the motorically and visually handicapped, with little attention being given to the hearing handicapped. With this lopsided beginning to the applications of technology to special populations, it is no wonder that more advanced devices exist for these groups than for the mentally retarded. The visually handicapped were among the first to benefit from new applications, and as a result, greater numbers of specialized devices and more widespread usage is common for this group.

Hardware

Special devices developed to assist the visually handicapped populations can be classified into five categories: (1) printed text to voice, (2) computer text to voice, (3) computer text to Braille, (4) the enlargement of text, and (5) devices to assist in mobility. Within these categories there exists a wide range of applications with an equally wide range of costs.

Print to Voice. In the first category, one machine stands out and may be unmatched in its capabilities. The Kurzweil Reading Machine, which was introduced in 1976, "reads" printed text and voices it using a speech synthesizer. It can transcribe a wide variety of type fonts, giving access to books, journals, and some columned materials that are not available in Braille for blind and visually impaired individuals. The speech synthesizer utilizes phonetic rules and 1500 rule exceptions to produce fairly accurate robot-like speech. Numerous controls allow choice of rate, volume, tonality, and other variations in the quality of speech output. Reportedly this is not a difficult machine to use, and it can be found in approximately 300 public and university libraries, schools for the blind, rehabilitation centers, state and federal agencies, and private corporations. At present the cost of the Kurzweil Reading Machine is prohibitive for individual ownership ($22,000 to $29,000), but costs are predicted to decrease in the future (Kurzweil, 1981).

Computer Text to Voice. Numerous talking terminals, the second category of devices, are now available to assist visually handicapped individuals in utilizing computer technology for work and study. These terminals range from simply incorporating a speech synthesis unit into a microcomputer to more sophisticated terminals that are specially designed for the purpose of translating computer text into voice outputs. An example of an adapted microcomputer speech application is the ECHO II speech synthesizer (Street Electronics). This device comes either as a peripheral card that plugs into a microcomputer or as a stand-alone device that can be interfaced with any microcomputer. Special software that is included with the synthesizer allows all text that appears on the computer screen to be spoken out as words or spelled, with or without punctuation. The voice is robot-like and uses a phonetic approach to translation similar to that of the Kurzweil Reading Machine, but with fewer exception rules, yielding less accuracy. This simple application is relatively inexpensive (approximately $170), but it is not as flexible and easy to use as more sophisticated devices.

A device of intermediate sophistication is the IBM Audio Typing Unit (ATU). This unit provides the blind user with a synthesized speech feedback to information typed on one of three IBM typewriters. It also has edit capabilities to make revisions and review of final copy possible without the assistance of a sighted person. Research has shown that the device is easy to learn to use. Over a 16 hour training period, the number of errors can be reduced significantly, and users have rated the ATU progressively easier to use and understand (Day, Gum, & DeGrasse, 1982). Another field trial resulted in no significant difference in the amount of assistance needed from a sighted person, but spelling errors decreased (Tyler & Gillman, 1982). In both studies, the attitudes of the individuals toward using the device were very positive, and it is believed that it could make a significant impact on a visually handicapped person's ability to be competitive in the job market.

Total Talk is highly specialized talking terminal that includes a Hewlett-Packard 2621A Interactive Terminal, a microprocessor, the VOTRAX VSB Speech Synthesizer, and software that integrates everything, creating an intelligent terminal that provides the user with auditory as well as visual feedback. This system is designed to be used with a main frame computer and will serve as the user's input and output device. All data entered or received by the terminal can be heard by the user, giving the visually handicapped individual access to large quantities of information as well as numerous capabilities for data management, computation, and word processing. Like the ECHO II it has various modes of feedback (for words, spelling, and punctuation), but it offers more flexibility in commands such as "Say the line," "Say the page," and "Say the memory." In addition to all the phonetic exception rules that the system utilizes, the user can also customize his or her own vocabulary to increase the degree of intelligibility (Blazie, 1981). Various options are now available for Total Talk, including the upgrading of the system to function as a stand-alone microcomputer rather than just a terminal, and specially designed software for information management and form generation.

Finally the Universal Laboratory Training and Research Aide (ULRA) has been developed in conjunction with a microcomputer to allow visually handicapped users to conduct their own chemistry experiments. This project allows the student to "make mistakes" like any other student. Plans exist to include voice activation and transfer to Braille (Hilldrup, 1984).

Text to Braille. The third category of applications available for the visually handicapped user takes computer text and translates it into Braille, and vice versa. These applications are generally based on software rather than on specially designed hardware (excluding a Braille embosser). The software acts as a translator or transcriber, moving information from English text to Braille code and back again. Common features of many of these programs include text editing capabilities, voice output as well as print, and the option of creating a hard copy via a Brailler or sending the braille code to the screen. This latter option is useful for sighted Braille users who need to transcribe music and mathematics into a more technical Braille code.

An example of a third category program is Braille-Edit. This program won national recognition in The Johns Hopkins First National Search for Applications of Personal Computing to Aid the Handicapped in 1981 (IEEE Computer Society, 1981). This program currently works in conjunction with the VersaBraille and provides a means by which Apple II microcomputer text can be translated into grade two Braille (a type of Braille shorthand) and transferred to the VersaBraille, or vice versa. The program provides many edit capabilities, such as cursor movement, merge, delete, and insert. Two systems of voice synthesis are supported allowing the blind user the opportunity for independent use of the Apple II microcomputer without the VersaBraille (Holladay, 1981, 1982).

Print Enlargement. There are two approaches to achieving print enlargement, the last category of applications for the visually handicapped. The first, software control, is a very inexpensive approach to altering the size of the text that appears on the computer screen. "Large Type," by N.I.R.E.,* is one such program for the TRS-80 microcomputer. Double width characters are displayed and some text editing capabilities are also provided.

A second approach is through specially designed hardware. Although more expensive, this offers a great deal more flexibility and utility. The DP-10 from Visualtek is a monitor and interface box that works with the Apple II microcomputer. It automatically enlarges the print display from 2 to 16 times its normal size. No alterations need to be made to a program to handle the 40 character line and 24 rows of print that normally appear on the screen. The DP-10 treats the screen as a window, and the user scrolls the text horizontally and vertically to see the entire screen. This technique makes the hardware software independent, and thus the majority of available software can be used (with the exception of programs that use graphics).

One additional program that is worth mentioning that falls under the more general category of computer assisted instruction (CAI) is "Braille Trainer" (Hoefer, Arnold, & Waddell, 1983). This program is designed to teach the skill of reading Braille. It is intended for sighted individuals who are interested in seeking certification for transcribing written works into Braille. The program follows a drill and practice format and is very simple to obtain; it is also free.

The voice synthesizer is a popular device in technologic applications for the visually handicapped. The most affordable type of voice synthesizer utilizes a text to speech phonetic approach which produces a robot-like

---

*National Institute of Rehabilitative Engineering.

voice as in the Total Talk talking terminal and the Kurzweil Reading Machine. It is not uncommon to experience difficulty in understanding this type of voice when heard for the first time, and many people seem to resist it because of its mechanical quality. Speech therapists question its use during language development years because it provides a poor human speech model. Many questions have not been answered related to its use, but research does indicate that with time, it becomes more understandable (Day, Gum, & DeGrasse, 1982; Rhyne, 1982; Tyler & Gillman, 1982). The use of the voice synthesizer has opened the door to employment for many visually handicapped individuals, as indicated by the testimonials of these users and statistical data gathered by developers (Maryland Computer Services (no date); *People*, 1979; *Star-News*, 1980).

Mobility Devices. The final area of hardware development for visually impaired individuals is in the assistance of mobility. Microprocessor-based devices, such as a laser cane that can detect obstacles and provide auditory feedback, are now available. Another, similar device has been developed by Pentad (Woodstock, VA). This relatively inexpensive handheld device uses sonar sent in a cone-shaped signal and is able to detect objects up to 20 feet away. It can provide a voice-synthesized auditory feedback through a set of headphones or through a Braille cell on the handle.

Hearing Impaired

The hearing impaired population frequently is isolated from information that is generally available to other people. This isolation is the major handicap related to a hearing loss, and this lack of information inhibits the development of language (Goldenberg, 1979; Withrow, 1978). Microcomputer technology can assist the hearing impaired individual with language development by providing an opportunity to "play" with the language, an opportunity often missed by this population. As Goldenberg points out, instruction in the classroom is usually presented in a directed response format, in which the child is requested to provide pat answers. To date, the majority of microcomputer applications have followed a format similar to drill and practice programs. These practices have denied the hearing impaired individual the chance to construct language hypotheses and test them in their environment, as young hearing children do naturally in their early learning years. One goal for the use of technology with this population must be language development and the provision of efficient means for using language to communicate.

The developments in the microcomputer technology have been broken into three categories for the purposes of discussing applications for the hearing impaired. First the hardware devices that serve this population will be reviewed. This will be followed by a discussion of software that is intended to serve as a tool, and finally a description of software with instructional goals will be given.

Hardware

Since the early 1960s when Weitbrecht developed a modem for converting key strokes to Baudot codes for transmission over telephone lines, the hearing handicapped have had a means for long-distance communication (Hagen, 1984). This vehicle was limited because few people in the general population were using Baudot code and fewer hearing impaired individuals could afford the equipment.

The use of microcomputers and telecommunications provides a similar means of long-distance communication but has the advantage of being a mainstream system, not a special use system. The code that is used with microcomputers in these telephone line transmissions is ASCII (American Standards for Communication Information Interchange). Unfortunately, this code is not compatible with the Baudot code and as a consequence all the hearing impaired individuals who bought the Weitbrecht system still cannot communicate with the majority of telecommunications users. Two of these were submitted to the Johns Hopkins National Search for Application of Personal Computing to Aid the Handicapped in 1981 (Bozzuto, 1981; Glaser, 1981). These two devices provide the Baudot user the option of transmitting or receiving information in Baudot or ASCII code by translating one to the other. A similar modem was developed by AmRAD (Amateur Radio Research and Development Corporation) using a standard Bell 103 modem but modifying it to detect both Baudot and ASCII code (Rinaldo & Bruninga, 1980; Taber, 1983). AmRAD also started a bulletin board and electronic mail service called HEX (Handicapped Education Exchange) to provide handicapped users access to education and communication in both ASCII and Baudot codes.

Levitt (1981) has developed a portable telecommunication system. Using a small handheld computer by Radio Shack, he has designed this system with a miniature telephone interface so that it can be used with any phone, including a public telephone.

These new developments in telecommunications technology for the hearing impaired can bring the mainstream world of information to that population that has been isolated from it historically. As with most new technologic developments, though, these are expensive, and users must often rely on industry assisting the handicapped. Northwestern Bell, the telephone utility company of the upper Midwest section of the United States, offers low cost loans to handicapped individuals to purchase communication hardware (Hagen, 1984). It is hoped that other industries will follow suit and make the world of information equally available to all.

Since the standard method of interacting with microcomputers is primarily visual and motor (keyboard and monitor), hearing handicapped individuals do not require major hardware modifications to interact with the microcomputer itself. The technology does, however, offer potential beyond the stand-alone machine. Watson (1978) describes two potential applications, the first of which is already available in a primitive form. In England a deaf member of the Parliament has the floor debates transcribed to a video screen. Based on device with a function similar to a stenotype, phonetic text is generated on a CRT. Developmental work is also being done to transform speech to visual cues using speech analyzer aids and displaying the cues for the hearing impaired individual on a special pair of glasses. While translating text into speech for nonvocal individuals is an available and affordable technology already, changing speech into text is not a simple process (see Chapter 12), and it will be a few years before this option is commonly available.

Tool Software

Software that can be used to assist an individual in performing a task efficiently can be considered tool software. An area of need for hearing impaired individuals is in the use of language for communication with nonhandicapped individuals. Hagen (1984) speaks of her experiences with her deaf son and his lack of desire to learn standard English. He seemingly had no use for it until he attempted to communicate with nonhandicapped people via telecommunications. He then became motivated by his desire to be understood. To practice his language he turned to word processing. This gave him an opportunity to "play" with language, manipulate it to test language hypotheses, and then send out his messages to his intended audience when he was ready.

Word processors can be important tools for the hearing impaired. They allow the chance to manipulate the language without being committed to what was said the first time. Use of word processors does not require lengthy rewrites, nor does it require lengthy work sessions. The communication produced can be sent to a printer, or it can be sent across telephone lines. The capability of communicating with nonhandicapped peers and receiving immediate feedback is important to language development and a motivating factor for improving writing skills (Goldenberg, 1979; Hagen, 1984; Watson, 1978).

In the same area of language, a second tool has been suggested, but yet not developed. As a result of not hearing language, severely hearing impaired individual frequently speaks in "deaf English," a form of English that does not follow all of the syntactical rules. Goldenberg (1979) suggests an appropriate use of the microcomputer would be a translation program from "deaf English" to a standard English. Programming a tool of this nature would be a difficult task but would be very helpful for this population.

Myers (1982) reports on another area of tool software in combination with special hardware. The environment can be monitored continuously by a microcomputer to sense auditory signals, such as doorbells, telephones, and timers. The program displays visual information to alert the hearing impaired individual of changes in status of all items being monitored.

Instructional Software

Computer assisted instruction (CAI) takes on many forms for the hearing handicapped population. The most common approach, teaching curriculum content, had early beginnings in education of the deaf. As early as 1970, CAI research was being conducted on deaf populations to measure the effects of CAI in mathematics. CAI was found to substantially increase computational skills (Watson, 1978). Later studies found CAI in combination with traditional teaching to be effective for deaf learners. These CAI uses do not require special software; deaf persons can use the traditional input and output modes of the microcomputer.

Another group of CAI programs use the microcomputer to teach skills that are specific to the hearing impaired population. The programs fall into three training categories: lip reading, signing, and vocalization (Hagen, 1984; Myers, 1982). The "Lip-Reader Trainer" is a program that teaches and drills the user in the 19 distinguishable lip positions of the English language speaker (Hight, 1981). The program converts typed sentences into appropriate sequences of mouth positions. The speed of presentations of these sequences is adjustable to allow the user to build up to "real life" speed.

Several programs are available to teach fingerspelling and signing. Four programs of this type were entered in the Johns Hopkins First National Search for Applications of Personal Computing to Aid the Handicapped in 1981. These programs are similar in that they use graphic representations of the alphabet signs and provide drill and practice for becoming efficient at recognizing them (IEEE Computer Society, 1981; Myers, 1982). Another interactive signing program resides on the "First National Kidisc" (Optical Programming Associates, 1981), an interactive video disc for children (see Chapter 12).

Vocalization trainers utilize special hardware in addition to software to analyze voice patterns, which are entered into the computer. Using a biofeedback approach, patterns are displayed on the video screen to provide the user with information for comparing their vocalization to that of a model pattern or a previous pattern of their own. By trying to match patterns, they can come to sound more natural in speaking. Two such programs were presented in the Proceedings of the Johns Hopkins First National Search (IEEE Computing Society, 1981). A program developed and tested much earlier comes from the Clarke School for the Deaf in Massachusetts (Watson, 1978).

In addition to content CAI and special skills CAI, some work has been done with deaf populations to develop thinking and problem-solving skills. Rose, Waldron, and Kolomyjec (1984) state an assumption that hearing handicapped have difficulty with problem solving because typically it requires language skills. They propose that the problems be presented in graphics, a highly visual medium that allows manipulation of the characteristics. Based on their study, they found that deaf individuals can solve problems and acquire rules through experimentation and deduction. Nugent and Stone (1982) base their program on a similar theory but incorporate an interactive video disc to present the visual information. The video disc provides motion and realistic information to assist the user in developing thinking skills.

The approach to using CAI with the hearing impaired population does not differ significantly from that for the general population. Comden (1981) illustrates several approaches using minicomputers and microcomputers for CAI and as tools. Several set-ups are described, including using minicomputers with several terminals dedicated to CAI alone and microcomputers networked together giving access to the capacity of a hard disc storage system. Computer literacy, CAI, telecommunications, tool uses, and vocational applications at the Western Pennsylvania School for the Deaf show the variety of applications for the hearing impaired population. While the basic system does not differ from that for the general population, the content of the software may require modification or specialization to meet the population's needs. Arcanin and Zawolkow (1980) describe their efforts to develop such software using an authoring system at their own school and then made the programs available to other schools serving deaf individuals. This type of sharing is exemplary and it is hoped that their efforts of dissemination will be duplicated by others.

Motor Impaired

Motor impaired (physically handicapped) individuals by definition do not have primary impairments of cognitive or sensory abilities but quite often these accompany the primary motor disability. Microcomputer technology has tremendous flexibility in addressing these multiple handicaps in their varying degrees. Adaptations can be made on either software or hardware and often are made on both.

Hardware

Hardware adaptations for motor impaired microcomputer users primarily involve the category of input devices, but secondary handicaps often require special output modes as well. For example, the individual with severe cerebral palsy, whose limited control affects the oral muscle groups, would require a special input mode and would probably desire a verbal output mode for assistance in communication. Combining adaptive inputs with adaptive outputs provides the user with a great number of options to meet individual needs.

Input devices. A variety of input alternatives were discussed earlier, and it was pointed out that the easiest and most common adaptations are switches. Burkhart (1980, 1982) has published two excellent books illustrating many inexpensive, easily constructed switches. Prentke Romich Company, Zygo Industries, and The Handicapped Source of Preston Corporation are three suppliers of commercially made switches. Switches often require custom modifications to the software, however. Several utility programs are available to assist the programmer in the process of customizing a program to help reduce the time and cost factors. These programs search the program code for all statements that require input of information by the user. Their locations or line numbers are fed back to the programmer, allowing them to quickly access the correct lines for change. Three example programs of this type are "Single Inputs Disk" from the University of Washington, "Handi-Routine Disk" from Input/Output Research (IOR) Enterprises, and "Florida Scanner" from G.E. Rushakoff at New Mexico State University. This method of changing code is limited to only those programs that have accessible code. Unfortunately, the majority of commercially available programs are copy protected and do not fall into this category.

A step beyond the software utility programs are hardware devices that convert single switch inputs into the appropriate keyboard information. One such device is the "Adaptive Firmware Card" from Adaptive Peripherals, Inc. (Schwejda & Vanderheiden, 1982). The advantage to adapting the hardware approach is that it is transparent (i.e., the software does not recognize its presence) and therefore it works with almost all software, code accessible or not. No customization is necessary for off-the-shelf software. This particular card also allows the user to set a number of parameters, like speed, selection method, and key presentation format to meet individual needs.

Switches and the Adaptive Firmware Card provide means for bypassing the keyboard. A second method for entering information into the computer, which was discussed earlier, is voice recognition. Special equipment is used to recognize and differentiate the various sound patterns. This type of device is particularly useful for quadriplegics with good verbal abilities. Several devices that perform this function are available commercially. Three of these are the "Voice Input Module" (VIM) from Voice Machine Communications, Inc., "Shadow/VET" from Scott Instruments Corporation, and "Waldo" from Artra, Inc. A dedicated or limited function device has been developed by Harris (1981) using the voice or sound recognition technology in an automatic phone dialer called "Yellaphone." Following a two second audible sound, the phone automatically dials one of the 16 numbers in its memory, allowing a no-hands telephone operation.

The second category of input devices, video pointing devices, differ from switches in the kinds of information being sent to the computer. The "Koala Pad" from Koala Technologies Corporation is an example of a touch tablet that requires holding and moving a stylus across a special surface; alternatively, the user's finger can act as the stylus. A light pen requires holding a stylus, but instead of working on an attached flat surface, the stylus is applied directly to the video screen. The mouse is another type of video pointing device that is coming into common use. Each of these video pointing devices allows faster responses than a switch. The ability to move the cursor directly to a desired position is more efficient than using a scanning or stepping process, but the increased efficiency requires more motor ability. Matching machine or device capabilities with those of the user is an important task for achieving maximum efficiency.

Another type of switch input device that is being introduced uses ultrasonic technology for determining X-Y coordinates and in that way is similar to the video pointing devices. Jaffe (1981) has applied this technology in developing an interface for wheelchair control. It is microprocessor-based and uses the ultrasound distance-ranging technology to track the user's head position and compute desired directions. The same technology permits obstacle detection, wall following, and cruising functions as well.

Keyboard emulation is another method of providing input to a computer. These emulators are devices that act as adapted keyboards. Users enter their input via these devices and the device generates the appropriate information for the computer, usually X-Y coordinates or ASCII code. Some of the more simple emulators consist of a matrix of connectors, which are activated with pressure. The X-Y coordinate of the pressure point is sent to the computer, and the specially designed software determines the meaning of the input. The "Presfax-100 Touch Key-Pad" from Computer Data Services is one such touch pad available for the Apple II+ or IIe. The Touch Screen from IIAT works on a similar principle. Instead of a matrix of connectors, infrared light beams form a matrix across the face of the monitor. When the monitor or screen is touched, the light beams are broken and the X-Y coordinates of that break are calculated and sent to the computer.

"Minspeak" from Prentke Romich Company is a highly specialized keyboard emulator. The system uses a modern linguistic coding system based on thoughts or ideas rather than words. Sentences are stored under a "set" of one to seven pictures, and when the user enters the sequence of pictures that represent the idea to be communicated (Fig.6-2), the corresponding sentence or phrase is recited verbally (Baker, 1982; Creech, 1983). The meaning of each key changes according to the sequence in which it is used, but this system allows the user to get maximum output with a minimum number of key strokes. For example, the sequence "apple, apple, turkey" would result in the sentence "Get the food out of my mouth" but the sequence "apple, apple, clothes" would produce "Look out: the food is getting on my clothes" (Table 6-1) (Baker, 1982). The voice output achieves fairly high intelligibility for analog speech because it incorporates a number of controls for pitch, inflection, and duration of individual phonemes.

Some manufacturers of electronic communication devices are now upgrading them to interface with microcomputers and serve as keyboard emulators. Zygo Industries, Inc., is one such company. Zygo's "TetraScan II" is a matrix display of information options in a research-proved "frequency of use" pattern. The scanning method (row or column or directed) and the number of switches used are two user options. In earlier models, the message was displayed on a small LED display or sent to an on-board printer, but now it sends the ASCII code for that message directly to the computer through the keyboard encoder. Using this method, the computer is not aware that the ASCII code is being sent from anywhere other than the keyboard, allowing the user to access to almost all commercially available software. Zygo has recently introduced a remote control option for the "TetraScan II" which uses ultrasonic and infrared signals to link the computer with the selection device. This allows the user more flexibility in positioning, and it interfaces with available BSR System X-10 environmental control systems (BSR [USA] Ltd.).

Output devices. The two common goal areas of communication and environmental control can serve as a framework for looking at output devices for the physically handicapped. With respect to communication, several forms of output are available. Print or hardcopy is one form. Printers can be easily interfaced with computers and physically handicapped users generally do not need to have these hardware devices adapted. Video output to a monitor is another standard output form requiring no modifications. If visual disabilities accompany the primary motor disability, some priorities may be set for the resolution or clarity of the video output. Voice output is an option generally not utilized by the nonhandicapped user. The options available and the two types of voice output were discussed earlier in this chapter. The applications of voice for this population do

Figure 6–2. The images on Minspeak keys represent neither letters nor words, but concepts. Because a picture is, indeed, worth a thousand words, the meanings of the symbols can change according to the order in which the keys are struck. Each image is rich in associations. In short and obvious combinations, they represent whole thoughts. When such combinations are actuated, sentences are spoken by the synthesizer. (See Table 6–1 for a description of the information on the keys.)

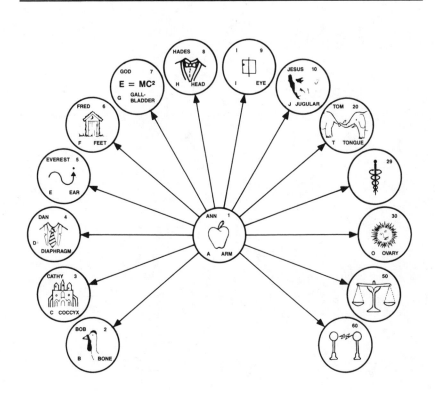

Table 6-1. Keys and meanings for Minspeak*

KEY #	Image	Theme	Letter	Anatomy	Person
1	apple	eating or food	A	arm	Ann
2	turkey	bad or danger	B	bone	Bob
3	cathedral	wheelchair	C	coccyx	Cathy
4	tie, shirt	dressing or clothing	D	diaphragm	Dan
5	directional arrow	transport or travel	E	ear	Everest
6	privy	ablutions, bathing, or water	F	feet	Fred
7	equation	philosophy or ideas	G	gall bladder	God
8	tuxedo	formalities, departures, or greetings	H	head	Hades
9	Chinese symbol, center	personal opinions or disclosures	I	eye	I
10	Bertrand Russell	logic or modality	J	jugular	Jesus
20	elephants	tag questions	K	tongue	Tom
29	caduceus	medical	—	—	—
30	sun	positive expression or happiness	O	ovary	—
50	scales	typing mode	—	—	—
60	electric current	electricity or control	—	—	—

* Each key may have several functions depicted. The majority of the keys have a number, a letter, a portion of human anatomy, a name, and an illustration. The theme of the key is the topic that is selected when the key is hit twice. The information in this table corresponds to the keys pictured in Figure 6–2. From "Minspeak" by Bruce Baker, appearing in the September 1982 issue of Byte Magazine. © 1982 Byte Publications, Inc.

not differ greatly from those for the visually handicapped. A fourth output mode is in the form of electrical code that can be rapidly transmitted across telephone lines. Telecommunications offers a wide variety of business, recreational, and communication options. Electronic mail and bulletin board services are available through a number of telecommunication services such as "The Source" and "SpecialNet." These new resources provide avenues for social interaction and communication with nonhandicapped peers.

Ultrasonic signals, radiofrequency waves, and electrical signals provide additional output modes for the motor impaired user which, while available to other people, will not impact their lives to the extent that it will this group of individuals. With appropriate software and hardware combinations, the physically disabled person can physically act on his or her environment by directing these nonstandard signals to specific electrical devices to control their operation. Three systems for this type of environmental control were entered in the Johns Hopkins Search (Campbell & Nieves, 1981; Holman, 1981; Launey, 1981). Launey's Motor-Handicapped Support System incorporates a number of technologies into one system. Voice recognition is available for the vocal severely handicapped user to direct commands to the computer for controlling devices. The system employs a real time clock, providing the option of scheduling routine operations for specific times. A sound generation system also provides numerous sound alarm options. Voice synthesis, either digitized or text to speech can be purchased and incorporated into any routine (Launey, 1982). A less comprehensive system that provides only the electrical control option is available from Bi-Comm Systems (the PC-1 Powerline Controller). Another system, available from the Prentke Romich Company, the N.U. Communication & Device Controller, utilizes two switch inputs for text generation and appliance control together in one system. An environmental control device that also features automatic telephone dialing and redialing is the AbilityPhone from Basic Telecommunications Corporation. The environmental control functions allow the user to operate up to 15 electrical devices. This battery-powered device can also store three emergency telephone numbers that will be dialed in sequence, delivering predetermined messages when activated either by the user or by medical, fire, or burglar alarms.

Environmental manipulation can be achieved sending these same types of signals to robots. While applications are not well developed yet, the technology is available to perform many self-help tasks for the motor impaired individual. Behrmann and Lahm (1984) have conceptualized the use of the Hero I robot from Heathkit in a sequence of teaching programs designed to teach multiply handicapped infants and toddlers to utilize the technology for environmental control and manipulation. By using a computer-generated picture menu, the children will be able to activate specific robot routines to assist them in such areas as retrieving objects for play or self-feeding. As the robotics technology advances, it will become affordable, and personal applications of robots will emerge. Smaller, scaled-down robots will have tremendous capabilities, which will offer many exciting options to the motor handicapped individual.

Tool Software

Verbal communication is a high priority goal for many motor handicapped individuals. Communication boards and electronic communication devices have existed for a long time and meet the needs of many individuals. Vanderheiden and Grilley (1977) provide an extensive overview of available devices. Additionally, Prentke Romich Company (1983) has developed a poster illustrating the features of most commercially available communication aids. Microprocessors are now being used to increase the speed and capacity of dedicated communication devices. One such device, already mentioned, is Minspeak from the Prentke Romich Company.

While dedicated communication devices have become increasingly more powerful, they still lack the flexibility of microcomputer systems (Lavine, 1980). Personal computers allow more individualization of communication content, the design of words and graphics, and devices interfaced for input and output (e.g., switches, voice, print, and so forth). In addition to the communication advantages, the user has a computer available for many other functions, such as instructional or vocational activities. Dollar for dollar, the computer seems the better choice, if programs exist or can be written to meet the user's needs.

Tool software for verbal communication usually approaches item selection in one of four ways: scanning, stepping, direct selection, or encoding. Scanning is defined by Vanderheiden as follows:

> Any technique (or aid) in which the selections are offered to the user by a person or display, and where the user selects the characters by responding to the person or display. Depending upon the aid, the user may respond by simply signaling when he sees the correct choice presented, or by actively directing an indicator (e.g., light or arrow), toward the desired choice. (1977, p. 21)

Microcomputer software generally relies on the visual or auditory display of the items for user selection. This eliminates the need for another individual to prompt the selection of a message. A typical procedure highlights the columns of a vocabulary or item matrix one at a time automatically, according to an adjustable timer. When the user activates the switch, the highlighting changes from columns to rows or the single choices that are available in the selected column. The user activates the same switch or another switch to make a final selection.

Stepping is another form of scanning used by many communication programs. The user activates a switch to move the highlighting from column to column, and when the desired column is lit, either a preset time delay activates movement down the row or a second switch can be used. As individual items of one column are highlighted, a second time delay or a switch makes the final item selection. Input Output Research Enterprises offers communication programs that use from one to five switches (incorporating line drawings, blissymbols, or words) in matrix presentations that use either the scanning or the stepping techniques. The user has the option of selecting the most efficient method without changing vocabulary content.

Direct selection is defined by Vanderheiden as follows:

> Any technique (or aid) in which the desired choice is directly indicated by the user. In direct selection aids there is a key or sensor for each possible choice or vocabulary element. (1977, p. 26)

This technique is more commonly used with simple picture communication boards but is being used more and more now with the touch tablets, such as the Presfax-100 Touch Key Pad described earlier. This selection technique generally requires custommade software because of the limited options available on the communication board. No one vocabulary would be appropriate for any two individuals.

The fourth and final method of item selection is encoding. Encoding has been defined as follows:

> Any technique or aid in which the desired choice is indicated by a pattern or code of input signals, where the pattern or code must be memorized or referred to on a chart.
> When an aid is used, any number of switches may be used (e.g., one, two, seven, etc.). The code may involve activating the switch(es), sequentially or simultaneously. (Vanderheiden, 1977, pp. 22,24)

With the memory capabilities of microcomputer communication systems, very few individuals need to rely on the memory needed for the encoding technique. At most, the user will have to know how to advance from menu to menu and not need to remember sequences or patterns for individual words or phrases. One exception to this generalization is the Minspeak system.

In addition to the communication programs just mentioned, three other programs illustrate different approaches available in communication software. First, the "Talking Blissapple" from the Trace Research and

Development Center (Kelso & Vanderheiden, no date) utilizes blissymbols as graphic representations of words. The program has a vocabulary capability up to 2000 words, 1400 of which have graphics already drawn and reside in a library. The user can choose as many of these words or create personalized symbols to include in the user library. Three selection techniques are available: (1) information can be put in through the keyboard, (2) the user can select symbol numbers by using a single switch and a scanning technique, or (3) a keyboard emulator can be attached for item selection. In all three cases, though, the symbols in the user's library must be memorized or available for reference because only the selected symbols are presented on the computer screen, and the numbers needed to retrieve them are not available except on a reference table. The options of voice and hardcopy or paper printouts are available if the user has the appropriate hardware.

The second program that illustrates a different approach to communication programming is the "The Talking Wheelchair" program by Dr. John Bennin (1984) from Baraboo, Wisconsin. The system was designed to provide a portable wheelchair communication system for one individual, using a car battery and battery inverter to provide power. Initially the user is presented a four item menu of (1) sentences, (2) words, (3) writing, and (4) basic options. The first two are preprogrammed sentences and words for use in verbal communication. The third option is a simple word processor that has been designed to use a minimum number of keystrokes to create written messages. The "basic" option allows the user to enter the BASIC language and do his or her own programming or run other software. The verbal communication options (i.e., sentences and words) present a second screen of environmental categories or a menu of options. The user selects a number by means of the direct selection technique and the keyboard. A third screen of phrases and sentences is presented. The user selects from them the item of his or her choice or chooses to create a new message. These messages can be sent to the printer or the voice synthesizer.

Buus (1981) uses a presentation method called "layered hierarchy." His initial menu is organized in categories by word types, such as people, places, verbs, and so forth. The scanning technique is incorporated for item selection in which a list of words is presented for sentence building. The user controls movement between menus. The speed of the scanning arrow can be controlled through the main menu, a very attractive feature.

Cohn (1981) presents a matrix of words or pictures. Buus (1981) and Bennin (1984) present a main menu with submenus of items. Both of these approaches are fixed, and unless forethought has been given in programming and the placement of the words, the user is stuck with limited access time, which is predetermined by the placement of vocabulary.

Randall L. Jones (Myers, 1982) takes a dynamic approach to presenting communication options. His program determines the probability of the next occurring letter and rearranges the menu so that letter is closest to the user's current location. In other words, if the user is spelling the word "cat," after the "c" and "a" have been entered, the program will guess that the "t" will be next and move the "t" next to the "a." The program uses the stepping technique and thus the user will only need one additional movement to reach the "t" and complete the entry. This approach can really speed up communication time, but the user must be able to handle a dynamically changing screen. A similar program, developed by Smallwood, predicts the next word or words in a sentence. This system provides auditory feedback for a nonreader as part of the selection process (Communication Outlook, 1982).

Computers can be used as tools in ways other than as verbal communication devices by the motor impaired. Written communication has already been mentioned as an option available with some of the programs. One specifically designed, written communication program for this population is the "Handicapped Typewriter" from Rocky Mountain Software. The program displays the keyboard on the screen and employs a scanning cursor to move through the keys. The user activates a switch to select the letter or symbol desired. The program also provides options for defining and a word or phrase dictionary, a calculator, telephone answering and dialing, a phone directory service, and environmental control. Other standard software tool packages, such as word processors, spread sheets, data base management programs, and address label programs can be accessed by the motorically handicapped by using the Adaptive Firmware Card or keyboard emulators that are transparent to the computer and its software.

Instructional Software

The motor impaired individual does not necessarily need special instructional software but does need to be able to access the software that is available. That access is gained through hardware adaptations described earlier. The utility programs that locate input routines to allow software adaptations for switch input are extremely useful.

A few examples of specialized instructional software do exist. The "Academics with Scanning: Language Arts" and "Academics with Scanning: Math" programs from Computers to Help People, Inc., are two examples. Single switches are used for input of worksheet information. Utility programs come with the package for the teacher to create new worksheets.

CONCLUSION

The purpose of this chapter was to review the learning needs and appropriate applications of technology to the population of physically and sensory impaired. The application of technology to this population has been increasing rapidly, and it is difficult, if not impossible, to review all relevant applications. The ones cited provide only a glimpse of what is possible.

Additionally, the complications of providing resources for multiply handicapped individuals cannot be addressed easily in a single chapter. For this population it is imperative to combine information given here with information from other chapters, particularly the one on computer use by young and cognitively low functioning persons (Chapter 7). It should be noted, however, that a number of multiply handicapped individuals may be gifted, learning disabled, and so forth, and their learning needs must be incorporated into any applications of technology.

REFERENCES

Arcanin, J., & Zawolkow, G. (1980, September). Microcomputers in the service of students and teachers. Computer-assisted instruction at the California School for the Deaf: An update. *American Annals of the Deaf*, pp. 807–813.

Baker, B. (1982). Minspeak. *Byte*, 7(9), 186–188.

Behrmann, M., & Lahm, L. (1984). Critical learn-ing: Multiply handicapped babies get on-line. In M. Behrmann & L. Lahm (Eds.), *Proceedings of the national conference on the use of microcomputers in special education* (pp. 181–193). Reston, VA: Council for Exceptional Children.

Bennin, J. (1984, January). *The talking wheelchair*. Paper presented at the Technology and Special Education Conference, Reno, NV.

Bigge, J. (1982). *Teaching individuals with physical and multiple disabilities*. Columbus, OH: Charles Merrill.

Blazie, D. B. (1981). Total talk: A computer terminal for the blind. In *Proceedings of the Johns Hopkins first national search for application of personal computing to aid the handicapped* (pp. 251–254). Los Angeles: IEEE Computer Society.

Boothroyd, A. (1982). *Hearing impairments in young children*. Englewood Cliffs, NJ: Prentice-Hall.

Bozzuto, R. C., Jr. (1981). The universal translating modem: An advanced telecommunication device for the deaf. In *Proceedings of the Johns Hopkins first national search for application of personal computing to aid the handicapped*. (pp. 62–64). Los Angeles: IEEE Computer Society.

Burkhart, L. J. (1980). *Homemade battery operated toys and educational devices for severely handicapped*. Millville, PA: Author.

Burkhart, L. J. (1982). *More homemade battery devices for severely handicapped children with suggested activities*. Millville, PA: Author.

Buus, R. (1981). A computer communication aid for the nonverbal handicapped. In *Proceedings of the Johns Hopkins first national search for application of personal computing to aid the handicapped* (pp. 131–135). Los Angeles: IEEE Computer Society.

Campbell, R.S., & Nieves, L.A. (1981). Communication and environmental control system. In *Proceedings of the Johns Hopkins first national search for application of personal computing to aid the handicapped* (pp. 114–115). Los Angeles: IEEE Computer Society.

Cohn, J.T. (1981). Microcomputer augmentative communication device. In *Proceedings of the Johns Hopkins first national search for application of personal computing to aid the handicapped* (pp. 43–44). Los Angeles: IEEE Computer Society.

Comden, T. (1981). The many uses of Apple computers at the Western Pennsylvania School for the Deaf. *American Annals of the Deaf, 126*, 591.

Communication Outlook. *The Jane Abler system: A single switch operated auditory-based scan portable communication system.* Vol. 4, No. 1, 14.

Creech, R. (1983). Rick Creech: Pioneer in technology for non-speaking individuals. *Rehabilitation Literature, 44*, 336–337.

Day, R.R., Gum, W., & DeGrasse, W. (1982, December). Implications of the IBM audio typing unit for blind word processors. *Visual Impairment and Blindness*, pp. 407–411.

Dearman, N., & Plisko, V. (1981). *The condition of education.* Washington, D.C.: National Center for Education Statistics.

Dykes, M.K. (1983). Using health, physical and medical data in the classroom. In Umbright, J. (Ed.), *Physical disabilities and health impairments: An introduction.* Columbus, OH: Charles Merrill.

Glaser, R. E. (1981). A telephone communication aid for the deaf. In *Proceedings of the Johns Hopkins first national search for application of personal computing to aid the handicapped* (pp. 11–15). Los Angeles: IEEE Computer Society.

Goldenberg, E.P. (1979). *Special technology for special children.* Baltimore: University Park Press.

Hagen, D. (1984). *Microcomputer resource book for special education.* Reston, VA: Reston Publishing.

Harris, J.D. (1981). Sound activated speakerphone and automatic dialer for individuals with severe motion impairment. In *Proceedings of the Johns Hopkins first national search for application of personal computing to aid the handicapped* (pp. 110–111). Los Angeles: IEEE Computer Society.

Hight, R. L. (1981). Lip-reader trainer: A computer program for the hearing impaired. In *Proceedings of the Johns Hopkins first national search for application of personal computing to aid the handicapped* (pp. 4–5). Los Angeles: IEEE Computer Society.

Hilldrup, R. P. (1984). The micro in the chemistry lab: An aid to the visually impaired. *Educational Computer, 50*, 52–53.

Hoefer, J. J., Arnold, P. F., & Waddell, M. L. (1983, November). A touch of Braille. *Microcomputing, 50*, 52–53.

Holladay, D. (1981). Braille-Edit program connecting an Apple II computer with a VersaBraille Paperless brailler. In *Proceedings of the Johns Hopkins first national search for application of personal computing to aid the handicapped* (pp. 231–233). Los Angeles: IEEE Computer Society.

Holladay, D. (1982). Computer applications to Braille. *Visual Impairment and Blindness*, pp. 324–325.

Holman, F. S., III. (1981). Communications, environment controller, and music synthesizer/color graphics generator. In *Proceedings of the Johns Hopkins first national search for application of personal computing to aid the handicapped* (pp. 138–139). Los Angeles: IEEE Computer Society.

IEEE Computer Society. (1981). *Proceedings of the Johns Hopkins first national search for application of personal computing to aid the handicapped*. Los Angeles: Author.

Jaffe, D. L. (1981). An ultrasonic head position interface for wheelchair control. In *Proceedings of the Johns Hopkins first national search for application of personal computing to aid the handicapped* (pp. 142–145). Los Angeles: IEEE Computer Society.

Kelso, D. P., & Vanderheiden, G. C. (no date). *Talking Blissapple Manual*. Madison, WI: Trace Research and Development Center.

Kirk, S., & Gallagher, J. (1983). *Educating exceptional children*. Boston: Houghton Mifflin.

Kneedler, R. D., Hallahan, D. P., & Kauffman, J. M. (1984). *Special education for today*. Englewood Cliffs, NJ: Prentice-Hall.

Kurzweil, R. C. (1981). Kurzweil reading machine for the blind. In *Proceedings of the Johns Hopkins first national search for application of personal computing to aid the handicapped* (pp. 236–237). Los Angeles: IEEE Computer Society.

Launey, R.O., III. (1981). The motor-handicapped support system. In *Proceedings of the Johns Hopkins first national search for application of personal computing to aid the handicapped* (pp. 104–109). Los Angeles: IEEE Computer Society.

Launey, R. O., III. (1982). The motor-handicapped support system. *Johns Hopkins APL Technical Digest, 3*(3), 255–258.

Lavine, R. A. (1980). *Personal computers serving people: A guide to human services applications*. Washington, D.C.: Hawkins & Associates.

Levitt, H. (1981). A pocket telecommunicator for the deaf. In *Proceedings of the Johns Hopkins first national search for application of personal computing to aid the handicapped* (pp. 39–41). Los Angeles: IEEE Computer Society.

Maryland Computer Service, Inc. (no date). *MCS develops ITS: What is ITS?* Vol. 3, No. 1.

Myers, W. (1982, February). Personal computers aid the handicapped. *IEEE Micro*, pp. 25–40.

Nugent, G., & Stone, C. (1982). The videodisc meets the microcomputer. *American Annals of the Deaf, 127*(5), 569–572.

Optical Programming Associates. (1981). *First National Kidisc*. New York: Author.

People. (1979, December 13). Blind operator at Yale works with a computer, p. 41.

Prentke Romich Company. (1983, February). *Features of commercially available communication aids*. Shreve, OH: Author.

Reynolds, M. C., & Birch, J. W. (1982). *Teaching Exceptional Children in All America's Schools*. Reston, VA: The Council for Exceptional Children.

Rhyne, J. M. (1982). Comprehension of synthetic speech by blind children. *Visual Impairment and Blindness*, pp. 313–316.

Rinaldo, P. L., & Bruninga, R.E. (1980). Microcomputers for the deaf. In *Proceedings of the IEEE computer society workshop on the application of personal computing to aid the handicapped* (pp. 22–27). New York: IEEE Computer Society.

Rose, S., Waldron, M., & Kolomyjec, W. (1984). Computer graphics and creativity and problem-solving skills with deaf and severely language-disordered students. In M. Behrmann & L. Lahm (Eds.), *Proceedings of the national conference on the use of microcomputers in special education* (pp. 116–131). Reston, VA: Council for Exceptional Children.

Schwejda, P., & Vanderheiden, G. (1982). Adaptive-firmware card for the Apple II. *Byte, 7*(9), 276, 278, 282–283, 286, 288, 291, 299, 302, 304, 306, 310, 312, 314.

Star-News. (1980, October 27). Pasadena has first blind claims report-taker in U.S., p. 5.

Taber, F. M. (1983). *Microcomputers in special education*. Reston, VA: Council for Exceptional Children.

Tracy, W. F., & Bevans, D. (1984). Switch rules and considerations for communicator use. *Communication Outlook, 5*(3), 7.

Tyler, C., & Gillman, A. E. (1982, December). A field trial of an IBM audio typing unit. *Visual Impairment and Blindness*, p. 410.

Vanderheiden, G. C. (1977). Providing the child with a means to indicate. In G. C. Vanderheiden & K. Grilley (Eds.), *Non-vocal communication techniques and aids for the severely physically handicapped* (pp. 20–76). Baltimore: University Park Press.

Vanderheiden, G. C., & Grilley, K. (1977). *Non-vocal communication techniques and aids for the severely physically handicapped.* Baltimore: University Park Press.

Watson, P.G. (1978, April). Utilization of the computer with deaf learners. *Educational Technology*, pp. 47–49.

Willis, D.H. (1976). *A study of the relationship between visual acuity, reading mode, and school systems for blind students.* Louisville, KY: American Printing House for the Blind.

Withrow, M. (1978). Computer animation and language instruction. *American Annals of the Deaf, 123,* 723–725.

CHAPTER 7

Using Computers with Young and Cognitively Low Functioning Children

This chapter represents a divergence from the traditional categorical approach for meeting the educational needs of handicapped individuals. Classically, children who were viewed as mentally retardated, physically handicapped, learning disabled, and so forth, have had separate (if somewhat overlapping) curricula due to the supposed "heterogeneous" instructional needs of these populations. The populations addressed in this chapter are quite heterogeneous in age, type, and severity of identified handicapping conditions. In spite of the apparent heterogeneity of the divergent groups that make up the young and cognitively low functioning population, there seem to be many similarities in learning needs, the computer and teacher assisted instructional methodologies and levels used, and the basic types of computer tool applications that are appropriate. These similarities provide a basis for classifying handicapped individuals according to "service needs" rather than characteristics relating to categories of handicapping conditions (Sontag, Smith & Sailor, 1977).

DEFINITIONS AND LEARNING NEEDS

In order to delineate the uses of computers with young and cognitively low functioning individuals it is necessary to operationally define the populations and explicate their learning needs. *Young children* include those children who are chronologically between the ages of birth and four years old. The primary characteristics of learning during this time span involve basic skill development that precedes academic learning. An enormous amount of learning takes place during this time span. Bloom (1964) postulates that 50% of all growth in intelligence takes place between birth and the age of four years.

This chapter was authored by Michael M. Behrmann and Elizabeth Lahm.

Young children learn by interacting with their environment. Initially they rely on and learn about perceptions of sensory stimuli. Soon they begin to differentiate similarities and differences between these stimuli, which they store in both short-term and long-term memory for later use. Eventually sensory inputs are combined with memory to be processed and produce complex cognitive structures. Finally, abstract thinking is developed (Bangs, 1979). From a curricular standpoint, learning in this population has been categorized by Bangs (1979) into the areas of language comprehension behaviors, language expression behaviors, problem-solving behaviors, social or personal behaviors, and motor behaviors.

The population referred to as *cognitively low functioning* has generally been considered "mentally retarded." However, for the purposes of this chapter, common definitions of mental retardation are not appropriate, mainly because of the changing learning needs and characteristics, depending on the age of the individual and severity of retardation. Additionally, since virtually every individual, retarded or not, at some time in life exhibits the same learning characteristics and needs (usually between birth and four years), it stands to reason that "mental retardation" is not an appropriate term. If, on the other hand, an operational approach is taken to defining this population, the concept of *functional retardation* can have more relevance. Thus, although a moderately retarded ten year old child with Down's syndrome might no longer be functioning at the preschool level, it would seem likely that a severely retarded adult may still exhibit many of the same learning needs as a preschool child (in terms of instructional methodology, not curricular content). The primary feature or characteristic of retardation is the "functioning level of each individual" and Sailor and Guess (1983) suggest that the definition of severely handicapped should be based on goals of programmatic instruction and environmental modification and adaptation.

The primary feature of learning needs of young and cognitively low functioning individuals is development of basic skills rather than academic skills. Primary skills can be defined as (1) self-help skills; (2) fine and gross motor skills; (3) early receptive and expressive communication skills; (4) early social skills; and (5) basic cognitive or preacademic skills (Sailor & Guess, 1983).

THEORIES OF EARLY LEARNING

In order to gain a perspective on early learning and the potential applications of technology to the learning process, it is first necessary to explore some major conceptual frameworks for developing learning environments in which computers might be utilized. The four major areas to be addressed are maturation learning, the cumulative learning model, social learning theory, and critical stages of learning.

Maturation Learning

The concept of maturation learning is based on the belief that psychological growth takes place similarly to the physical growth process—that is, it is developmental in nature, and a child passes through a series of stages, each being prerequisite to the next. Gesell, Ilg, and Ames (1974) note that all growth, whether physical or mental, implies organization, and environmental factors support, inflect, and modify but do not generate the progression of development. The developmental sequence comes from within the individual.

Piaget's cognitive developmental theory has become very popular for describing the stages of learning, even though the theory puts more weight on development than on learning (Klausmeier, 1979). According to the Piagetian developmental concept, during the first year of life, the child develops the skills of attending to stimuli, discriminates many separate features of them, and formulates representations of the concepts that may be recalled for later use. Instinctual and sensorimotor actions on the environment are refined to become intentional actions that are used for testing the concepts attained. During the second year of life, development is characterized by refinements of object identity, that is, objects are separate from their environment and have permanence. Objects are also used as tools to extend experimentation on the environment. The last stage of development in the second year is the invention of new means, as characterized by the ability to combine previous learning in new ways and predict reactions before testing them. As more concepts are stored in memory, more background information is available for arriving at new decisions about the world or, in Piagetian terms "accommodation." Strategies for storing information are developed that make the process more efficient. Language is just one of these strategies.

During the next stage of development, the preoperational period (ages two to seven years), the child moves from sensorimotor activities to representative symbolic behaviors. The behaviors associated with this period are characterized by language development, imitative play, perceptual confusions, basically egocentric thoughts, centering attention on the most compelling attribute of a stimulus, and inability to move back and forth along a train of thought (Mori and Masters, 1980). Rowher (1979) summarizes the value of a developmental stage perspective in that it provides a summary of a child's capabilities as he or she matures, which, if the stage of functioning is known, provides the teacher with an idea of what the child can and cannot do.

Recent research has questioned these stages as Piaget orders them, and many researchers can no longer accept this as a working model. One of the bases for this needed change is the amount of research showing innate abilities of infants, abilities that do not fit into Piaget's stages. Gelman (1982) suggests that infants have an innate ability to classify objects as animate or inanimate. In Piagetian terms, this skill does not develop until much later. Moore and Meltzhoff (1978) report that infants have the capacity to construct internal representations that are used for cognitive development. Again Piaget does not acknowledge that skill until the child is approximately eight months of age. Moore and Meltzhoff suggest that a fundamental reorganization of Piaget's conception of the infant is required. This would include the innate perceptual abilities, representational abilities, and the capacity to conserve the identify and permanence of objects and formulate rules to allow this even as the perceptual world changes.

Cumulative Learning

The research cited earlier suggests that a second perspective of developmental change be investigated. Gagne (1970), in a "cumulative learning" approach, believes that, apart from the limits imposed by physical growth, a child can learn virtually anything at any age. This theory assumes that the child has accomplished all necessary prerequisite learning. Rowher (1979) notes that the implication here is that, rather than information about a child's developmental stage, the educator needs to know what the child has learned previously. This approach is consistent with that supported by advocates of a functional approach to learning (Brown et al., 1978). Advocates of a functional approach stress teaching skills to disabled individuals that will meet the "criterion of ultimate use" or the "criterion of use in the next setting" (Sailor & Guess, 1983). It is possible to separate content from method, and this chapter addresses instructional technology and learning needs, not curricular content. Table 7–1 illustrates how a developmental basic skills curriculum can adjust content to cover skills from preschool to adult ages for severely handicapped individuals.

Social Learning Theory

Since the developmental theory of Piaget is based primarily on naturalistic observations of children, it is completely possible that very young children may not have the physical capabilities to express all they

Table 7-1. Skills for Severely Handicapped Individuals from Preschool to Adult Age

	Preschool	School-age	Adult
Sensorimotor	Sensorimotor stimulation, including developing sensory responses and encouraging exploration	Sensorimotor development including the identification of objects, sounds, and textures	Sensorimotor integration, involving skills such as sorting, pulling, folding, making choices, and discriminating between sizes, weights, and colors
Language	Language stimulation, including attention, localization, and vocalization	Language development, including name recognition, identification of objects and body parts, speech imitation, and the use of gestures, words, or phrases	Language and speech, including listening, using gestures and words, and following one or two step directions
Social	Interpersonal responses, including recognition of people, manipulation of objects, and demanding attention from other people	Social behaviors, involving requesting attention, parallel and cooperative play	Work and self-direction, including sharing, taking turns, traveling with or without supervision, and completing assigned tasks

From Luckey, R. E. (1974). The profoundly retarded: A new challenge for public education. *Education and Training of the Mentally Retarded, 9*(3), 125. Reprinted with permission.

have learned. Thus, observable behaviors that provide evidence of learning accomplishments may not be present. Very often this also appears to be the case with severely physically disabled individuals who often are perceived as low functioning. For both young and severely handicapped individuals, then, the major problem is finding a methodology of allowing the individual to express what has been learned. It is in this area that the computer's ability to maximize minimal physical inputs and collect and analyze large amounts of data may be a valuable tool in learning and expressing what has been learned in very young and severely physically disabled individuals.

The behavioral concepts and research principles developed under operant conditioning (Skinner, 1953), social learning theory (Bandura & Walters, 1963), and applied behavior analysis (Alberto & Troutman, 1982) provide a framework and methodology for establishing that learning has occurred in very young children. Using these principles, it is necessary that an observable behavior occur in such a way that a functional association with learning can be made. It is therefore necessary to provide a systematic approach of teaching, observing behavior, and collecting data to identify that causal relationship.

There are two principles of learning under social learning theory that need to be highlighted for young and cognitively low functioning individuals. The first is the principle of modeling and imitation. There is considerable evidence that learning occurs through observation of the behavior of others even when the observer does not reproduce the model's behaviors. By seeing what reinforcement the model receives, the observer's behavior may be modified. This is referred to as vicarious reinforcement and vicarious learning. The concept of vicarious learning is of extreme importance to severely physically disabled individuals since in many cases they will be physically unable to perform the behaviors modeled. This does not mean, however, that they will not be able to learn a concept.

Just as the concepts of imitation and learning through modeling are of critical importance in the learning process of very young children, so too is the concept of vicarious learning for cognitively low functioning individuals. Mercer and Algozzine (1977) in a review of research on observational learning have found that modeling and imitation can be effective with even severely retarded individuals. If such learning does take place might not the computer assisted manipulation of the environment provide a more reinforcing learning tool for the young or cognitively low functioning individual? As he or she experiments and manipulates the environment, behaviors that are necessary to establish a causal relationship are exhibited, therefore allowing observational learning to occur.

A second important principle is that of operant conditioning. When applied to human beings, operant conditioning is called behavior modification (Alberto & Troutman, 1982). The computers can provide consistency of stimulus inputs, schedule reinforcement, control environmental response stimuli, and, probably most important, collect and analyze data. These capabilities of computers make behavioral constructs for learning important in the application of technology to learning with handicapped individuals.

Critical Periods for Learning

There remains one more question to be addressed before moving on to what role technology can take in the education of young and cognitively low functioning children. This is the question of whether or not there are critical periods for learning in children. Animal research strongly suggests that there are critical or sensitive periods during which certain important processes are developing most rapidly. Disturbances during these periods may alter the development of these processes in critical ways. For example, if an animal is raised in darkness during the first year of the life its vision may be permanently impaired. The first year, then, is critical for normal visual development. Hunt (1961) has drawn upon such research with animals as a compelling reason to support the concept of early intervention. Rowher (1979) suggests that early formal control over the child's learning environment may be highly desirable. This concept has been supported by a number of studies (Gulley, 1982; Stevens, 1982; Scarr-Salapatek & Williams, 1973) and is demonstrated by the Colorado Department of Education findings that at least one third of the handicapped children who receive services before they are three years old do not need special education after their preschool years (Lloyd, Kauffman, & Hallahan, 1983).

However, the question of critical periods of learning in human beings remains unanswered because of inability to conduct controlled experiments on ethical grounds. An additional, related question in the education of severely handicapped is, "Do we teach children to be dependent?" That is, do children learn at an early age that others will take care of their every need and learn that they do not have to exhibit any of the behaviors that we perceive as learning. Since it is not ethical to evaluate critical learning experimentally, and it is surely not desirable to teach dependency, it would seem that the best policy would be early intervention and the development of systematic teaching procedures for children who may not be able to follow the normal progression of learning. Additionally, the inability of handicapped individuals to learn normally or act upon the environment may create secondary handicaps because they are not able to have the normal experiences of the world to build information upon (Goldenberg, 1979). If these secondary handicaps can be prevented the attempt should begin at an early age in order to take advantage of this critical learning period. The prevention of lags in conceptual development will facilitate both language development and development in other learning domains. The microcomputer and related technology can be utilized in this prevention process. Such methods can provide a reliable means for a young child to control and manipulate the world and explore it as nonhandicapped children do (Vanderheiden, 1981). To do this we can combine the advantages of technology and the systematic instructional procedures provided through the principles of social learning theory and applied behavior analysis so that physically handicapped young children become effective learners.

IMPLICATIONS OF THE TECHNOLOGY
Accessing The Technology

Computer assisted instruction (CAI), communication, and environmental control programs can be beneficial uses of the technology for the young and low functioning populations. (See Chapter 3 for a description of these types of programs.) The common skills needed by this population fall into the learning categories of social, language, self-help, motor, vocational, recreational, and basic cognition. While the computer has the potential of offering valuable learning experiences in each of these areas, the young and cognitively low functioning user must have a means of accessing the medium. An assumption made in defining this population is that they are nonreaders. Therefore, the keyboard is for the most part useless. The challenge, then, is to create and provide ways of bypassing the keyboard to give access to the powerful teaching potential of the microcomputer.

Standard applications on the microcomputer use the keyboard for input and the video screen and printer for output. In order that these and low functioning people might have successful interactions with computers, adaptations of the inputs and outputs are necessary. These adaptations were described in Chapter 6 as they applied to the populations with sensory and motor impairments but the devices developed for those groups can also be applied to the young and cognitively low functioning. These input and output devices will be reviewed briefly.

Input devices. Switches are the easiest adaptations for information input into the computer. Most microcomputers have game I/O ports or ports designed to accept game paddles and joysticks. These are types of switches and video pointing controls housed in one device. The young or low functioning user may not have enough fine motor control to use these popular devices, but constructing a switch with the same electrical qualities to meet the user's individual's needs is a relatively simple and inexpensive matter. Burkhart (1980, 1982) has published two books illustrating numerous ways of building simple switches.

Video pointing devices also allow the user to move the cursor around the screen through an external device such as a touch tablet, joystick, or mouse. This provides the user with a faster and more direct mode for selecting from options displayed on the screen—for example, selecting individual words in a communication program. These devices can also be used by for this population for creative arts. Software packages exist for most video pointing devices that allow the creation of drawings using very simple commands or selecting the options from a menu. One package for the "Koala Pad" from Koala Technologies Corporation is particularily appropriate for the nonreading population because it presents the options or menu in icons or pictures as well as in words. This touch tablet also allows the child to use a finger instead of the stylus if desired.

Several programs are available to teach the use of switches and adapt programs to accept switch inputs. The "Single Switch Assessment Program" from E.G. Rushakoff at the New Mexico State University assists the teacher in deciding appropriate switches for each student. Key information about the switch used and its placement are entered before beginning the program. Several parameters are adjustable; for instance, the teacher can select the content of the stimulus (words or letters). Response time is collected to help determine which switch and what position are the most efficient for the user. "Motor Training Games" from Computers to Help People is a series of motivating activities to help the student become more proficient at using a switch.

Utility programs that search the program code for input statements that must be modified to accept single switches are reviewed in Chapter 6. These programs assist the teacher who knows enough about programming to change the code to fit individual needs. The "Adaptive Firmware Card" from Adaptive Peripherals, Inc., overrides the input statements in almost any program by presenting the keyboard options in a menu that is scanned to allow the use of a single switch. These two approaches to adapting software for the young and low functioning users contribute greatly to providing access to the technology.

Output Devices. The standard nontext outputs of video and print are generally appropriate for the young and low functioning population. Adaptations may be required to alter the size of the text, when text is appropriate, especially on the video screen. Both hardware and software alternatives are available to perform this function. The hardware adaptations, such as magnification of the screen, make the required alterations possible without need for special software. Software approaches to altering text size are generally program specific—that is, they are built into a specific program and are not usable with other programs.

Adding the option of voice output is very desirable for this population. Nonreaders can access many more programs if the directions are presented verbally than if there were only displayed visually. Two types of voice output are available for use with microcomputers. Digitized voice generally requires more memory capacity of the computer and is less flexible than the second type because it is limited to its "dictionary" of words. Digitized voice is more "human-like" than its analog counterpart, text-to-speech voice synthesis. This second type has a "robotlike" quality to its production of words but allows all text to be spoken, even student input.

Environmental control as a possible output for the young and low functioning can be important for providing temporary control to individuals not yet able to perform tasks independently. Ultrasonic signals are generated by the computer to turn electrical devices on and off. While many of the people falling into the category of young and low functioning will eventually be able to perform these tasks without computer assistance, they miss learning opportunities and opportunities for the development of self-concept by being dependent on others for such functions. Computer assisted environmental control can help continue appropriate learning through environmental interactions and maintaining of self-esteem while the necessary motor abilities are being developed.

Instructional Applications

The push to provide early learning opportunities via the computer emanates from both the professional and the commercial worlds. Major computer manufacturers are promoting their hardware through advertisement campaigns that suggest that good parents should be providing computers for very young children to get ready for school. Commercial software houses are beginning to create programs for audiences as young as three years old (Moritz, 1983). These programs typically cover the early academic skills of letters and numbers. Atari's "Learning With Leepers" uses the graphic capabilities to teach colors, numbers, and the alphabet. "Stickybear A B C" from Xerox Educational Publications focuses only on the alphabet but provides supplemental storybooks and stickers to enhance the computer activities. Spinnaker has several programs available for the young child. "Kindercomp" has programs for matching shapes and letters, writing names, drawing, and filling in missing numbers. "Facemaker" allows the child to create animated faces that wink, smile, and wiggle their ears. While most of these programs have been developed for nonhandicapped children aged three years and up, like toys they are often introduced to children younger than intended. These commercially available programs are most of what is available for young and low functioning handicapped children.

Evidence of the professional world's endorsement of computers for very young children is found in the number of specialized preschool and camp programs springing up around the United States and in other countries. The Byte Sized Computer Acquaintance Center in Oakville, Ontario, Canada, has organized classes for two and three year old children (Paul, 1983). The Capitol Children's Museum in Washington, D.C., runs a three session "CompuTOTs" programs for three and four year olds (Wrenge, 1982). Preschoolers of ages three to six can participate in computer activities while attending one of the 54 Kindercare centers operating in Minnesota, Texas, and Alabama (Classroom Computer News Directory, 1983). These programs indicate support for the theory that microcomputers can be useful devices for teaching young children.

These programs will probably teach us something about children and computers. What they do and accomplish will in part influence the direction taken in special education for implementing the computer technology in the classrooms of the young and low functioning handicapped population. The software developed for them will be a major portion of the materials for this special population as well. Commercial developers will undoubtedly not be interested in investing their time and resources in developing special software for such a low functioning population. It will be up to the classroom teacher to take what is available and make it appropriate to the handicapped learner.

In many cases, commercially available software can be modified for special input and output modes. The gaps that are not filled by these programs will require specially designed software. This software should be designed to meet instructional needs and methodologies that are significantly different from those for other populations. There is a significant amount of literature on the design of instructional software for nonhandicapped audiences that can be applied to special education software. Goldenberg (1979) and Papert (1980) advocate interactional computer environments for handicapped students. Damarin (1982) has developed a matrix for determining the level of interaction appropriate for achieving types of cognitive goals. For example, to introduce concepts the user would need to have a minimum of computer interaction because the initial appropriate level would entail "watching" a demonstration of the concept which—if we consider how early learning takes place—is what very young children do first. As the cognitive goal changes, the additional interaction levels of "finding," "doing," "using," "constructing," and "creating" should be employed to be successful in using the concept in problem-solving situations. Instructional software for handicapped students should strive to achieve this cognitive goal–interaction level match.

To ensure that interactions will be beneficial experiences for a student, basic instructional principles must be applied in the program design. Behavioral principles, incorporating reinforcement, creating motivational tasks, and providing guidance through cuing and shaping can easily be incorporated into programs. The ability of the computer to provide immediate feedback based on real time analyses of performance, resulting in sequencing the presentation of information, allows data-based decisions for instructional changes (Lesgold, 1982; Park, 1982). Software that incorporates these principles utilizes the sound instructional strategies of pretest, teach, test, teach, posttest on an ongoing basis, continually monitoring performance and branching to appropriate levels of teaching.

The versatility of the microcomputer allows for incorporating more than one instructional strategy simultaneously. In addition to the behavioral principles, discrimination learning strategies can be employed easily by using the many graphics features of microcomputers. Concept learning by attribute isolation is one example (Hall, Comer, & Merrill, 1982). Coupled with the continuous monitor and feedback methods of the behavioral principles, a concept such as "round" can be defined, demonstrated, and isolated in a variety of applications that can be easily manipulated. With appropriate interaction levels, the concept of "roundness" can be taught from its introduction to its use in problem-solving situations.

Another important instructional methodology is the presentation of learning experiences in more than one modality (Goldenberg, 1979). Computer assisted instruction is a logical medium for meeting that requirement. The ability to use motor, tactile, and auditory inputs to achieve tactile, visual, motor, and auditory outputs either simultaneously or individually provides flexibility for teachers in how to present materials to meet the needs of a variety of different individuals. The emerging video disc technology enhances the multiple modality approach because of its ability to not only present visual and auditory information but to simulate motor actions while still being accessible to the feedback and branching capabilities of the standard microcomputer.

Research. While the mechanical capabilities of microcomputers can be easily cited, their benefit in instruction for the young and low functioning population has not been satisfactorily demonstrated as yet. The technology as applied in special education is very new, and adequate time has not elapsed to produce the quality and extensive research necessary to completely justify its use in the classrooms for this population. Some isolated research is beginning to surface in the literature, often with conflicting or inconclusive findings. Swenson and Kingman (1981) found CAI a feasible method of instruction, showing that 12 mentally retarded subjects made substantial learning gains after daily use for nine months. Research of a more specfic nature was conducted by Jenkins at the

University of Wisconsin, Stout. He examined the relationship between IQ and the ability to use the keyboard and found that there was no statistically significant correlation with a group of 30 subjects ranging in IQs from 30 to 80 (Hagen, 1984). On the lower end of the IQ scale, work is being done in a Pennsylvania state institution with nonambulatory, profoundly mentally retarded residents. These researchers have found that some subjects show no consistent increases in rate of responses, some show transient response rates, and others have definite increases (Bourland, Jablonski, Allen, & White, 1984). As yet, they have no way of predicting how a person will perform.

One of the initial skills any computer user must have is the capability of entering information into the computer. Brinker and Lewis (1982) have been working on that task with handicapped infants in their Contingency Intervention Project. By using various adaptive switches they have found that they can teach infants as young as three months to activate a microcomputer. These infants have learned the concept of cause and effect and practice environmental interactions similar to those described in Piaget's primary and secondary circular reactions. These basic skills are prerequisite to other skills more traditionally associated with instructional curriculum for the young and low functioning population.

Similar research in a less clinical setting was conducted by Behrmann and Lahm (1984). Multiply handicapped infants and toddlers under the age of 30 months are being taught to interact with a microcomputer using adaptive switches. Once these children have learned the cause and effect relationship between the switch and the computer output (visual, auditory, or both), they are taught through a sequence of instructional programs to use a microcomputer for communication and environmental control. The programs move through a teaching hierarchy that begins with experiencing the technology in a fairly unstructured format to very structured formats requiring responses to verbal commands. Each level develops skills required to understand that the picture on the screen is a representation of an object, action, or speech output. The relationship between these pictures and the effect they can cause on the environment by selection of the picture is of utmost importance. Initial phases of the research have indicated that handicapped children as young as 11 months' mental age can consistently interact with a microcomputer when prompted verbally.

Working with handicapped children who are a little older, Myers teaches preschool children language by allowing them to control their environment through the microcomputer (Trachtman, 1984). Two approaches were compared, one with the child controlling graphics and the second with the child controlling synthesized speech output. It was found that children are more motivated to stay on the task when they can control the voice rather than when they control the graphics. Other findings indicate increased attempts to use oral language as well as an increase in level of comprehension. The key, according to Myers, is giving complete control to the child and letting him or her learn by experimentation.

MCE, Inc., has focused their research on the young adult population in the areas of vocational and self-help skill training. While their research has involved field testing and validating software for commercial distribution, their findings are valuable information for determining the value of microcomputers for this population. With a group of subjects ranging in IQ from 32 to 47, they found a minimum growth of 20% to 30% for the skills presented in their programs, with some programs resulting in gains of 20% to 70% (Hagen, 1984). On a more subjective note, they cite the motivational advantages of computer assisted instruction as a possible explanation for their findings.

Despite these few findings, it seems logical to incorporate microcomputers into the classrooms for young and low functioning individuals. The capabilities of the machines suggest their appropriateness as teaching tools. Teachers will have to participate in the research on their effectiveness and will be instrumental in the success or failure of computer applications based on how they utilize them and demands they make for appropriate instructional software.

Applications in Specific Instructional Areas. CAI applications specific to the young and low functioning population can be organized by the following categories: language, perceptual motor, cognitive, leisure or recreation, vocational, and creative arts. A number of programs are available in each of these categories, some more appropriate than others. A few programs will be described here to illustrate each category and stimulate thoughts about other applications.

Language. Wilson and Fox (1984) have developed several programs for early language development. Each program uses the color graphics and animation capabilties of microcomputers coupled with voice synthesis and single switch inputs to provide auditory language development opportunities. "First Words" teaches nouns through six teaching levels. Each noun is presented through two pictures to assist in generalizing the word. "First Categories" includes some text on the screen to introduce the categories of animals, body parts, clothing, food, utensils, and vehicles. "Micro Lads," through the use of animation, assesses and teaches beginning syntax such as noun-verb agreement.

Perceptual motor. "Motor Training Games" from Computers to Help People has already been mentioned. This series of programs teaches visual tracking and motor coordination necessary for using a single switch. Skills often incorporated into other software are taught, too, such as the concept of a scanning cursor or arrow.

Cognition. Drill and practice programs exist for some early cognitive skills. One example is the "Early Learning Games" disc from Learning Tools, Inc. Counting, simple addition, and letter identification are some of the skills covered. A series of programs developed by Lahm and Behrmann have been designed to teach the concepts of cause and effect, matching, and picture identification for preparing the child to use the computer as a tool for communication and environmental control.

Leisure or Recreation. The "Motor Training Games," while designed for teaching motor skills, can double as recreational software. The programs are all presented in a game format, some with scoring features. "Facemaker" from Spinnaker can serve as recreational or cognitive skill development. The student contructs faces from a variety of choices available in each category (e.g., eyes, mouth, nose).

Vocational. MCE, Inc., has a variety of vocational software available for the low functioning adult. Their programs cover such skill areas as money, time, and work habits, each with data collection procedures to assist the teacher in monitoring skill development.

Creative Arts. The "Koala Pad" comes with software that provides easy access to many drawing methods, such as fill-in, background, and erasing. Figures such as circles and squares can easily be drawn and used to contruct pictures. With programs and devices such as this, the creative abilities of the child do not have to be inhibited by limited motor abilities.

Computers as Tools

Enormous potential exists for improving the life style and level of independence for the young and low functioning population if all the capabilities of microcomputers are harnessed and directed toward the goal of environmental assistance. The term "environmental assistance" is used very broadly to include verbal and written communication, environmental manipulation, and self-help assistance. Both young and cognitively low functioning individuals can use computers as tools for accommodation to handicaps in recreation and learning. Older low functioning individuals may use them in vocational settings. The point must be made, however, that appropriate application programs and devices to attain these goals are few, but the potential is enormous even with the currently available technology.

That potential is being investigated by the Association for Retarded Citizens Bioengineering Project (Kneedler, Hallahan, & Kauffman, 1984). To begin with, they have identified a list of devices that assist this population in accessing the technology. Beyond what is currently available, they have investigated sensors that can be used to train attention by monitoring physiologic signs that indicate attention and then activate various stimuli for feedback and positive reinforcement. Automatic memory devices have been investigated for their potential for providing cues or prompts to individuals while performing a task. Additionally, self-help devices have been reviewed, such as the Bladder/Bowel Sensation Exaggerator and the Self-Feeding Tray. Although these examples go beyond microcomputer technology, certainly the advances in microcomputer technology have influenced a great number of other technologic developments.

Developments in the area of environmental control probably have paid more attention to the needs of the physically and sensory handicapped populations than the young and cognitively low functioning, but the functions performed by this technology are applicable to the lower functioning group. "Waldo" or the "Motor-Handicapped Support System," two systems that are essentially the same but developed for use with different computers, from Artra, Inc., are multiple-function devices that provide the means for controlling electrical appliances, generating sounds for alarm systems, and voice synthesis. Any of these options can be activated by using the keyboard or by using the on-board voice recognition capabilities. Many low functioning individuals do not understand the operation of electrical devices but can benefit from the self-help and recreational functions of such devices. For example, tape recorders and radios for listening pleasure or yard lights and alarm systems for safety could easily be activated using such a system.

Communication is a necessary life skill, and a computer system can assist the nonverbal or individual with unintelligible speech in that area. Two approaches are appropriate to this population. The Echo II Voice Synthesizer from Street Electronics (previously mentioned) comes with a program that is loaded into the computer and continues to be available for speech output until the computer is shut off. This allows the user to enter unstructured text into the computer and have immediate feedback. A child can experiment with sounds in a self-teaching process similar to that done by very young children. A more structured approach requires whole words to be used instead of individual letters. Since this population generally consists of nonreaders, a modification of this approach is necessary to make it useful. The "Picture Communication Program" from Input-Output Research Enterprises is an example of such a modification. Sixteen pictures with the written word are displayed in a four-by-four matrix on the video screen. Rows and columns of pictures are highlighted according to either a scanning or a stepping procedure (see Chapter 6 for definitions of these procedures). By controlling the position of the highlighting with single or multiple switches, the user selects a word or picture. Sentences can be constructed if desired, and when the user is ready, the entire sentence, a phrase, or just a single word can be sent to a voice synthesizer.

Written communication is seldom considered an achievable skill for the young or low functioning individual. Fine motor control, a necessary component, is often not refined enough to be successful at manipulating a writing instrument. With minimal fine motor skills, the writing task becomes a long and laborious process. Microcomputers have brought the advantages of electronic word processing to the general population, and there is no reason why the low functioning population cannot take advantage of this technology as well. The available editing capabilities, combined with the devices designed to provide alternative ways of accessing the computer, can make the writing task achievable, more gratifying, and successful. When the child is not inhibited by fine motor problems, his or her potential in this area may be more freely demonstrated. One of the easier word processing programs available is "Bank Street Writer" from Bank Street College of Education. A simple menu of options is clearly displayed at the top of the screen at all times, and simple procedures are used to access the edit features. Written communication will not be viable for most of this population, but having access to the benefits of word processing will allow the teacher some flexibility in presenting the skill.

CONCLUSION

As was noted at the beginning of the chapter, early learning is built upon motor experimentation with the surrounding environment (Goldenberg, 1979; Behrmann & Lahm, 1984). Computerbased technology can provide a means of allowing more normalized and extended interactions with the environment for individuals who have "bodies that don't work" or have limited cognitive abilities. It is hoped that this technology, applied early in life, may provide alternatives to experiential learning that will reduce the occurrence of secondary handicaps. For older, cognitively low functioning individuals, it must be remembered that learning is a lifelong process, and the goal of instruction utilizing technology should address the concept of developing more independence and a better quality of life.

REFERENCES

Alberto, P.A., & Troutman, A.C. (1982). *Applied behavior analysis for teachers.* Columbus, OH: Charles E. Merrill.

Bandura, A., & Walters, R.H. (1963). *Social learning and personality development.* New York: Holt, Rinehart & Winston.

Bangs, T. (1979). *Birth to three: Developmental learning and the handicapped child.* Boston: Teaching Resources.

Behrmann, M., & Lahm, L. (1984). Critical learning: Multiply handicapped babies get on-line. In M. Behrmann & L. Lahm (Eds.), *Proceedings of the national conference on the use of microcomputers in special education* (pp. 181-193). Reston, VA; Council for Exceptional Children.

Bloom, B.S. (1964). *Stability and change in human characteristics.* New York: Wiley.

Bourland, G., Jablonski, E.M., Allen, G. B., & White, J. (1984). On microcomputers, institutions, and the severely developmentally disabled. In M. Behrmann and L. Lahm (Eds.), *Proceedings of the national conference on the use of microcomputers in special education,* (pp. 135-153). Reston, VA: Council for Exceptional Children.

Brinker, R. P., & Lewis, M. (1982). Making the world work with microcomputers: A learning prosthesis for handicapped infants. *Exceptional Children,* 49(2), 163-170.

Brown, L., Branston, M., Hamre-Nietupski, S., Pumian, I., Certo, N., and Gruenewald, L. (1978). A strategy for developing chronological age-appropriate and functional curricular content for severely handicapped adolescents and young adults. *Journal of Special Education, 13,* 81-90.

Burkhart, L. (1980). Homemade battery powered toys and educational devices for severely handicapped children. Millville, PA: Author.

Burkhart, L. (1982). *More homemade battery powered devices for severely handicapped children with suggested activities. Millville, PA: Author.*

Classroom Computer News 1983 Directory. (1983). Watertown, MA: International Educations.

Damarin, S. (1982, March). Fitting the tool to the task: A problem in the instructional use of microcomputers. Paper presented at the American Educational Research Association, New York.

Gagne, R. (1970). *The conditions of learning.* New York: Holt, Rinehart & Winston.

Gelman, R. (1982). Recent trends in cognitive development. In J. Schierer & A. Rogers (Eds.), *The Stanley Hall Lecture Series, 3.* Washington, D.C.: American Psychological Association.

Gesell, A., Ilg, F., & Ames, L. (1974). *Infant & child in the culture of today.* New York: Harper and Row.

Goldenberg, E.P. (1979). *Special technology for special children.* Baltimore: University Park Press.

Gulley, S.B. (1982). The relationship of infant stimulation to cognitive development. *Childhood Education, 58*(4), 247-254.

Hagen, D. (1984). *Microcomputer resource bool for special education.* Reston, VA: Reston Publishing.

Hall, K.A., Comer, R.C., & Merrill, J.A. (1982). Taxonomy of instructional strategies for computer-based education. Paper presented at the American Educational Research Association, New York.

Hunt, J. (1961). *Intelligence and experience.* New York: Ronald.

Klausmeier, H.J. (1979). Introduction. In H.J. Klausmeier & associates (Eds.), *Cognitive learning and development: information processing and Piagetian perspectives,* (pp. 1-27). Cambridge, MA: Ballinger Publishing Co.

Kneedler, R. D., Hallahan, D.P., & Kauffman, J.M. (1984). *Special education for today.* Englewood Cliffs, NJ: Prentice Hall.

Lesgold, A.M. (1982, March). Instructional principles for computer-based learning. Paper presented at the American Education Research Association, New York.

Lloyd, J.W., Kauffman, J.M., & Hallahan, D.P. (1983). *Special education today,* Inaugural Issue, 2.

Mercer, C., & Algozzine, B. (1977). Observational learning and the retarded: Teaching implications. *Education and Training of the Mentally Retarded, 12,* (4), 345-53.

Moore, M.K., & Melthzoff, A.N. (1978). Object permanence, imitation, and language development in infancy: Toward a Neo-Piagetian perspective on communication and cognitive development. In F.D. Minifie & L.L. Lloyd (Eds.), *Communication and cognitive abilities—early behavioral assessment* (pp. 151-184). Baltimore: University Park Press.

Mori, A., & Masters, L. (1980). *Teaching the severely mentally retarded.* Germantown, Md.: Aspen Systems.

Moritz, M. (1983). Education: *What can a computer do? In Money Guide: Personal Computers,* New York: Time, Inc., (pp. 67–68).

Papert, S. (1980). *Mindstorms: Children, computers and powerful ideas.* New York: Basic Books.

Park, O.C. (1982, March). Computer-based adaptive instructional models: A critical review. *Paper presented at the American Educational Research Association,* New York, NY.

Paul, M. (1983). *Child's play: Preschoolers and PC's. PC, 2*(5), 349–358.

Rowher, W. (1979). Cognitive and perceptual development in children. In A. Lane, (Ed.), *Human growth and development of the exceptional individual.* Boston: Special Learning Corp.

Sailor, W., & Guess, D. (1983). *Severely handicapped students: An instructional design.* Boston: Houghton Mifflin.

Scarr-Salapatek, S., & Williams, M.L. (1973) The effects of early stimulation on low-birth-weight infants. *Child Development, 44,* 94–101.

Skinner, B.F. (1953). *Science and human behavior.* New York: Macmillan.

Sontag, E., Smith, J., & Sailor, W. (1977). The Severely Handicapped. Who are they? Where are we? *Journal of Special Education, 11,* 5–11.

Stevens J. H., Jr. (1982). From 3 to 20: The early training project. *Young Children, 37*(6), 57–64.

Swenson, R.P. & Kingman J.C. (1981). Computer assisted instruction in special education. *In the Proceedings of the Johns Hopkins First National Search for Application of Personal computing to aid the handicapped* (pp. 76–77). New York: IEEE Computer Society Press.

Trachtman, P. (1984). Putting computers into the hands of children without language. *Smithsonian, 14*(11), 42–51.

Wilson, M. S., & Fox, B. J. (1984). Using audible microcomputer software in special education. In M. Behrmann and L. Lahm (Eds.), *Proceedings of the National Conference on the Use of Microcomputers in Special Education,* (pp. 132–134). Reston, VA: Council for Exceptional Children.

Wrenge, R. (1982, July). Hands on. *Popular Computing* pp. 110–114.

Vanderheiden, G.C. (1981, January). Practical application of microcomputers to aid the handicapped. *Computer,* pp. 54–61.

CHAPTER 8

The Computer as a Management Tool for Teachers and Administrators

Paper, paper, paper. A major impact of P.L. 94-142 and the ensuing delivery service plans of the states has been a dramatic increase in the information gathering, record keeping, and reporting responsibilities of both the special education teacher and the administrator. They are required to maintain information about and report on individual students, curricula, materials and supplies, and programs. The organization and maintenance of these records using traditional paper and pen or pencil methods can be an overwhelming and extremely time-consuming task. As increased time is spent in record keeping, less time becomes available for these professionals to teach, supervise, and plan.

The dynamic qualities of the computer provide the special educator with a viable and important alternative for coping with these record-keeping responsibilities. Not only can data be maintained and updated more easily on a computer, but in addition the information recorded can be more easily manipulated in order to provide the educator with useful and timely analysis.

A computer is most commonly described as an electronic information processing machine. It is designed to accept and remember large amounts of information. The data can be evaluated and used to solve a problem at an extremely high rate of speed. Finally, the results of the information analysis can be reported in a variety of formats, including print and graphics. All of these dynamics of a computer make it an important tool for special educators in order to assist in meeting their planning, evaluating, diagnosing, record keeping, and reporting responsibilities.

The management applications of the computer in special education can be summarized under two categories: computer managed instruction (CMI) and computer assisted management (CAM). The first, CMI, refers to the use of the computer to systematically monitor, plan, and report on the instructional process. CAM is a more global use of the computer for management and implies the use of the computer to analyze, manage, and

This chapter was authored by Joel E. Mittler and Edward Cain.

report on programs. The emphasis in CMI is on the individual learner, as opposed to program or school management applications in CAM.

COMPUTER MANAGED INSTRUCTION (CMI)

A major premise in the field of special education is that an individual education program will be developed for each student. Implicit in the IEP process is a continuous cycle of testing, diagnosis, prescription, individualized instruction, and monitoring of progress. The use of the computer to assist in the prescription and monitoring of individual student programs is one of the oldest and most effective uses of computers in special education.

The successful provision of instruction to exceptional students is based upon sound decision making. The special educator must constantly monitor information about the individual pattern of learning strengths and weaknesses of students and their levels of mastery in order to make decisions about when to change an instructional approach and, more importantly, what kind of change to make in student's individual programs.

CMI refers to the use of the computer as a record keeper, diagnostic tester, test scorer, pupil progress monitor, and prescriber of what each student should study. The intent in CMI programs is to provide the teacher with information necessary about each child in order to assist the instructional decision-making process and enhance the individualization of instruction. It is most basically a computerized inventory program, maintaining records about instructional objectives, individual student learning strengths and weakness, instructional methods and materials employed, and pupil mastery.

Cluster or Mastery Learning Systems

Cluster or mastery learning CMI systems are criterion-referenced computer data bases of instructional curricula that permit the monitoring of individual pupil progress. The curriculum is defined as a scope and sequence of instructional objectives stated as behavioral goals or skills. These goal statements are grouped into clusters representing the hierarchy of skills that must be mastered in order to learn a concept. Skill clusters are arranged into strands that represent the major components of a particular curriculum sequence. These strands are then organized into major curriculum domains or goals.

Following is an example of this organization of criterion-referenced behavioral objectives in the subject of reading. "Word Attack" represents a domain of skills that permeates the scope and sequence of the curriculum entitled reading. It is a basic skill essential to the decoding and comprehension of written language. "Phonics," "structure," and "context" are major strands contained within the area of word attack. The strand of phonics could be subdivided into the following hierarchy of skill clusters: consonant identification, consonant substitution, consonant variants, and vowels. Within the cluster of skills called consonant substitution would be the hierarchy of skills: consonants, beginning-single; consonants, beginning-blends and digraphs; and consonants, ending-single. Each of these skills would be stated in terms of an objectively stated behavioral goal; for example: "The student will indicate the placement of a word: before, between, or after a pair of guide words."

Cluster or mastery computer learning systems permit the monitoring of individual students regarding the mastery of the skills contained in the taxonomy data base. The management system makes pertinent information about each student available to the teacher through a series of reports and allows the teacher to maintain information on each child. Most CMI systems provide the teacher with at least the following types of reports.

Student Progress Reports. These reports provide a teacher with information about each individual student. The data provided include information about the number and type of skills a student was assigned (Table 8-1), the skills that were mastered, and the date when the skills were mastered. These reports are particularly helpful in evaluating pupil progress and placement and in planning for parent conferences; they can be used as a part of a student's permanent record. A typical student progress report would look like that given in Table 8-2.

Enrollment or Class Reports. These reports provide the teacher with the same types of information as the student reports except that data are provided for all pupils in a particular program or class. Often the management system offers the option of reporting this information in an alphabetical list format or graphically in a chart. An example of a class report is given in Table 8-3.

Current Assignment Report. This type of report lists all students who may be working on the same skill, cluster, and strand. This information is particularly useful in grouping and regrouping students in a class. Table 8-4 is an example of such a report.

Correlation Reports. Correlation reports permit the information about student skill assignment and performance to be cross-referenced to instructional materials used or to the textbook page reference for the skill. Information reported in this manner assists in the evaluation of the

Table 8-1. Assignment Status Report

Language Arts
CLASS #1:

ASSIGNMENT STATUS REPORT
Teacher: R. MARTELLI

PAGE 2

ST. #	STUDENT NAME	REFERENCE NUMBER	CURRENT SKILL	TOTAL SESSIONS	DATE OF LAST ACTIVITY
	Anne MICHAELS	768483	501	80	04-Feb-82
	SKILLS ASSIGNED				
501	SESS-3				
502	503, 504	463, 465	464, 562	466	440
441	442, 443	444, 445			
	SKILLS BYPASSED				
404	BYP-0, 406	BYP-5, 414	BYP-8, 419	BYP-5, 420	BYP-4,
505	BYP-8, 508	BYP-3, 562	BYP-1, 462	BYP-3, 513	BYP-1
	SKILLS MASTERED				
401	PRE-1, 402	PRE-3, 403	POST-1, 405	PRE-5, 411	PRE-#,
412	POST-5, 413	POST-#, 418	POST-5, 421	POST-1, 422	PRE-1

Table 8–2. Student Progress Report

**SPECIAL PROGRESS REPORT FOR: Tim PUTNAM Date: 14-Dec-81
PREPARED BY: MS PEREZ**

Language Arts PROGRESS REPORT

Tim has been working with a special Language Arts program since 02-Oct-81. This computer program helps students master their basic skills. This report tells you how Tim is doing.

As of 04-Dec-81 Tim has successfully completed the assignments in these skill areas.

     SIMPLE SUBJECT
     COMPOUND SUBJECT
     PERSONAL PRONOUNS

Additional work has been assigned in the following areas:

     VERB TENSE
     DID, DONE
     CAME, COME
     INDIRECT OBJECT
     PREPOSITIONS
     PREDICATE ADJECTIVE

Should you like more information about this report, please contact MS. PEREZ.

---

instructional programs and also provides important information to the regular classroom teacher when the student is mainstreamed. A correlation report might look like that given in Table 8–5.

Survey Statistics Reports. These reports permit the analysis of student progress by skill descriptions and the number of students mastering or failing the skills. Data can be combined for analysis in a survey report on the basis of individual classes, schools, or a school district as a whole. Table 8–6 is an example of a survey statistics report.

Table 8–3. Enrollment or Class Reports

MATH
Class #1:

STUDENT LIST REPORT
Teacher: MR. JOHNSON

PAGE 1

ST. #	STUDENT NAME	REFERENCE NUMBER	GRADE	TOT. SES.	ACCUM. PCT.	LAST ACTIVITY
		GROUP #1:				
31	Ken ASHLEY	24441	4	5	82%	20-Jul-81
23	Rose COOK	21234	5	2	87%	23-Jul-81
24	Carl JOHNS	23123	4	1	63%	23-Jul-81
27	Ralph LANNON	23165	4	5	75%	21-Jul-81
25	Rebecca LYONS	23156	5	1	—	23-Jul-81
28	Shannon MOORE	23189	5	3	91%	22-Jul-81
32	Warren VOGEL	22210	4	4	84%	21-Jul-81

Reading
Class #1:

WORK REPORT
From - 04-Jan-83   To - 27-Mar-82
Teacher: S. THOMPSON

PAGE 1

ST. #	STUDENT NAME	REFERENCE NUMBER	SKILL NUMBER	RESULT	DATE OF SKILL ACTIVITY
		GROUP #1			
28	Andrew BUTCHER	87509	501	PRE-1	22-Jan-82
			502	PRE-1	25-Jan-82
			503	SESS-2	26-Jan-82
3	Connie GODIN	87123	SURVEY		04-Jan-82
			461	PRE-1	15-Jan-82
			462	BYP-1	26-Feb-82
			463	SESS-1	27-Mar-82
4	Peter KATZ	87503	510	SESS-#	05-Jan-82
			511	POST-1	07-Feb-82
			512	PRE-1	14-Feb-82

Table 8–4. Current Assignment Report

Language Arts
Class #1:LA 7-2

CURRENT ASSIGNMENT REPORT
Teacher: K. WINTER

PAGE 1

ST. #	STUDENT NAME	CURRENT SKILL	SESSION NUMBER	DATE OF LAST ACTIVITY	NEXT SKILL
		GROUP #1			
5	Jesse BEVERLY	701	0	04-Mar-82	702
9	Brenda CHASE	726	0	02-Mar-82	727
12	Elsa PRESSMAN	714	#	30-Mar-82	715
38	Rodney RICHARDS	704	1	20-Apr-82	705
6	Martha SELZNICK	770	1	02-Mar-82	771
7	Anthony SMITH	703	2	18-May-82	702

Table 8-5. Correlation Report

Reading   SKILL LIST   PAGE 1

SKILL	DESCRIPTION	CURRENT REFERRAL AND LOCAL OBJECTIVE*
	COMPREHENSION/INTERPRETIVE	
741	MAIN IDEA	WORKBOOK P. 34 EX. 3-9 SEE MS PORTER FOR ADDITIONAL HELP.
742	TONE/FEELINGS	READ PP. 43-45 IN YOUR POETRY BOOK AND DO THE EXERCISES.
743	TONE/CHOICE OF WORDS TO EXPRESS MOOD	SEE MR. YEE FOR HELP ON TUESDAY DURING 5TH PERIOD STUDY.
744	TONE/SENSORY WORDS	WORKBOOK P. 23-34. WORKSHEET #32

Table 8-6. Survey Report

Problem Solving
Class #1:

SURVEY REPORT
Teacher: MISS LEWIS

PAGE 1

GROUP #1

ST. #	STUDENT NAME	GR.	DATE	SURVEY	S1	S2	S4	TOTAL
56	Ken ASHLEY	5	24-Jul-81	A	80%	90%	60%	76%
60	Carl JOHNS	5	24-Jul-81	B	90%	70%	90%	83%
47	Cheryl JOHNS	5	24-Jul-81	A	90%	70%	90%	83%

Language Arts
Class #3:

SURVEY REPORT
Teacher: S. STONE

GROUP #1

PAGE 1

Melissa CHIRIACKA

SKILL #	DESCRIPTION	PASS	FAIL	NOT TAKEN
440	STATEMENTS			
403	QUESTIONS	X		
404	COMMANDS	X		
405	EXCLAMATION		X	
406	COMPLETE SUBJECT		X	
408	COMPOUND SUBJECT	X		
409	COMPLETE PREDICATE	X		
415	COMMON AND PROPER NOUNS		X	
419	ACTION VERBS			X
421	CONTRACTIONS			X

Cluster or mastery learning CMI systems have as a common element preprogrammed formats for the input of student data and for the format of the reports. The teacher has certain flexibility to modify a specific report format within prescribed limitations. The more complex versions of these systems contain large data banks of sequentially listed instructional skills and usually require the memory capabilities of minicomputers. Less intricate versions are available on microcomputers and these systems permit the teacher to determine the instructional program sequence. The following will provide a brief description of these two types of CMI systems.

DOLPHIN. DOLPHIN is a comprehensive CMI mastery learning system produced by the Time Share Corporation, a division of the Houghton Mifflin Company. Four instructional programs are offered in the subject areas of reading, language arts, mathematics, and problem solving. Each subject area program has a large data base of skills organized into a scope and sequence of instructional skills. The management system includes a criterion-referenced survey test used to identify each student's level of mastery, a computer assisted instruction (CAI) drill and practice program for each of the skills, a post-test, and a comprehensive program of different reports available to the teacher. Records can be maintained for approximately 2000 individual students in all subject areas. Correlations are available to textbook series, to other instructional materials, and to local objectives. Since this is a comprehensive CMI system, it requires an interactive minicomputer system.

The element that makes DOLPHIN somewhat unique from other comprehensive mastery learning CMI systems is the fact that all functions are performed on computer terminals. Students take the survey, pretests, and post-tests on the terminal. The drill and practice experiences are also on terminal. The teacher enters student data, makes individual student assignments and requests reports on the computer terminal. The DOLPHIN CMI programs, therefore, not only use a computer to maintain student information, but also provides pupils with structured learning experiences on a computer. They combine CMI mastery learning with the elements of CAI drill and practice.

DOLPHIN has been designed to assist the teacher in making instructional decisions for individual students. Although the program contains a sequentially structured list of skills for each curriculum, the management program does not attempt to make student assignments. The teacher must assign specific skills to each pupil based upon historical data and the results of the criterion-referenced pretest. Thus, the teacher, not the CMI system, is making decisions about students.

The reporting component of DOLPHIN permits the teacher to select a variety of options in order to analyze the data. Information can be obtained about individual pupils historically and by subject area. Skill performance can be analyzed by cluster, strand, class, teacher of record, or any group of students as a whole. Thus, the data maintained on the system can be used to assess individual student progress, class performance, or regrouping of students or to report about the instructional program as a whole. The data base is updated each time a teacher makes a student assignment and every time a pupil uses the system to take a test or for drill and practice. Table 8–7 shows the management options that are available to the teacher for DOLPHIN.

The DOLPHIN system is representative of the large CMI mastery learning program. The complexity of the program and hardware requirements necessitate its use in a school or school system in order to be cost-effective.

AimStar. AimStar is a less complex CMI mastery learning system designed for use by special education teachers on a microcomputer. It is constructed to provide the teacher with student performance data in order to improve the decision-making ability of the practitioner concerning when and what kind of change should be made in an individual student's instructional program by providing data on a decision-making flowchart.

AimStar is designed to be used by persons with no computer experience and allows the user to manage student performance data and carry out the graphing and flowchart analysis without the associated paper and pencil tedium. The use of this microcomputer CMI system permits the teacher to enter and store daily data on each instructional program for each pupil and then carry out formal decision-making on each program in a matter of minutes.

AimStar is an open-ended CMI structure, one that requires the teacher to create student data files and to define the components of the instructional program. The user must define the target instructional program in terms of the program name, aim date, criterion level, and data type. Data files must be set up for each instructional program. Once they have been constructed, they can be revised and edited at any time.

The AimStar program is designed to permit the entry of large amounts of information about student performance in the shortest period of time. Once the data have been collected and entered, the program allows each set of program data to be evaluated using decision-making rules. The user has the option of running decision rules on one, some, or all of the programs for a group of students. AimStar can also be used to graph the data in order to determine if a student's instructional program should be altered.

AimStar does not permit the maintenance and analysis of data for a large number of students. School and district surveys cannot be obtained from this program. Its advantage is that it is easy to use and requires only a microcomputer and a printer. It is a CMI system designed for use by

Table 8-7. Available Management Options for DOLPHIN

---

1. CLASS Maintenance
2. STUDENT Maintenance
3. ASSIGNMENT Maintenance
4. REFERRAL Maintenance
5. CLEAR Work
6. MONITOR
7. REPORT
8. SKILL REVIEW
9. STUDENT SESSION
10. END

WHICH OPTION? 8

---

an individual teacher or a small group of teachers. It provides curriculum flexibility since the instructional skills are not defined in the management program.

Computerized Test Scoring. Another area of CMI, which is of particular help to the special education practitioner, is computerized test scoring. This service is available in two types of formats: scoring services and test scoring computer programs. Both systems are designed to provide the teacher with criterion-referenced test analysis in order to assist in the diagnosis, prescription, and placement of exceptional children.

All of the major achievement test publishers now offer criterion-referenced analysis reports for their achievement batteries; examples are the Iowa Test of Basic Skills (ITBS) and the Metropolitan Achievement Test (MAT). The reports generated identify the skill mastery levels of individual pupils in the major subject areas for the items tested. This profile report quickly identifies for the teacher the areas of academic strength and weakness. Summary reports are available for classes, grades, and schools. Certain test scoring services, such as Riverside Publishing Company (Iowa Test of Basic Skills) will also generate a computerized analysis of each student's performance in a parent letter form.

There has been a dramatic increase in the last few years in the number of microcomputer test scoring software programs available to special educators. These programs are designed to provide individual pupil profile reports identifying learning strengths and weaknesses, cluster scoring for both grade and age, and standard scores. Programs are now available for ability tests such as the WISC-R and diagnostic instruments such as the Woodcock-Johnson, Peabody Individual Achievement Test, and Test of Syntactic Abilities.

A generic scoring program, Microcomputer Scoring System from Tescor, Inc. (Herndon, VA), can be used to score any standardized achievement or ability test, criterion-referenced-test, or teacher-made test Using an optical reader, the Tescor software computes a variety of scores, including raw and standard scores, national percentiles and standings, and grade equivalents. Additionally, the program is designed to generate administratively useful reports (e.g., pupil profiles, class lists, item analyses) and test labels for permanent student records. Potentially, a system such as this can be coordinated with a curriculum or program of studies allowing individual student progress to be monitored. It can be predicted that the number of diagnostic-prescriptive test scoring programs available for use on microcomputer systems will continue to increase in the future.

Computerized IEPs. As with test scoring programs, there has been an increase in the number of computerized IEP programs available for use by the special educator. These systems are also available in two formats: large comprehensive minicomputer systems designed for use by a school system, and microcomputer software programs designed for use by an individual teacher or an individual school. Both types of systems are designed to create, monitor, and evaluate student IEPs based upon P. L. 94-142 regulations, state procedures, and local school district objectives.

Insight Unlimited, Inc., is an example of a company that provides a comprehensive computerized IEP program to school districts. The company provides a computerized pupil tracking and IEP service on either a minicomputer or, in an abbreviated version, a microcomputer. The Insight program is designed not only to print students' IEPs but also to analyze test scores and monitor both long-range and short-range instructional goals.

Insight will customize its software to reflect local curriculum objectives, state reporting requirements, and local standardized testing calenders. All special education pupils are tracked regarding their short-term and long-term IEP goals. New short-range goals are generated by the computer, based upon the local objectives, when pupils have displayed mastery of previously generated goals. The program provides individual student, class, school, and district reports.

As with other CMI microcomputer software, there has been a significant increase in the last few years in the number of IEP programs available for use by special educators. All permit some flexibility to the user in listing local objectives and related service options. A variety of report options are also included in most programs.

Project IEP, produced by Evans Newton, Inc., is one example of a CMI IEP program designed for use on a microcomputer. Data can be stored on a floppy disc or on a hard disc. Hard disc storage provides enough memory capacity to store the records for a moderate sized school district. Project IEP will print 15 different reports for teacher, parent, student, and special education administrative review.

COMPUTER ASSISTED MANAGEMENT (CAM)

Computer assisted management (CAM) is a term used to identify computer software that has been designed primarily for administrative and management purposes, rather than for instruction, as is the case with CMI software. These microcomputer systems provide the administrator with fast and accurate information that can be analyzed in a variety of manners to assist in the administrative decision-making process. They are designed for use by the individual with little or no computer experience. Most of these programs were originally designed for use in business, rather than being specially produced for educational use as is the case with CMI software.

There are three basic types of CAM software that are particularly useful to the special education administrator: data base management systems, word processing, and electronic spreadsheet. Versions of these three types of CAM systems are available for use on almost all types of microcomputers. The minimum hardware requirements to use these products fully as administrative tools are a microcomputer with at least 16K of memory, a dual or hard disc drive, and a printer.

Data Base Management Systems. Data base management programs were originally developed for small companies to help them with inventory control. They were designed to permit the user to customize and refine their program by selecting options from a menu. No programming experience is necessary, therefore, to use these systems.

Data base management is a systematic approach to storing, updating, and retrieving information stored as data items, usually in the form of records in a file. Information is organized into files. Each of these files consists of a series of records which are made up of a number of fields. Each field represents one type of information contained in a record.

Data base management programs permit the user to sort records by one or more fields in order to analyze the information contained in a file. They permit the user to design how they want to report the results of the computer analysis by designating the specific fields to be printed, the order of their presentation, and the records to be included in the report.

Suppose that we wanted to design a student file for all pupils in a district's self-contained special education program. We might want to have each student record to include the following fields (individual units of information): last name, first name, date of birth, street address, town or city, state and ZIP code, parents' names, handicapping condition, school assigned, special education teacher's name, related services, date of admission into the program, date of transfer out of the program, where transferred, and date of last psychologic examination. Once this file format was established, the appropriate information would be entered for each student in the self-contained program.

The administrator could then analyze all students in the program by sorting the records by one or more fields (category of information, such as school assigned or related services). Once sorted, a report could be written using some or all of the fields. For example, asking the computer to sort by last name and teacher would provide an ALPHA list of students for each teacher. Likewise, asking the computer to print parents' names, street address, city or town, state, and ZIP code would permit mailing labels to be printed for all students.

The major advantage of data base management systems is that they allow the user with no computer experience to develop powerful record-keeping programs. The information contained in the files can be manipulated in a variety of ways to provide the specific data needed upon demand. Files are quickly and easily updated by changing only the specific field containing the information that has changed. Records can be deleted from a file and new records can be added as needed.

Some of the various files that can be designed for use by the special educator on a data base management program include permanent records, student program records, personnel files, attendance, equipment and materials inventories, scheduling, budget information, and administrative schedules. This list is by no means comprehensive and is used only as an example. The variety and types of files that can be designed are limited only by the needs and imagination of the user.

Some of the most popular data base management systems used by educators are INFOPRO, PFS (Personal Filing System), D-B (Data Base) Master, and Quick File. A key consideration in selecting a data base system is the type of microcomputer and disc capacity, the ease of use, and the flexibility for record analysis.

Word Processing. Word processing is a computer-based system for writing, editing, and formatting letters and reports. These systems permit the user to type, print, and revise documents with minimal effort. A few commands permit the user to insert and delete text, rearrange text within a document, and move text for later revision or printing. The use of word processing as an administrative tool implies that letters, reports, and documents can be updated, altered, or revised without manually retyping the entire document.

All word processing systems contain two major functions: formatting and editing. Formatting refers to the computer program's ability to alter the appearance of the text by changing items such as the line spacing, justification, and column width. The user can examine a variety of formats prior to deciding which to print as the final copy. Once the material that has been written is saved on a disc, it can be reformatted at any future date.

The editing capability of word processing permits the user to alter or delete any letter, line, or section of text without having to retype the entire page of print. Material can be inserted at any point in the existing material. Sentences, paragraphs, and sections can be moved and inserted at any time. Thus, the editing function permits the user to compose written material without ever using an eraser. The final copy, which is printed, is the corrected copy. Should an error be found in the printed copy, the user simply has to make the correction on the computer and let the machine print out the revised copy.

A number of microcomputer word processing softwares are designed to be used with data base management systems. The combination of these two CAM functions means that a letter or report can be designed on the word processor. Specific data can then be added by selecting fields from the data base file to be inserted at specified points in the written material. For example, a letter to the parents of all special education students could be composed on the word processor. Individual letters to each parent could be printed by inserting the parents' names and addresses from the data base file. The students' names could also be inserted into the body of the letter.

Word processing is the most commonly used CAM system in education. Unfortunately, it is all too often used only by secretaries. When special education teachers and administrators begin to use this flexible tool to cope with their record keeping and reporting responsibilities, they find these tasks greatly simplified. The more this tool is used, the more uses that are found for it.

A few of the most commonly used microcomputer word processing softwares are WordStar, The Bank Street Writer, Word Pro, The Quick Brown Fox, Edix, and Easy Writer. Some of the key considerations in selecting word processing software are the type of hardware, particularly the memory requirements, the ease of use, and the documentation (instructional manuals and reference cards).

Electronic Spreadsheet. Electronic spreadsheet microcomputer programs represent the third major type of CAM system useful for administration and management. These programs provide the user with the ability to process hundreds of numbers at once, to find patterns, draw conclusions, and explore alternatives suggested by any type of numerical data. They are most simply flexible and versatile programs that permit the user to explore "what if" alternatives by changing the variables on the computer.

Electronic spreadsheet programs allow the user to organize numerical information into the categories and define how these categories are to interrelate. Once the display has been designed and the numerical data entered, the information can be manipulated in an almost unlimited variety of ways. With the electronic spreadsheet, paper, pencils, and calculators are replaced by the computer. The paper is the computer display, pencils are the keyboard keys, and the calculator is the computer. Each time you wish to recalculate the results, you simply change the appropriate numbers on the screen and the computer carries out the calculation for all sections affected in the formula.

Electronic spreadsheets are, of course, most helpful in solving the accounting problems faced in administration. Budget projections, inventories, and service fee analysis are just some of the tasks that can be performed using these systems. They can also be most effective in other administrative reporting and record-keeping activities. Test scores can easily be analyzed on them. Enrollment projections can be made for a school, program, or district. Student and teacher scheduling alternatives can be reviewed on them. Almost any analysis requiring the manipulation of numerical data can be performed on these versatile electronic tools.

The most popular electronic spreadsheet is VisiCalc, published by VisiCorp (formerly Personal Software, Inc.). Versions of this system are available for all major microcomputer systems. Other electronic spreadsheets include Multiplan and SuperCalc.

A new generation of electronic "what if" problem-solving programs have begun to be published. They permit the user to solve problems for any set of unknowns without using the spreadsheet format. TK!Solver is one of these new problem-solving systems.

SUMMARY

The electronic information processing aspects of computers make them powerful and important record keeping alternatives for special educators. There are two types of management applications that are of particular use to both teachers and administrators: computer managed instruction (CMI) and computer assisted management (CAM). Both are available for use on minicomputer and microcomputer systems.

CMI refers to using the computer to monitor and plan for individual students. These types of softwares are designed to assist in the decision-making process. The three major types of CMI discussed were cluster or mastery learning systems, computerized test scoring, and computerized IEP systems.

CAM was defined as the use of the computer to analyze, manage, and report on programs. Three types of CAM systems were identified as being of particular use to the special educator: data base management, word processing, and electronic spreadsheets.

Part III
Getting On-Line:
Using Technology to
Benefit Exceptional Learners

CHAPTER 9

In-Service and Preservice Training

"The need for including computer education in teacher education is obvious." (East, 1983, p. 56)

As East points out, computer technology has become part of our society. As such, our schools, which reflect societal events, must respond by including computer technology within their walls. Among other things, educators will discover the importance of teaching students about computers and how to use them, and they will also discover the application of computer technology to the many functions served by the schools. As this textbook has clearly demonstrated, the application of microcomputers to one of these functions, special education, is significant.

This application will not occur automatically. The entire field of special education has just recently gone through a period of rapid growth, with many newly certified teachers now providing instruction on a daily basis. These teachers have had to be provided with the necessary attitudes, knowledge, and skills to adequately instruct the exceptional child. They are just beginning to develop the techniques they will employ to accomplish their goals. The adoption of the microcomputer will be impossible for many of our teachers without the acquisition of additional skills.

East (1983) has pointed out that teacher education for the regular educator assumes that considerable knowledge of the subject matter (e.g., reading, mathematics science, social studies, and so forth has been acquired prior to entering college. Even in the field of special education, considerable previous experience of academics, children's behavior, daily living skills, and so forth, provides the basis upon which new information and techniques are applied that will assist the teacher to work with handicapped learners. In addition, the common tools of the classroom (e.g., chalkboard, film, books) are relatively familiar to most prospective teachers prior to entering a training program.

Unfortunately, this is not the case with the application of computers to special education. Current trainees in special education as well as those working within the field have little, if any, experience within this new technology. Of course, this is a temporary situation, as computers will

This chapter was authored by Joel E. Mittler.

become increasingly familiar within all levels of education and in the home. It is hard to imagine a teacher trainee 10 years from now who has not been exposed to a microcomputer. But the trainee, both now and in the future will have little understanding of the integration of this technology to the existing curriculum.

As the complex material of this textbook suggests, the application of computers to special education is neither a simple nor unidimensional process. Teacher training in special education and computers, whether it be a preservice or in-service situation, must be prepared to address the novice who desires to incorporate the microcomputer in the classroom, as well as the "expert," who will design the entire system for the school district. In addition, such training must be adequate for the special education administrator, the evaluator or any other individual that is part of the special education system.

WHO IS TO BE TRAINED?

The preparation of competent users of computers within special education can be accomplished by providing training to one of several possible groups. Some of these are listed in Table 9-1.

This diversity of need suggests that any preservice or in-service program should to be broad enough to meet the needs of all trainees yet specific enough to be appropriate to the individual training needs. It is the purpose of this chapter to describe the content and implementation of training programs to assist in the preparation of individuals who will employ computer technology in their professional special education efforts, not to discuss the training of computer science majors to be special educators nor to train special educators to be computer scientists.

Competencies

The competencies required for any education program to meet the needs of a diverse group must also be broad and varied. Students will enter a program with differing backgrounds in computer familiarity. An additional variable in any preservice or in-service program that will influence the attainment of competencies is the amount of time available for training. Time is limited by the fact that training will have to occur while professional responsibilities are still being met, as in an in-service program, or as part of a comprehensive preservice program preparing special educators. Priorities must be established that suggest which

Table 9-1. Groups Requiring Training

---

1. Preservice students without any previous training in special education or in computers.
2. Preservice students already trained as special educators but without any training in computers.
3. Preservice computer science majors who want to become special educators.
4. Special educators, currently employed, who desire to develop skills in computers for use in the classroom.
5. Computer teachers, currently employed, who want to apply their skills to exceptional children.
6. Special education administrators, currently employed, who want to develop computer skills.
7. All other professionals and paraprofessionals working within the field of special education who desire to learn about computers.

---

competencies are of greatest importance. Rogers, Moursand, and Engel (1984) have suggested a priority listing of competencies for educators. Using a similar model, Table 9-2 suggests competencies for special education teachers in terms of the time available for training.

Of course, competencies can be added to these as technologic advances dictate. It is not expected that all special education teachers will achieve all of these competencies in a given program, unless considerable time is spent on computer training. Yet, as has been previously pointed out, most preservice teachers have minimal time available in their program for computer training, and most in-service programs also have limited available time.

Another factor that can dictate additional competencies is the individual's purpose in obtaining training. While these competencies are sufficient for the special educator to become proficient in the use of computers in most special education settings, there are professional roles that might dictate the learning of other skills. For example, the special education administrator would need additional skills in areas such as creating an overall system for a school district, advanced skills in spreadsheet analysis, and so forth. The specialist in teaching others about computers would need greater knowledge of available hardware and software, some ability to make minor repairs on hardware, the ability to organize and run in-service program and more. The diagnostic specialist would require thorough knowledge of assessment via the computer, familiarity with computer-generated Individual Education Plan, and so forth.

Table 9-2. Prioritized Competencies for Computers in Special Education

---

Highest Priority (with limited time)

1. Learn to operate a computer, load and run commercially available software.
2. Be able to select appropriate software for classroom usage.
3. Learn to perform basic utility functions, such as formatting disks, copying files, printing, etc.
4. Understands the role that the computer has in special education.
5. Know the major types of application of computers to special education, i.e., CAI, CMI, simulation, etc.
6. Know related resources and how to obtain access to them.

Medium Priority (with somewhat longer time)

1. Experience a substantial variety of computer assisted instructional programs applicable to various handicapping conditions.
2. Be familiar with a variety of computers and peripherals appropriate for exceptional individuals.
3. Know the current potential impact of computers on society, education, and special education.
4. Know specific computer assisted instructional software representing various types, i.e., tutorial, drill and practice, simulation, etc., and their application to handicapped learners.
5. Know specific computer assisted instructional software in specific content areas and appropriate for exceptional learners.
6. Have knowledge and use of educational programming languages, such as BASIC, LOGO, and PILOT.
7. Knowledge of computer assisted prosthetic devices for handicapped learners.
8. Know related technologies, such as video discs, various video displays, robotics, etc.
9. Know and use graphics for instructional purposes.
10. Know the roles of computers in work and careers and be able to prepare handicapped students for the possible vocational uses of computers.
11. Be able to use the computer to assist in the diagnosis of handicapped learners.

Lower Priority (for extended training)

1. Ability to use programming languages to write instructional programs to meet the needs of students.
2. Ability to use word processing, data base management, and spreadsheets in special education.
3. Ability to perform the technical tasks necessary to modify the hardware to meet instructional needs.
4. Advanced programming techniques in BASIC, LOGO, PILOT, or Pascal.
5. Ability to consult with other school personnel, i.e., administrators, school nurse, etc. on the possible use of computers with handicapped learners.

One additional area that must develop its own competencies is that of the educational researcher investigating computers and special education. The suddenness with which this field has emerged suggests that there are many questions that must be answered. Zinn and Berger (1983) have suggested several areas of study in computers and general education. These can be modified and enhanced for special education as indicated in Table 9-3.

CONTENT OF COMPUTER TRAINING PROGRAMS

At the present time, most special education teachers are being introduced to computer technology during their preservice training or while actually teaching. Their needs are similar, in many ways, to those of general educators who are first being exposed to computers during their professional training. It can be envisioned that, 20 years from now, all college students will be thoroughly familiar with computers from their elementary and secondary school years. Until then, however, basic computer literacy will have to be taught prior to teaching applications to specific job training. It is therefore apparent that there may be extensive similarity between training programs for general educators and special educators. Although other training programs may vary their offerings, Burke (1983) provides a listing of over 30 courses offered by a university in its computer education program. These courses are listed in Table 9-4.

Although it is not recommended that all special education teachers be required to take all of the courses listed in Table 9-4, it is obvious that since most special education teachers have not developed computer related skills prior to beginning an in-service or preservice program, many of the topics listed for general educators might prove useful. In fact, a careful review of the competencies listed in the beginning of this chapter would indicate that there are many similarities in competencies needed by general and special educators. Emphasis for special educators, however, is on specific applications to students with handicapping conditions.

Preservice Training

The task of training special education teachers is already difficult and complex. For example, students must be introduced to the foundations of the educational system, be provided knowledge and skills to teach several academic subjects to a variety of exceptional students, be provided skills to manage a class, and much more. Any attempt to also provide opportunities for students to acquire the additional competencies described

Table 9-3. Possible Research Areas in Computers and Special Education

1. Studying attitudes of students, teachers, administrators, parents and others in special education toward learning, technology in special education, family activities, careers, handicapped students, etc.

2. Studying computer assisted learning in relation to specific handicapping conditions, efficiency, effectiveness, long-term effects, thinking and problem-solving, learning skills, generalization to areas not taught with computers, specific uses of the computer to assist instruction, etc.

3. Studying the social structure relating to the computer, including classroom organization, friendships, integration with nonhandicapped students, teacher-student relationships, teacher roles, parent roles, implications for the family, student expectancies, etc.

4. Studying innovative uses of the computer with special populations, including speech synthesis and nonvocal populations, robotics and students with limited mobility, word processing and students with written language difficulties, etc.

5. Studying the training of special education teachers and others in the field in the use of computers with reference to who does the training, where it should be done, the content of the training, the integration of training into traditional special education courses, etc.

earlier must be extremely difficult. Yet it is obvious that some proficiency in the use of computers in the special education classroom is certainly desirable and may soon be mandatory for employment in this field.

There are several difficulties in attempting to accomplish this task. As mentioned previously, most teachers enter preservice training with little, if any, familiarity with computers. Thus, the first step of any program would be to have the student acquire basic computer literacy. Fortunately, many colleges and universities are making computer literacy part of their required core topics for all students. Thus, many preservice students will become computer literate prior to entering their professional training. For those students who are not required to take such courses or who are being trained as special education teachers at the graduate level, a course in computer literacy should be offered as a required course. Traditionally, such courses are taught by members of the computer science department and typically cover the following (Rogers, Moursand, & Engel, 1984):

What computers are and how they work.
The basic skills to operate a computer.
A history of computers and technology.
An introduction to programming.
An overview of the application of computers to society.
A discussion of the social issues generated by computers.

The resources of computer science departments around the country are currently being strained to provide computer literacy to a generation of students who have not been exposed to computers prior to entering college. Since most universities realize this is a temporary condition that

Table 9-4. Sample University Computer Courses

Computer Literacy
Operating Microcomputers
Teaching Computer Literacy
Computer Programming in PILOT
Computer Programming in Pascal
Computer Programming in LOGO
Computer Programming in BASIC I
Computer Programming in BASIC II
Program Generator
Teaching Computer Programming
Computer Assisted Instruction I
Computer Assisted Programming II
Computer Managed Instruction
Interactive Intelligent Simulation
Interactive Intelligent Graphics
Communication and Intelligent Electronics
Managing the Computer Education Environment
Computing Hardware
Software Search and Evaluation
Administrative Applications of Computers
Data Base Management
Word Processing
Computor Applications in Business Education
Computer Applications is Teaching English
Computer Applications in Math Education
Computer Applications in Science Education
Computer Applications in Social Studies Education
Computer Applications in Teaching Reading
Computer Applications in the Teaching of Writing
Computer Applications in Special Education
Practicum
Internship
Thesis

will undoubtably change as today's computer trained elementary school students enter college, they are unlikely to expand their resources sufficiently to meet this need. It is therefore possible, and perhaps advisable, that such computer literacy courses be offered by Schools of Education and be taught by qualified teacher educators who would stress educational implications.

It will not be sufficient to merely train special education teachers to be computer literate, expecially if that training is provided by members of a computer science department, who may not be in a position to stress the educational aspects of computers in the classroom. Furthermore, just as it is necessary for all special educators to understand general education and its systems and goals, it is imperative that all special education teachers understand the place that computers have in general education. It is therefore essential that all Schools of Education also provide all special education teachers with a course in computers in education, which includes at least the following (Rogers, Moursand, & Engel, 1984):

Familiarity of the goals of computers in education.

Knowledge of when it is appropriate to use computers in education.

Knowledge of the effects of computers on curriculum content
as well as instruction and learning.

Knowledge of current and future hardware, software, and computer-related educational materials.

After an introduction to basic computer literacy as well as the role of computers in education, the preservice special education student would receive training in computer technology as it relates to the exceptional individual. The content of the courses might correspond to the competencies listed in Table 9-2 and be offered either in a program consisting of several courses specifically relating to computers and the handicapped or as part of a overall program preparing special educators. A sample program in Computers and the Handicapped is presented in Table 9-5. It assumes previous training as a special education teacher has been completed.

Teachers who are receiving their computer training as part of their special education teacher preparation would still require a sequence of courses to acquaint them with computers. It is recommended that the introductory courses in computer literacy and in computers in education be included for all preservice teachers. In addition, an introductory course on computers in special education, as described in Table 9-6 should be included.

Such a course would be taught through three modes. Each idea would be presented in lecture format with description of the related research. This would provide the theoretical base for the discussion of the topic. Next, each lecture would be accompanied by a laboratory session in which the instructor would demonstrate the necessary software without student

Table 9-5. Sample Program in Computers and Special Education

Introduction to Computer Literacy (3 credit hours)
Introduction to Computers and Education (3 credit hours)
Introduction to Computers in Special Education (3 credit hours)
Selecting and Evaluating Software for Exceptional Learners (3 credit hours)
Using Computer Technology to Assist the Disabled (3 credit hours)
Teaching Computer Literacy to the Mildly Handicapped Learner (3 credit
    hours)
Programming for the Special Education Teacher (3 credit hours)
The Use of LOGO in Special Education (3 credit hours)
Research in Technology and the Exceptional Learner (3 credit hours)

Table 9-6. Introduction to Computers and Special Education (3 credits)

I.	Review of Computer Fundamentals
II.	Theoretical Basis of Computers and Special Education
III.	Computers and the Assessment of Handicapped Learners
IV.	IEP Preparation and the Computer
V.	Computer Assisted Instruction and the Exceptional Learner
VI.	Computer Managed Instruction and the Exceptional Learner
VII.	Vocational Training in Microcomputers for the Handicapped Student
VIII.	Programming for the Special Educator
IX.	LOGO and Special Education
X.	Authoring Languages for the Special Educator
XI.	Computers and Special Education Administration
XII.	The Computer as a Prosthetic Device for the Disabled
XIII.	Computers and the Language Impaired
XIV.	Computers and the Sensory Impaired

involvement. This is best accomplished in a laboratory in which there is one computer and several large screens to show the output. In this way, students do not have machines directly in front of them, which often provides a temptation to play and not watch the demonstration. Finally, the students are provided with computers or terminals with which they would work on relevant course assignments. This practice would give the student the necessary "hands-on" experiences to reinforce the learning accomplished through lecture and demonstration.

Introducing computer technology into a program preparing teachers of exceptional children presents an additional problem. The question is whether computer skills should be taught through a series of stand-alone courses similar to those previously described or technologic skills should be integrated into existing courses, i.e., assessment, methods, curriculum, and so forth. Although it is generally believed that a course introducing the area, similar to that already described, is necessary, it appears that integration of technology is the preferred approach. The successful implementation of computer technology will occur when these skills are used with special education students in classrooms. The integration of these skills into existing courses will assist the teacher trainee in deciding on how to best select hardware and software, how to evaluate it, and most importantly, how to integrate it into classroom instruction.

The next several years, however, will necessitate an alternative approach. As described earlier, many teachers will not be entering preservice training programs with basic computer skills. Thus, mandatory computer literacy courses will necessarily have to be included in a preservice program. It is also anticipated that sufficient special education faculty members with the ability to teach an integrated approach to computer usage are not currently available. This will necessitate an increased dependence on stand-alone courses, such as those described previously, until such faculty are available. It can be anticipated that both of these situations will be greatly alleviated over the next 10 years.

In-Service Training

In-service training for special education teachers in the use of computers in their classrooms will be a critical and necessary step in the implementation of technology with handicapped learners. It will be impractical to wait for an entire generation of teachers to be trained during their preservice years. Furthermore, many of those individuals who are being trained in computers in their preservice years will be employed by private industry at more attractive salaries and not enter the teaching field.

Despite the desire for a similar end result—that of an integrated use of computers in a special education classroom—in-service training must be significantly different from preservice training. Dennis and Steinberg (1983) suggest that although the preservice teacher will spend three to four hours per week in class studying computers and then spend 20 to 25 hours per week practicing these skills, working teachers do not have 20 to 25 hours available per week over a sustained period of time to learn anything. The content of the training for working teachers must, therefore, be different as well as the process of that training.

The content of an in-service program for working special education teachers must emphasize practical applications of computers in their classrooms. Computer familiarity must be the initial objective, followed by the demonstration of specific software applications. Emphasis must be on the use of existing hardware and software resources and the evaluation of such resources for use with the student population. Information should be provided for the teacher to either obtain help or obtain further training in computer technology. It is best to provide content in areas that will be most inviting to teachers. For example, introducing word processing to teachers often gets them "hooked" on the benefits of computers and encourages further exploration. Another incentive to the development of interest is introduction of a time-saving IEP writing package, which can relieve the teacher of some of the more demanding aspects of the job. On the other hand, it is recommended that in-service trainers avoid teaching an area in which they are most proficient, assuming that the working teacher will share their interest. For example, the classroom teacher may be only mildly amazed at the use of video discs, which is the current interest of the overzealous in-service trainer. In such a situation, it is more likely that the classroom teacher will become convinced that this new technology is much too difficult.

The process of providing in-service training to special education teachers must be different from many existing in- service training programs. It will not be sufficient to provide teachers with a short series of lectures or a "conference" day. A comprehensive, well-developed sequence of workshops that may spread out over a few years will be necessary to train the neophyte. As with preservice training, hands-on experiences will be crucial and should be implemented using the hardware and software currently available in the school. It is unreasonable to expect the working teacher to generalize skills to another computer. Initially, resources may be poor. However, schools cannot wait for the ideal situation to occur before initiating their in-service

In many situations, it will also be most helpful if the school district has identified a source for information and support. Another school district, a consortium of several districts or a local university may be able to organize and run the in-service program. In addition, these courses may provide further consultation, short-term loan of equipment for trial use, advice on highly specialized equipment, or other assistance. School districts cannot forget that there currently exists a much greater demand for training about computers and the handicapped than can be met with adequate training programs.

RESOURCES REQUIRED FOR TRAINING

Unlike many other staff development programs, in-service or preservice training in computers in special education is dependent upon the availability of resources that are costly or scarce. It is necessary to have sufficient hardware, consisting of microcomputers or terminals hooked up to a larger system, plus adequate peripheral devices to fully apply the computers. Equipment needs will differ according to the training purposes. In a preservice program that will prepare teachers to work with students with a variety of handicapping conditions, it is obvious that a more extensive library of software must be available. This library should include samples of software that is appropriate for children with various intellectual abilities, of differing ages, and for differing instructional purposes. In addition, examples of different computers commonly found in special education settings might be included. Also, samples of computer assisted prosthetic devices could be demonstrated.

In an in-service program, the equipment needs would, in many situations, be much more limited. The hardware and software would consist of that which is already present in the schools. In the event that new equipment was obtained by the school, special inservices might have to be offered. The content of in-service programs would most likely be limited by time constraints. This would minimize the need to have as varied a repertoire of equipment for an in-service program.

The physical setting for a preservice or in-service program would allow for thorough lecture, discussion, demonstration, and hands-on practice. Ideally, such a setting requires two rooms. In one room, students sit in a regular pattern of rows of desks. In addition to a desk in the front of the room the instructor would have a computer terminal on which computer skills could be demonstrated. Large terminals, similar in size to 25 inch television sets, should be suspended from the ceiling at appropriate intervals so that each member of the class can see what appears on the screen as the instructor works at the keyboard. The computer at the front of the room should be the only terminal in the classroom. This will prevent the trainees from being distracted by having terminals in front of them. The second room should be set up as a computer laboratory. Terminals should be situated around the room so that all students face the front. The instructor should also have a terminal, and large monitors should again be suspended from the ceiling. This room is to be employed as a site for hands-on use during class and should be available at other times for practice.

Another resource critical to a successful in-service or preservice program is adequate instruction. It is only recently that specialists in the application of computers in special education have become available in colleges and universities or in schools. Previously, the most knowledgeable computer experts were computer scientists who had little, if any, understanding of the role of computers in the education of handicapped individuals. The individual chosen to instruct preservice and working teachers should be thoroughly familiar with the role of computers in education, be knowledgeable about the many potential applications, be familiar with various pieces of hardware and software, be able to perform simple repairs on hardware, and be an excellent teacher of adults.

It is impractical to expect that every college faculty will harbor such individuals or that such persons are available to every school district. It is equally impractical to expect hardware and software availability to meet the levels previously suggested. This does not mean, however, that staff development should not begin with less than desirable equipment and staff. Schools cannot afford to wait for ideal situation before they initiate staff development programs. They must begin now and allow their staff to develop the skills necessary for the future.

SUMMARY

Preservice and in-service training of special education teachers in the use of computers in their classrooms will be necessary if the current developments in technology are to be applied to the lives of exceptional individuals. Such training must be capable of providing the unsophisticated computer user with the many skills required for successful integration into the classroom. Preservice teachers, working teachers, and special education faculty members must find the time and the resources to accomplish this task. The time is here for special education to avail itself of the advantages offered by the use of computers in the classroom.

REFERENCES

Burke, R. L. (1983). Graduate degree programs in computer education for elementary and secondary teachers. In J. B. Rogers (Ed.), *Topics: Computer education for colleges of education* (pp. 36–44). New York: Association for Computing Machinery.

Dennis, J. R., & Steinberg, E. (1983). Computers in the College of Education, University of Illinois. In J. B. Rogers (Ed.), *Topics: Computer education for colleges of education* (pp. 50–55). New York: Association for Computing Machinery.

East, J. P. (1983). Computer education for elementary schools: A course for teachers. In J.B. Rogers (Ed.), *Topics: Computer education for colleges of education* (pp. 56–63). New York: Association for Computing Machinery.

Rogers, J. B., Moursand, D. G., & Engel, G. L. (1984). Preparing precollege teachers for the computer age. *Communications of the Association for Computing Machinery, 27*, 195–200.

Zinn, K. L. & Berger, C. F. (1983). Computers for teachers: Activities at the University of Michigan School of Education. In J.B. Rogers (Ed.), *Topics: Computer education for colleges of education* (pp. 105–111). New York: Association for Computing Machinery.

CHAPTER 10

Software Evaluation

Microcomputers in education can no longer be considered a technology of the future. Statistics for 1980 showed that approximately 50% of the nation's school districts already had microcomputers and that by 1990, all schools will have enough computers available to allow each student 30 minutes of interactive computer time for each of the 40 million elementary and secondary school children (Pitts, 1982). Although special education often lags behind regular education in terms of computer availability and access time, the technology is still of the present and many issues must be dealt with now.

Some critics of this new technology warn of the misuse of microcomputers, recreating the expensive experimentation and resulting disillusionment with mainframe and computer assisted instruction applications that education experienced in the 1960s and 1970s (Hofmeister, 1982; Hofmeister & Thorkildsen, 1981; Lambert, 1982). Unfortunately, their predictions could very easily come true as there is a severe lack of appropriate, educationally sound software available for classroom use. The prevention of such historical repetition is the responsibility of the consumers: teachers, administrators, teacher educators, and students. Users of special education software must become intelligent consumers.

Until recently, much of the available software was created by computer programmers, with no educational background, much less knowledge of the learning characteristics of exceptional individuals (Hannaford & Taber, 1982; Taber, 1983). The programs they marketed were worthy from a technical standpoint but seldom offered educators materials that utilized the theories and concepts of education that have long been used successfully by educators. Software publishing houses are becoming aware of this shortcoming and are beginning to employ individuals with dual capabilities, but it is still up to the educators to effect a real change in the industry. Educators must evaluate software before purchasing it to determine its soundness, cost-effectiveness, and benefit as a supplement to the existing curriculum (Dean, 1982; Lambert, 1982). If software users do not scrutinize the available programs and selectively purchase quality materials, poor

---

This chapter was authored by Elizabeth Lahm and Michael M. Behrmann.

programs will continue to infiltrate the educational system and may result in the abandonment of microcomputers as an instructional medium in education (Taber, 1983).

Special educators have additional responsibilities in the evaluation process because of the multiple and individual differences of their students. Programs must be more flexible to meet the learning needs of students, their specific instructional objectives, and the related data collection requirements of the teachers. They must fit into an appropriate instructional hierarchy, such as that proposed in Chapter 3. For example, purchasing 10 programs that present a single concept in 10 different ways to meet the needs of 10 students is not cost effective and will not be cordially accepted by administrators. Special requirements of adaptability make software evaluation an even more important area of competency for special education personnel.

EVALUATION OF SOFTWARE

Comparison of Available Tools

Computer assisted instruction (CAI) is the most common type of educational applications software. CAI can be found in all areas of education from preschool through post-secondary, as well as in specialized areas, such as vocational and special education. The criticism of the lack of educationally sound software spans all these areas. Educators have responded to the dilemma by incorporating systematic evaluations of software before purchasing and have begun demanding excellence in programs both technically and educationally. Some of the evidence for this lies in the numerous evaluation devices that are now appearing in the literature. To effect change, though, commitment is required, not just a fancy tool or checklist that may never be used.

To be effective, Taber (1983) suggests that the evaluation process must be conducted in two parts, external and internal. External evaluations involve gathering information from people outside the user's environment as to the value of a program. This may range from using software reviews published in appropriate journals to seeking information from a neighboring district that is already using the program. More and more districts are hiring computer specialists to coordinate the incorporation of computers into their schools. The external evaluation process generally falls into their hands. The internal review requires more time on the part of the staff in the home district. Each piece of available software should be evaluated by potential users. The commitment comes in the amount of time that must be devoted to that process. Examination of the *internal review process* is the focus of this chapter.

Instrument developers have been conscious of the need for efficient tools to assist teachers in the evaluation process. Many available instruments are formatted on one page, and others allow multiple evaluations on one form. The merits of each of these features can only be decided by the individual user or the computer specialist responsible for the task of software evaluation. Regardless of which form is chosen for what reason, it must be viewed as easy to use while still yielding enough information to make the final evaluation worthwhile. In many cases, an alternative form may be constructed utilizing the ideas of several forms. The software evaluation process should be an individualized process.

A comparison of seven evaluation devices will be presented to note similarities or the consensus as to what should be considered when evaluating educational software. The seven tools, their sources, and the abbreviations that will be used to reference them hereafter are found in Table 10-1.

Five of these tools were designed to evaluate educational software in general, whereas two, CEC and MCE, were designed more specifically with special education software as the focus. As a result, major differences are evident between the two groups of instruments. Specifically, these differences are in the areas of "curricular content" and "methodology." The differences are not in the evaluation of these areas in general but rather in the degree to which they are evaluated. In the special education evaluations, the areas of curriculum and methodology are emphasized to evaluate the finer points of instructional strategies and methods necessary for special needs students. One example is in the general area of content. While all seven evaluations examine content, at least in terms of its usefulness, MCE and CEC expand content into five individually rated subareas: (1) validity, (2) timeliness, (3) representativeness, (4) completeness, and (5) utility. Other, more precisely evaluated concerns are in the areas of utilizing behavioral principles within the program for the delivery of feedback and the teacher's ability to alter the key parameters of the program to tailor it to meet individual needs.

While all seven instruments initially examine the descriptive information provided by the author, some do not evaluate this information. For example, NCTM and ESEF only request the evaluator to record the ability levels; the instructional objectives are not even listed for consideration, much less evaluated for clarity. Each program must be evaluated in light of the intended audience and rated on whether stated objectives can be met using the program. Unless that information is clearly stated, the rest of evaluation is of little value. The evaluator cannot know what to look for. Additionally, the methodology used to achieve the

Table 10-1. Software Evaluation Devices

1. CEC Software Search Evaluation Form (CEC)
   Council for Exceptional Children
   Reston, VA (Council for Exceptional Children, 1983)

2. Courseware Evaluation Form (CWF)
   Microcomputer Resource Center
   Teachers College, Columbia University
   New York, New York (Naiman, 1982)

3. Educational Software Evaluation Form (ESEF)
   Educational Alternatives, 1981 (Naiman, 1982)

4. MicroSIFT Courseware Evaluation (MicroSIFT)
   International Council for Computers in Education
   University of Oregon, Eugene (MicroSIFT, 1982)

5. Modified MCE Program Evaluation Form (MCE)
   MCE, Inc.
   Kalamazoo, MI (Taber, 1983)

6. School Microware Evaluation Form (SMEF)
   School Microware, Vol. 1, No. 1 (Naiman, 1982)

7. Software Evaluation Form (NCTM)
   The National Council of Teachers of Mathematics, Inc.
   Reston, VA (National Council of Teachers of Mathematics,
   1981)

objectives must be compared to the target audience. This is an especially critical issue for special education software. Only NCTM, ESEF, MCE, and CEC include appropriateness of methodology on their instruments.

Three general points covered by all seven instruments were the motivational aspects, the humanizing qualities, and the use of appropriate levels of content and vocabulary for the target audience. SMEF extended this last item to include the appropriate level of input required. Only two instruments questioned the appropriate length of a program or program module: CEC and MCE. Some included the ability of the user to get help with the program without stopping the program sequence. This becomes an important feature when the teacher would like to remain free of interaction with the students during a given program. Ideally if the student realizes that he or she needs to review a piece of material or needs the directions repeated, the opportunity should be available without necessitating entering wrong answers to trigger a lower or repeat branch of the program.

Some technical issues that most instruments cover well are screen formatting, ability to set key parameters, beneficial use of technology, and the ability for teacher and student to progress through the program without total dependence on the documentation. Another important feature overlooked by some is the consistency of the inputs and outputs. Too often programs change the type of input required or change feedback midstream and confuse the learner.

With the exception of one type of software evaluation tool, each of the tools reviewed here considered it important to go beyond the software itself and evaluate supplemental materials and how the programs would fit into existing curricula. MCE, the only special education tool that covered this area, extended it to include the program's usability within IEPs.

FIVE SOFTWARE CATEGORIES

Most evaluation tools available have been developed for educational or instructional software. In addition to *computer assisted instruction* (CAI), special educators must be aware of four other types or categories of applications software for handicapped users, and each must be evaluated differently. A second is *recreation*. Like CAI, recreation software is commonly used by nonhandicapped individuals, but it also is an important area of application for users with special needs, as it provides the only opportunity for normalized recreation for some individuals. The applications include both solitary and group uses of games. A third category is *utility programs*. These are software programs that make existing hardware and software more accessible to handicapped users. For example, altering the way a program "looks" for student inputs may allow switch inputs rather than keyboard inputs. *Environmental control or self-help* software constitutes the fourth category. The computer is utilized as a tool or assistive device by a handicapped individual to perform some skill more efficiently or to provide skills ordinarily unavailable to him or her without the computer. The final category is *computer managed instruction* and includes measurement and data base systems to evaluate student progress toward stated goals and objectives.

In order for the education profession to effect a change in the quality of computer software for use with handicapped users, standards must be set and definitions created to guide the commercial software industry. Some guidelines and general points that pertain to all software as well as specific guidelines for the five categories follow. By creating standards and adhering to them, quality software will become the rule, not the exception.

General Criteria

Although each of the five categories of software must ultimately have different evaluation criteria, there are some general criteria they must first all meet. The three evaluation areas that are common to all software include the quality of descriptive information, technical soundness, and program flexibility. These were evaluated to varying degrees in each of the seven CAI tools reviewed and must also be evaluated in the other categories of applications.

Descriptive information items related to software programs that need initial scrutiny are the following: (1) Has the target audience been specified for (a) the learning characteristics or exceptionality it intends to serve, (b) the chronologic age, and (c) the requisite readability level (if any) of the intended user? (2) Is the purpose of the software clearly presented? Are there clear learning objectives, and achievement levels in the software, and are they appropriate for the targeted audience? (3) Is the documentation organized and complete? That is, does it cover all the objectives, rationale, and prerequisites, as well as the possible options available in the instructional and operational procedures?

The second area that teachers need to be critically aware of is the technical aspect of the software. (1) Will the program "crash" if wrong information is used, intentionally or unintentionally? A simple example of this is spelling numbers out (e.g., "twenty") rather than using numerals. If the programmer has not anticipated such a response, this can create student frustration and cause problems in maintaining instructional data. (2) Does the software use the technology to its benefit (i.e., use the strengths of the computer, such as data collection, patience, branching, and so forth) rather than present material that is done well by traditional print media. Criticism of much of the current instructional software or CAI is that it does not appropriately or adequately use the strengths of the technology. Many programs rely solely on drill and practice methods or present computerized textbooks. These probably are better presented in a traditional printed format. When evaluating the use of technology, the stated objectives and the intended target audience should be considered. The teacher should ask, "Does the program use the data collection and analysis, graphic, and audio capabilities of the computer to supplement or create methods of presenting materials which enhance the teaching of handicapped children?"

Other items to examine under the technical area are (1) whether the program allows the user to work independently without constant teacher supervision, (2) whether the screen is aesthetically formatted, including the amount of information presented and figure ground considerations, and (3) whether the response or input required of the user is consistent and logical in terms of type and location (e.g., numerals versus written number words accepted or the "return" or "enter" key is consistently required or not required for each input).

The third general software evaluation area is program flexibility — the ability to individualize instruction through altering the key parameters.

Is the teacher able to adjust parameters such as the speed at which the program moves through the content? Are the number of trials to reach mastery criterion alterable? Can the vocabulary utilized in the program be individualized to meet the needs of a particular child? Three ways a teacher may be able to adjust these parameters are (1) through a menu of choices presented by the program, (2) through direct input of content and information, or (3) through the ability to change the program code (i.e., the program is not "locked" and a programmer has access to the code). Ability to alter the key parameters offers flexibility to a program to better meet the individual educational needs of handicapped children.

Educational and Instructional Programs

In addition to the general evaluation of software, there exist some specific items that should be examined when selecting educational or instructional programs (CAI) for handicapped individuals. The six areas to evaluate this software include (1) motivation, (2) format, (3) level of content and vocabulary, (4) instructional methodology, (5) interactiveness, and (6) curricular content.

Generally, these programs should be *humanizing and motivational*. They should use appropriate rewards and reinforcements within the program and recognize the user as an individual with individual differences. In short, the program should leave the user with a good feeling about himself or herself (Hannaford & Taber, 1982).

A second criterion area relates to the *formatting of the material*. Is the program an appropriate length for its intended audience? For example, a program for a preschool child should probably not be more than 5 minutes in length, whereas a program for a junior high school student might be 20 minutes. If it is modular (i.e., small independent lessons that form a unit), does it offer logical breaks during use? These breaks should be options to stop the program without "losing the student's place" so that he or she does not have to start from the beginning again.

The teacher should also evaluate educational software for its *level of content and vocabulary*. Does it match the learning characteristics of the target audience, reading levels, and the interest levels of the chronologic and mental ages for which it was designed or is being marketed? If it is for young children, does it use graphics, or artificial voice, or does it interface with a tape recorder to present directions and instructions (to circumvent lack of reading skills)? Finally, does the program offer opportunities for the user to get help? That is, does it demonstrate a concept and provide additional instruction within the program so that if the child has a problem, he or she can elect a demonstration mode to review the concept and then return to the problem and give it a try?

The *instructional methodology* used by the software is the fourth evaluation area. Are prerequisites stated or does the program allow a pretest to let the user enter at the appropriate level rather than having to go through an entire sequence of previously mastered skills? Is the software truly tutorial, allowing the instruction to continue based upon the student's responses? Related to the tutorial concept, does the program continually collect and analyze data on the student's answers and then use that information to determine the instructional sequence? These features permit the highly desirable characteristic of individualization sought by special educators.

The *interactiveness* of the program is yet another aspect to be evaluated. Damarin (1982) has developed a matrix to assist in evaluating the match between interaction levels and the stated cognitive goals (Table 10-2). For example, if the program objective is problem solving, the type of interaction should not be limited to watching (demonstration) and finding (multiple choice or matching), but should incorporate activities such as manipulating and creating as types of interaction. An example of these would be moving puzzle pieces to fit the appropriate space or drawing lines to simulate an electrical connector between two points.

The last, and probably the most critical area of evaluation for educational or instructional software is that of *curricular content*. Teachers have extensive training in curriculum, and they should determine if (1) the content is valid, (2) the content is up-to-date, (3) the scope of the content is representative of what the child needs to learn, (4) the program teaches the entire concept in terms of the stated objectives, (5) the information being presented is useful and important to the targeted audience, and (6) the sequence of the program proceeds in a logical instructional order.

Utility Programs

The next category of software applications for handicapped users is referred to as utility programs. Utility programs make existing software and hardware more accessible to handicapped users and are quite different from other programs. There are five evaluation areas, technical in nature, that are specific to this category (1) accessibility, (2) range of application, (3) ease of use, (4) individualization, and (5) hardware universality.

First, does the program make other programs or hardware more accessible to handicapped users? Many software programs that are currently available are content appropriate but inaccessible to handicapped users. Programs that can bypass that accessibility barrier are of tremendous value.

Table 10-2. Matrix Supplement

1. Watching: directed attending to a computer display, frequently animated graphics
2. Finding: examining computer display or printout in search of a predetermined object or event
3. Doing: performing a requested operation
4. Using: using a computer generated object in the performance of a task
5. Constructing: causing the computer to produce a specified object using simpler computer generated objects
6. Creating: causing the computer to produce an object (graphic display, printout, etc.)

Cognitive Goal	Watching	Finding	Doing	Using	Constructing	Creating
Concept Development						
Practice with Concept						
Application of Concept						
Problem Solving						

Notes

Second, is this accessibility offered to a wide range of hardware and software or is it limited, for example, to one series of programs, one publisher, or one computer? A utility program that only interfaces with DLM (Developmental Learning Materials) software, for example, would be of less value than one that adapted three or four publishers, or better yet, any commercially available program. Third, is the routine or sequence required to use the utility program so complicated that it does not make the effort worthwhile, it or is it easy enough that the handicapped user can install and use it without help? The general idea is to increase accessibility while maintaining or increasing independence. The value of accessibility is lost when too much dependence is required. Fourth, are there options available that allow the individualization of the program? More than one person may need to use the program, and each user has individual needs. Examples might be requiring adjustment speed or print size. Fifth, does the program run with a number of hardware configurations and commercially available interfaces, such as joysticks, light pens, and paddles? It is important to realize that whenever custom hardware is required, the affordability of the program greatly decreases.

Recreational Programs

Although recreational software for handicapped users may not differ significantly from that designed for nonhandicapped users, there are some important points to evaluate before purchasing recreational software. In addition to the three general criteria that pertain to all software, descriptive information, technical sound, and flexibility, some general points relative to recreational software must be considered. The first point is its humanizing quality. As with CAI, it is important to present a program without stereotypes and consider its overall contribution to making the user feel good about himself or herself (Hannaford & Taber, 1982). Second, motivational levels and techniques should be examined. Are appropriate rewards and reinforcements used? Are the content and goals intrinsically motivating? Is the level or type of competition appropriate? The third general point is the length of the game. Does the length match the attention level of the intended audience or can the length be controlled to fit different audiences? The last consideration relates to the appropriateness of the content and vocabulary level. Again, the evaluation decison should be based on the intended audience. As with CAI, incompatibilities often exist in this area, especially if the chronologic ages of the users are not similar to their mental ages and interests.

A second group of evaluation questions could be labeled "individualization concerns." A major criterion here is the ability of the user to set the key parameters of the program to meet individual needs. These parameters include speed, level of difficulty, length, input mode, number of players, and display format specifications such as text size. The more options available to the user, the more flexible the program becomes and more individualized the needs that can be met. A related criterion is that of branching. Is the program sensitive to the success and failure of the user and able to adjust for it? Many handicapped individuals have experienced much failure and frustration in so many aspects of their lives that adding another is not needed. Reducing frustration should be a consideration of the software purchaser, especially in a program that is intended to be recreational.

The final evaluation concerns in the recreation category examine the interactiveness of the program. Similar to CAI, the evaluator must look for the program's ability to handle a variety of inputs and provide an appropriate response to incorrect inputs. Additionally, the appropriate use of both auditory and visual outputs should be examined. Recreation software, by its nature, is highly interactive. Its success or failure may lie in its ability to be truly and appropriately interactive.

Environmental and Self-Help Programs

Environmental and self-help programs are those that are designed to be tools or provide assistance to handicapped individuals. With their use the microcomputer becomes a prosthetic device. There are eight criteria that teachers need to evaluate when selecting this type of software: (1) flexibility for adjusting to different ability levels, content, and environments, (2) contribution to normalization, (3) multiple functions ability, (4) independent usage, (5) hardware availability, (6) hardware affordability, (7) portability, and (8) hardware durability. These eight evaluation areas can be grouped into two categories for environmental and self-help programs: content and technical.

Content. In the content category, the first area to look at is the program's capacity to handle many levels of user abilities. This can be provided for in a manner similar to the educational programs by presenting menus that allow the user to change key parameters such as changing the screen letter size to accommodate the visually handicapped or change the speed of a scanning option for input selection by the physically handicapped. Each user's environment and needs will be different so that the content itself must also be alterable. The vocabulary in a communication system is an excellent example of content that must be alterable to fit the individual and the environment.

As a second consideration, these types of programs and associated hardware are used in an environment in which they are likely to be noticed and judged by nonhandicapped individuals. The teacher must determine whether the program reduces the impact of the user's impairment enough to warrant the use of the assistive device. If so, do the program and accompanying hardware requirements contribute to the normalization of the user as much as possible? These factors must be weighed against the intended user's ability to tolerate curiosity and the reactions of nonhandicapped individuals.

Third, does the program allow multiple functions? Current developments in integrated software are based on the premise that the needs of users must be emphasized more than requirements of computers. Some types of functions that a user may need within a short time period are means of controlling appliances (e.g., television, toaster) while answering the telephone. He or she must be able to perform both tasks without changing programs. Once a function is being used and it becomes necessary to perform a second function, an extremely important consideraton is whether the user can easily get back to where he or she was. For example, if the phone rings while using a word processing program, is it necessary to shut the word processing system off to answer the phone and then have to return to the original task by starting at the very beginning? Programs that allow the user to move between frequently used functions without losing place are certainly of higher value than those that do not provide this flexibility.

The fourth consideration for environmental or self-help programs is whether the handicapped user will be able to use it without great amounts of additional help from other individuals. The primary purpose of these programs is to give the user maximum independence. Is this independence impaired by requiring another person to set up and supervise the program?

Technical. The final group evaluation topics are related to the hardware necessary to run the program and thus are more technical in nature. Is the hardware available commercially? Special order equipment often escalates the cost enormously and can lead to maintenance and reliability problems. The cost of hardware is important as well. "Affordable" is a relative term and should be judged on what one might expect the user to have to pay for other adaptive equipment or for attendant care considering his or her handicap. Another issue is whether the equipment is portable or available in multiple environments. An ethical issue can be raised in relation to this question. If an individual is provided with a system that gives added independence can it be "taken away" by not transporting or providing it in all appropriate environments? Should a child only be able to communicate effectively in the homeroom and struggle or be silent elsewhere? The final question that must be addressed is whether the equipment is durable. A system that requires frequent repairs can frustrate the user in the same way as lack of portability. These items, although related more to hardware, must be of major concern when evaluating software in this category because of the hardware-software interdependence.

Measurement and Data Base Systems

When evaluating measurement and data base systems, teachers must again look at content and technical criteria. Within these two categories there are eight areas of evaluation that assist in the selection of software designed for managing instruction: (1) flexibility or multiple options, (2) quality of data collected, (3) ease of use, (4) information storage format, (5) hardware availability, (6) hardware affordability, (7) hardware universality, and (8) information storage options.

Content. The first four points are grouped in the content category. Flexibility or multiple options, or the degree to which the user can select options to make programs fit their individual needs, should be evaluated. It will often be necessary to delete and create categories (e.g., groupings of students) and edit information on student performance or instructional objectives in these types of programs. Any program that allows access to confidential information must provide for guarded access. Is there a password system, coded data, or file numbers that protect individual student information? Many programs are designed for very specific applications, and the decision to market them comes later without thought to generalizing capabilities. Programs limited in application to one type of facility, such as a residential setting, are less valuable than those that the user can adjust to meet the needs of several settings. These content features make a program flexible enough to meet the varied and changing needs of service providers.

A second evaluation point in the content category addresses accuracy, type, and the completeness of the data collected by the program. The evaluator must determine the appropriateness of the data collected and decide if sufficient amounts are collected to meet user needs. Evaluations of the accuracy of the data analysis should be based on a review of formula and statistical methods used to yield the answers.

Programs that leave the user bewildered as to what to do next are of little value. Accompanying documentation may provide all the necessary answers but if one must continually refer back to the manual, the program will be a frustrating experience. "User friendly" software, that which actually assists the user through the correct sequence, is desirable, especially for nonspeaking technical users. Ideally, adequate instructions will be embedded in the program to allow ease of use once the teacher is familiar with the program. A final consideration in the content area is the storage of information. Is it stored in an organized manner and is it readily retrievable? Do category headings make the program easy to use? Are they logical to the intended application? Does retrieving information by a category or heading yield the expected information?

Technical. The technical area of evaluation specific to measurement or data base systems examines four additional points: (1) If hardware other than the standard system of computer, disc drive, monitor, and printer is necessary (e.g., card scanning device), is that hardware readily available? (2) Similarly, is additional hardware affordable (i.e., available at reasonable cost)? (3) Will the program run with a number of different peripherals? That is, will it adapt to or accommodate various popular brands of printers, monitors, and disc drives? (4) Does the user have the option of storing information on either disc or paper? These four technical features add to the flexibility of the program and allow the user to incorporate the program into a number of settings. It may prevent the obsolescence of the program if the user must change hardware for any reason.

SUMMARY

As a result of the multiplicity of learning needs of handicapped children, the field of special education has made significant contributions to the development of new instructional techniques and materials to educate children. Among others, these methods and techniques include individualizing and setting instructional objectives according to learner characteristics, developing data-based instructional and record-keeping systems, such as precision teaching, task analysis, and skill sequencing techniques, engineering and adapting the learning environments for achievement, and using equipment and materials for self-paced programmed instruction to supplement direct teacher instruction. Teachers in this field are trained to be logical problem solvers in educating children, and they are taught to give children individual attention where appropriate. They set criteria for achievement and try different ways of teaching if the child is unable to reach appropriate goals. Finally, they are taught to be objective and collect and analyze data on student progress. These are all tasks that are consistent with computer programming and the capabilities of computers in instruction.

The introduction of the microcomputer into the classroom is adding another powerful tool to the special education teacher's materials. There are strong parallels between the way special educators are trained to teach and the beneficial aspects of computer technology applied to the teaching process. Special educators who already have these instructional skills can be readily trained in software evaluation. Training should involve the application of these curriculum and instruction skills to form a basis for expectations of quality in computer software. Not only can this reduce the "threatening" aspect of evaluating new technology, but it will also help to establish high standards for developers and publishers. If special educators act now to set high standards of expectation for computer software, the entire field of education stands to benefit.

ACKNOWLEDGMENTS

The authors would like to thank members of The Johns Hopkins University and staff of The Council for Exceptional Children who participated with the authors in the development of the first CEC software competition. The discussions by this group on software evaluation led in great part to the development of this article.

REFERENCES

Council for Exceptional Children. (1983). Software search evaluation form. Unpublished manuscript.

Damarin, S. K. (1982, March). *Fitting the tool with the task: A problem in the use of microcomputers*. Paper presented at the Annual Meeting of the American Educational Research Association, New York.

Dean, J. W. (1982). What's holding up the show? *Today's Education*, 74(2), 21–23.

Hannaford, A. E., & Taber, F. M. (1982). Microcomputer software for the handicapped: Development and evaluation. *Exceptional Children*, 49, 137–142.

Hofmeister, A. M. (1982). Microcomputers in perspective. *Exceptional Children*, 49, 115–121.

Hofmeister, A. M., & Thorkildsen, R. J. (1981). Videodisc technology and the preparation of special education teachers. *Teacher Education and Special Education*, 4(3), 34–39.

Lambert, F. L. (1982, March). The classroom computer is naked. *Interface Age*, pp. 84–89.

MicroSIFT. (1982). *Evaluator's guide for microcomputer-based instructional packages*. Eugene, OR: International Council for Computers in Education.

Naiman, A. (1982). *Microcomputers in education: An introduction*. Cambridge, MA: Technical Education Research Centers.

National Council of Teachers of Mathematics. (1981). *Guidelines for evaluating computerized instructional materials*. Reston, VA: Author.

Pitts, M. R. (1982, March). *R & D's contribution to technology's use in schools: A view from the schools*. Paper presented at the Annual Meeting of the American Educational Research Association, New York, NY.

Taber, F. M. (1983). *Microcomputers in special education: Selection and decision making process*. Reston, VA: Council for Exceptional Children.

CHAPTER 11

Hardware Selection and Evaluation

The proliferation of computer technology into seemingly every facet of our society has begun to impact significantly on the field of education. Whereas some large school districts have been involved in complex computer systems for a number of years through timesharing arrangements (Bork & Franklin, 1979), the reduced costs associated with the microcomputer explosion has put technology within reach of a greater number of school systems. Several recent surveys regarding computer use in the schools verify this trend. Although descriptive data are quickly outdated in this area, recent estimates indicate that computers are located in one third (Ingersoll, Smith & Elliot, 1983) to one half (Schiffman, Tobin & Cassidy-Bronson, 1982) of the school districts across the country. Approximately one third of the special education teachers in the United States report that they have access to microcomputers (Hanley & Yin, 1984).

Unlike previous timesharing systems, in which individual schools had little direct control in the selection of the educational material available for the system (Joiner, Sedlak, Silverstein & Vensal, 1980), the use of microcomputers in the schools demands a greater degree of participation on the part of the user in determining the specific applications of the technology in a setting. With all indications that the proliferation of microcomputers in the schools will continue (Hanley & Yin, 1984) it is clear that information must be provided to assist educators without computer expertise in making sound decisions regarding the purchase and use of this equipment.

The purpose of this chapter is to discuss considerations in the purchase of computer hardware for use within the public schools. Steps in conducting a needs assessment, and factors to consider in comparing equipment will be reviewed. Finally, a systems development approach to hardware selection will be proposed. The model is described and recommended for the purchase of equipment for both group and individual applications.

There is little information available regarding the means by which school districts acquire computer equipment and supervise its use. One comprehensive report (Hanley & Yin, 1984), based on case studies in 12 school districts across the country found no pattern with respect to the

---

This chapter was authored by Elizabeth Lahm and Gail McGregor.

personnel involved in these activities. In districts that were highly centralized, district level administrators played a major role in the adoption and implementation of microcomputer applications. A decentralized pattern was evident in other sites in which district level personnel were involved in approval and funding decisions, whereas school-based personnel determined the specific uses of the system.

Taken to an extreme, each approach presents a different set of problems. In an overly centralized system, the individual needs and interests of the intended users may tend to be disregarded, resulting in an underutilization of the equipment. On the other hand, isolated users were found to engage in redundant and inefficient operations. In an unusual case, a district-wide moratorium on the purchase of new hardware and software was imposed in response to problems of incompatibility resulting from different hardware purchases.

Due to the limited resources of educational agencies, the wide range of available equipment from which to choose the rapidly developing and improving technology, and the general lack of knowledge about computers among educators, it is important that prepurchase planning be systematic. Whereas schools frequently begin with the purchase of a computer and then determine how to use it, careful planning will reverse that sequence of events.

CONDUCTING A NEEDS ASSESSMENT

Several models have been developed to guide a needs assessment related to hardware purchases (Matthews, 1979; Thomas & McClain, 1979; Tinker, 1982). A comparison and synthesis of these approaches yields five steps, which appear to be essential in selecting the right equipment for a given setting.

1. Identify the areas in which the use of a computer is targeted. As described in Chapter 3, the range of computer applications in both administrative and instructional domains is great. A cumulative list of the intended purpose(s) of the system should be established by the people who will be the users of the equipment.

2. Determine the hardware requirements. At this point, someone knowledgeable about computers should assist in the identification of equipment that is needed to perform the functions delineated above.

3. Survey the capabilities of currently available hardware. A wide range of characteristics have been suggested as issues to consider when comparing hardware for educational applications (Braun, 1979; Jongejan & Johnson,

Table 11-1. Considerations in Selecting a Microcomputer System

	System A	System B (etc.)
Technical		
Portability		
Memory		
Read only memory (ROM)		
Random access memory (RAM)		
Expansion capabilities		
Graphics capabilities		
Screen size		
Colors available		
User-definable graphic characters		
Keyboard		
Layout		
Size		
Quality		
Number of keys		
Music capabilities		
Reliability of equipment		
Access to servicing		
Training		
Ease of use		
Quality of documentation		
Support from dealer		
Software		
Quality of available software		
Future potential for software		
Cost of software		
Program languages available		

1978; Naiman, 1982; Ricketts & Seay, 1979; Zinn, 1978). They are summarized and presented in Table 11-1. The information is organized within the three categories identified by Taber (1981) as the major considerations in hardware acquisition.

4. Determine the system prices. Gather the cost information about each system that fits the specifications established in the second step. If the costs exceed available resources, some modification of the plan will be required.

5. Select the hardware. After comparing the equipment on the basis of the criteria listed in Table 11-1, an analysis of the price and performance features of each system should lead to the final selection.

SYSTEMS DEVELOPMENT PERSPECTIVE

The approach to hardware acquisition described earlier emphasizes the characteristics and application of equipment in a particular setting. The human component of a setting, on the other hand, was not a focal point in this needs assessment process. According to DeGreene (1969b), this is a common characteristic of organizational behavior. In his view, individual needs, rewards, expectations, and attitudes of the people interacting with the system *must be considered* in the planning process in order to create an effective system.

Systems psychology, a relatively new specialty within the field of psychology, provides a theoretical basis for a more systematic and comprehensive approach to the integration of technology into an environment in which humans must function. A systems development approach has been used by the military and major engineering firms since the end of World War II. Systems developers, or "human factors engineers," strive to find a match between human capabilities and limitations and the development of machines, tasks, and work environments (McCormick & Saunders, 1982).

An overview of the systems development process is presented in Figure 11-1. As depicted, there are five levels through which a developer must proceed to complete the software selection process. They are requirements analysis, functions analysis, task analysis, interface analysis, and field evaluation. Each level will be considered individually. For ease of reading, the term "client" is used in the following section to refer to both individuals and groups involved in a systems development project.

Requirements Analysis

Four steps are involved in analyzing the basic requirements of a computer system. The first, determination of general systems goals, corresponds to the procedures described by DeGreene (1969a), Gagne (1962), and Meister (1971) in projects within larger systems development projects. In this application, input from a client regarding the goals for a system is gathered through an interview or questionnaire format. The second step is an extension of the information-gathering process. General client abilities and resources are assessed. Relevant documents are examined to provide detailed information. For an individual user, this might include test results and Individual Education Programs, while inventories and staff training reports are examples of documents of interest in organizational planning. Clients are also asked to provide any additional information related to their performance capabilities and resources that will assist in the planning process.

Figure 11-1. Handicapped user's method for analyzing needs-systems development.

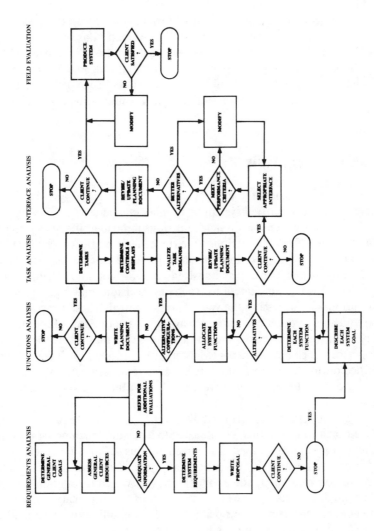

A determination of the general system requirements is the third step of the requirements analysis. In other words, how well will the system have to perform to meet its stated goals? "System requirements" may include specifications regarding performance speed, storage capacity, or memory of the system.

The information gathered thus far provides the basis for completing the last step—development of an initial proposal for a specific system to meet the established goals. The system is described in as much detail as possible, including estimates of cost and time required for consultation, equipment, and training (Chapanis, 1969). In addition, suggestions for at least one alternative system should be provided (DeGreene, 1969a). At this point, the client must make a decision regarding continuation of the systems development project.

Functions Analysis

If a client indicates the desire to proceed, the second level is begun by describing the identified system goals in a detailed fashion (DeGreene, 1969b). This process enables system functions to be identified (DeGreene, 1969b; Meister, 1971). "Functions" are the general means or actions that contribute to the system's ability to meet its requirements. For example, an individual's goal of using synthesized voice for communication might be broken down into functions such as decision making, input of information, and accessing the voice output control. These functions are then sequenced in order of occurrence and analyzed in terms of the client's ability to perform them, environmental factors that may affect them, and their performance requirements (Meister, 1971). If any new functions are identified during the analysis they are included in the sequence. If potential alternatives are identified, they are incorporated into the systems plan as well.

After all systems functions have been identified, sequenced, and analyzed each function must be allocated to a person, machine, or person-machine combination based on considerations of the most efficient utilization of resources. In order to allocate system functions, a determination must be made about the way in which a function will be implemented. For example, will the function of communication occur in written or spoken form? A comparison of the capabilities of the intended user and those of the machine will assist in this process (Chapanis, 1965; Kennedy, 1962; Meister, 1971). A guide for this type of analysis, compiled by McCormick and Saunders (1982), is contained in Table 11-2. When all functions have been delegated, each should be evaluated in terms of the client's ability to perform the function as implemented and the degree to which the performance meets system requirements (Meister, 1971).

Table 11-2. Relative Capabilities of Humans and Machines

Humans are generally better in their abilities to:

Sense very low levels of certain kinds of stimuli: visual, auditory, tactile, olfactory, gustatory.

Detect stimuli against high "noise" level background.

Recognize patterns of complex stimuli, which may vary from situation to situation.

Sense unusual and unexpected events in the environment.

Store (remember) large amounts of information over long periods of time (principles and strategies more than details).

Retrieve pertinent information from storage (recall), frequently retrieving many related items of information; but reliability of recall is low.

Draw upon varied experience in making decisions; adapt decisions to situational requirements; act in emergencies.

Select alternative modes of operation if one fails.

Reason inductively, generalizing from observations.

Apply principles to solutions of varied problems.

Develop entirely new solutions.

Make subjective estimates and evaluations.

Concentrate on most important activities when overload conditions require.

Adapt physical response (within reason) to variations in operational requirements.

Machines are generally better in their abilities to:

Sense stimuli that are outside the normal range of human sensitivity.

Apply deductive reasoning, such as recognizing stimuli as belonging to a general class.

Monitor for prespecified events, especially when infrequent.

Store coded information quickly and in substantial quantity.

Retrieve coded information quickly and accurately when specifically requested.

Process quantitative information following specified programs.

Make rapid and consistent responses to input signals.

Perform repetitive activities reliably.

Exert considerable physical force in a highly controlled manner.

Maintain performance over extended periods of time.

Count or measure physical quantities.

Perform several programmed activities simultaneously.

Maintain efficient operations under conditions of heavy load.

Maintain efficient operations under distractions.

From McCormick, E.J., & Saunders, M.S. *Human factors in engineering and design.* New York: McGraw-Hill, 1982, pp. 489-490. Reprinted with permission.

In addition to the evaluation of individual functions, assessment should also include the performance of functions in the sequence in which they are ultimately intended to occur. Alternative configurations that are possible to achieve the system requirements are handled in a similar fashion. The evaluation of each alternative should include both performance and cost effectiveness (Meister, 1971). The information derived from this process is then incorporated into a second planning document, along with a more complete description of the system and an estimate of total client costs. Once again, the choice to continue or terminate the process must be made by the client.

Task Analysis

The third level of a systems development approach is task analysis. In this application, a task is defined as "a composite of related (discriminatory-decision-motor) activities performed by an individual and directed toward accomplishing a specific amount of work within a specific work context" (DeGreene, 1969a, p. 21). Since each function has already been allocated to person, machine, or a person-machine combination, the tasks required of the handicapped user can be specified in detail. For example, the system function of displaying a menu of choices can be described in the following steps: visually discriminating that the current monitor display is not the menu, making the choice to display the menu, and selecting and activating the appropriate interface to display it. Task descriptions should include the purpose of a task, the form in which input and output occurs, and the points at which the user must make a decision (DeGreene, 1969b, Meister, 1971). The end product of this analysis is a verb-noun description of each task (e.g., "display menu" to request the display of choices) and the equipment required to perform it (Meister, 1971).

The second step of the task analysis process requires a determination of the appropriate controls and displays to facilitate task performance (Chapanis, 1965; DeGreene, 1969b). In order to make this determination, each task is analyzed in terms of what is required to perform the task, how it is performed, time requirements, frequency of performance, and type or category of behavior that is required to perform it. The tasks are then listed and sequenced in order of their performance, and the interrelationships are assessed and matched to client abilities (DeGreene, 1969a; Meister, 1971). A tentative list of control and display devices can then be generated to match these specifications. At this point, the planning document is revised to incorporate this additional information, with approval to proceed sought from the client.

Interface Analysis

The last level in the planning process is the interface analysis. An interface is the piece of equipment that assures that the handicapped user will be able to operate a system efficiently. The tentative list of controls and display devices has previously been identified, but their placement on a panel or piece of equipment that can be manipulated by a user must be evaluated. Once the equipment design has been developed for efficient access, a mock-up or prototype of the system is constructed, and the client is asked to perform the identified tasks (Chapanis, 1969; DeGreene, 1969b). As a client performs the tasks, his or her behavior is carefully evaluated. The amount of time required to perform each task, as well as the performance errors that occur, are noted and classified so that modifications to remedy the problems can be planned (DeGreene, 1969b; Kidd, 1962; Meister, 1971). Mock-ups of alternative system configurations are assessed in a similar manner in order to identify all viable options.

The last step of the interface selection process is a determination of the cost-effectiveness of each alternative system that meets the basic system requirements. Specific system characteristics are compared, including technical performance, quality of interaction, economic benefit, psychological satisfaction, and overall satisfaction. This information is integrated into a final version of the planning document.

Field Evaluation

If the client elects to complete the systems development process, the last level of assessment relates to the construction of the system and the ensuing field testing. All intended uses, situations and environments are considered in relation to system requirements, task performance, and client satisfaction. This should lead to the identification of all facets of the system that require modification. Ideally, field testing should incorporate three, six, and 12 month follow-ups to ensure the continued proper performance of the system.

The remainder of this chapter will focus on an instrument that was developed to assist in the acquisition of computer hardware for handicapped users. Although the tool is generic, it is especially useful for handicapped users or organizations that serve students with handicaps because it focuses on specific human capabilities and limitations, not the abilities of the mainstream population. The instrument matches these qualities with existing hardware and software in order to identify a system configuration that meets the goals established for the system prior to its purchase. The HUMAN-SD (Handicapped User's Method for Analyzing Needs—System Development) outlines a procedure for identifying equipment that meets the needs of an individual user or group of users, such as a special education classroom, a school, or a school district. Using the HUMAN-SD for designing systems for individuals and groups will be described in greater detail in the next section.

HANDICAPPED USER'S METHOD FOR ANALYZING NEEDS—SYSTEMS DEVELOPMENT (HUMAN-SD)

Systems for Groups

The HUMAN-SD is designed to assess the system needs of a group of users or an individual user. A school is one such organization or group of users that could benefit from the systematic approach reflected in this instrument. Based on the framework established in the previous section, the application of this process to a group situation will now be described.

Requirements Analysis

Goal Determination. There are many possible uses of computer hardware in a school setting. Table 11-3 presents specific questions to assist in identifying possible applications, environments, resources, and requirements. Potential applications generally fall within the categories of computer assisted management, computer managed instruction, computer literacy, computer assisted instruction, tool use for individuals, recreation, and reinforcement. As specific goals are identified for computer use, further consideration must be given to the intended setting(s) of each application.

In a school, target sites may include the office, library, classrooms, or a computer laboratory. Depending on the financial limitations of the school, one or more systems may be needed to meet all or combinations of identified goals. If an analysis of settings and applications indicates that the equipment will be moved from place to place, the concepts of durability and portability may be important considerations in the final equipment selection. The number of students and staff that will use a given system is another important setting variable which will impact on the number of systems required to meet an organization's goals. A realistic expectation must be established early in the analysis. Similarly, all limitations that could possibly inhibit the achievement of the goals should be identified. These include financial constraints, physical space limitations, scheduling restrictions, and time limitations for implementation. It is possible that "adjustments" may be needed with regard to the use-system ratio or the number of system goals that realistically can be achieved.

For the purposes of illustration, consider a small special education facility that is located within a regular secondary school. The program supervisor would like to purchase one computer system and has identified three goal areas for that system. These are computer assisted management (CAM), computer managed instruction (CMI), and computer assisted

Table 11-3. 1.0 Requirements Analysis

1.1 General Client Goals

What are the client's goals or reasons for seeking a computer system?
In which area(s) are the goals classified? (e.g., communication, home control, CAI, CAM, CMI)
In what specific environments would the client like the system to function? (e.g., home, school, office, library)
How portable should the system be?
Will the user mind an equipment intensive system? (i.e., how unobtrusive should the equipment be?)
What are the general financial limitations of the client?

1.2 Assess General Client Abilities And Resources

What is the client's mode of communication? (verbal, vocal, gestural, assistive device, interpreter, none)
What are the client's present capabilities?

Information from school/work/medical records
Current resources being used to achieve goals

If this information is not adequate, refer for an evaluation

1.3 Determine System Requirements

What is the mission (purpose) of the system to be developed? (e.g., to control electrical appliances)
Where will the system be used? (home, school, etc.)
How will the client operate it? (hand, foot, voice, etc.)
What are the specific goals of the system? (e.g., independent operation, multiple tasks, multiple or alterable functions, etc.)
What are the performance requirements of these goals? (speed, portability, flexibility, etc.)

---

instruction (CAI). The school has three special education classes for the students, who range in age from 12 to 21 years and who have disabilities ranging from severe to moderate. Approximately 15 staff members serve that population, and each will need to access and use information on the computer system at some point or another. When both staff and students are expected to use the same equipment, multiple environments are usually indicated. The abilities of the staff are significantly different from the students, which means that the system will have to be very flexible. If financial limitations permit the purchasing of only one system, this will have a dramatic impact on the final system recommendation. This school, its situation, and its goals will continue to be used as an example throughout this discussion to illustrate the process of the HUMAN-SD.

Analysis of Resources. A consideration of the existing resources and current strategies for meeting the desired computer system goals is the second major step in the requirements analysis. Frequently, small computer systems may already be in place, acquired by an organization in the absence of a comprehensive plan. In the example, knowledge of systems currently being used by the regular education or district level staff is valuable information. Equipment and other resources, such as trained users and technicians, should be inventoried to obtain the complete picture of available resources, which may maximize the cost-benefit of a system. Finally, the commitment of staff to the use of a computer system should be assessed. For example, if the supervisor intends to rely on a data base as a source of official information, he or she must be certain that the staff is willing to continually update the data base files. An unmotivated staff will never yield a successful system.

In addition to consideration of the equipment, software, and staff resources already present in a setting, available commercial software that may meet needs should be identified. In this case the computer system will be required to run standard and specialized management programs as well as a wide variety of educational software. These requirements severely restrict the range of equipment options available. While functionally comparable software may be available for different hardware systems, each package has unique features, which may not suit the user's preference for file handling, ease of use, content, methodology, and so forth. One dramatic example is the icon menu approach of the new Macintosh computer (Apple, Inc.) versus the standard text approach. The former may provide opportunities for nonreaders to access the computer for vocational training. These differences should be noted and added to the information to be considered during the decision making process.

While potential computer applications that a school might identify may be novel, i.e., applications that presently are not being performed in another way, at present most functions are probably being handled traditionally. The expectation generally is that a computer system will be more time- or cost-efficient than present practices. For example, all special education programs develop Individualized Education Programs in some form or another, and some type of data are collected to support the identified plans. These are tasks that can be assisted by the computer. Some key questions included in analyzing current practice, which may be computer assisted, include the following: (1) How is the goal being accomplished now? (2) What resources are presently being used? (3) Within the organization, how are decisions made for the implementation of new ideas? (4) What is the general feeling toward the present strategy? This information (i.e., current costs and efficiency) will be used next to evaluate the cost-benefits of a computer system.

Determination of System Requirements. When all information from the previous step has been gathered, three additional tasks will assist in the determination of system requirements. The first is a comparison of existing and desired strategies to achieve each specified goal (cost-benefit).

Next, a discrepancy analysis will identify existing gaps in goal delivery (e.g., all IEPs need to be completed by the end of September and up to now have not been completed until mid-November). Finally, a comparison should be made between current resources and those needed to fill the gaps. The result of this process enables the system designer to realize the overall system requirements, and provides enough information to describe a potential system.

Planning the Document. The final step in the requirements analysis component of the HUMAN-SD yields the first of five reports to the organization. The designer summarizes the findings of the process thus far in the form of a planning document. This document describes a potential system that would achieve the goals stated by the group. The feasibility of the plan to the present can then be discussed. Within the document, all information necessary for making an informed decision to continue, discontinue, or revise the plan are provided for the client. The progression to the second level is contingent upon the organization's desire to continue.

Functions Analysis

The functions analysis process begins with a detailed description of each of the system's goals. This is achieved by examining input and output requirements, performance requirements in terms of speed and accuracy, and environmental factors or user limitations that affect the achievement of each goal. Table 11-4 presents guidelines for this level of analysis to assist in sensitizing the designer to the numerous factors that must be in place in order for a system to meet its stated goals successfully. The specific goal of utilizing a computer system for the collection of classroom data will be followed to help illustrate the points.

The next step involves a determination of who or what is best suited to perform each identified function. Table 11-2 can be used to assist in this process. While these guidelines may appear to reflect no more than common sense, it is critical to verify that individuals in the target setting have the ability to perform the functions assigned to the human component. This is particularly important when handicapped users are involved. A more complete set of questions to guide you in this process are presented in Table 11-5. A major question for our example is whether it is better for the computer to collect the data directly or for the human to enter it.

Task Analysis

The third level of the HUMAN-SD is a further refinement of the description of potential system(s) to address the needs of the target organization. Each of the functions designated previously as a human

Table 11-4. 2.0 Functions Analysis

2.1 *Describe Each System Goal*

For each identified goal (e.g., data collection):

What is the system output for this goal? (e.g., reports)
What input does the system require for this goal? (e.g., classroom data)
What system capabilities are demanded by this goal? (e.g., sorting and filing data)
What performance requirements are demanded by this goal? (e.g., accuracy, speed)
What environmental factors potentially affect this goal?
Do client limitations (financial, psychological) restrict this goal?

2.2 *Determine the System Functions*

What are the major operations (actions) of the system? (e.g., data entry, data analysis, report
    output)
What sequence will these operations follow? (e.g., data entry, data analysis, report output)
Do client limitations affect the functions? (e.g., financial, psychological)
Do environmental factors affect the functions?
Do the performance requirements of the system affect the functions? (e.g., speed—ease of
    data entry)
Were any additional functions identified in the above answers?

> If yes:

>> Include on the list of major functions
>> Where do they fit in the sequence?
>> What limitations, environmental factors, or performance requirements
>>   affect these new functions?

2.3 *Describe Each System Function*

What information does the user require for this function? (e.g., data entry—information format
    required)
Will it be directly or indirectly sensed? (e.g., direct—shown on monitor)
Will it require relative or absolute descriminations? (e.g., absolute—specific format)
Will it be dynamic or static in nature? (e.g., dynamic—change for each data type)
What responses are required of the user for this function? (e.g., keyboard use)

> Will some equipment need activation? (e.g., keyboard)
> Will a discrete setting with a control have to be made?

Will a quantitative setting have to be made?

> Will data entry (keyboard or switch) be necessary? (e.g., yes—keyboard)

What information processing or decision-making will be required between the receiving of
    information and the response? (e.g., determine if available data fit the format)
Are additional functions required to achieve these inputs or outputs?

> If yes, include them in Section 2.2 and analyze each

What alternatives can be designed to achieve this same function?

> Complete 2.3 for each alternative

Table 11-5. 2.0   Functions Analysis

2.4   *Allocate System Functions*

How will each function be implemented?
What will the configuration look like?

> Refer to "Relative Capabilities of Humans and Machines" (Table 11-2)
> What are all the probable equipment functions?
> What are all the probable client functions?
>
>> Which can the client perform?
>> Can the client perform these well enough to meet performance
>>   requirements?
>
> In what sequence will the functions be performed?
> Are additional functions identified as a result of this analysis?
>
>> Return to Section 2.3 for each new function

What alternative configurations could achieve the same goals?

> Complete Section 2.4 for each alternative

> Rank the alternatives by estimated cost-effectiveness

>> Estimate cost of consultant and training time
>> Is hardware available to perform the functions identified?
>> Will the hardware meet the client requirements?

---

function is task analyzed by following the line of questions in Table 11-6.
An example of the application of human factors research findings to the
designation of controls and displays is presented in Table 11-7.

Following each task analysis, controls and displays must be identified
that will assist the user in performing the task efficiently. Each task is
analyzed with reference to the specific control or display. Table 11-8 should
assist in that analysis.

Interface Analysis

The ability of a user to perform not only single tasks but also a series
of tasks in real and simulated situations is an important evaluative question.
Since specific controls and displays can be varied in terms of their size
and spacing, mock-ups of potential systems must be created to identify
combinations that will match system requirements. As in the case of our
small school–one system example, the secretary may have different size and
spacing requirements than the lowest functioning mentally retarded
students. The best system for "all goals and users" must be identified. The
mock-up provides an opportunity to evaluate all users performing all tasks
when they are arranged in their proper sequence. Table 11-9 presents factors

Table 11-6. 3.0   Task Analysis

3.1 *Determine Tasks*

What functions will the client perform? (e.g., data entry)
What sequence of activities achieve each function? (develop a flow chart)
Describe each activity or task (e.g., read and interpret the display to know data format)

What is the purpose of the activity?
What information will the client need to complete this activity? (e.g., visual information from monitor)
Is a display necessary?

If indirect sensing is required:

What type of information must be displayed?

quantitative? (e.g., level of volume)
qualitative? (e.g., approximate level of volume)
status indication? (e.g., on/off)
warning/signal? (e.g., flashing light to indicate that the stove is on)
visual/representational? (e.g., international symbols for the menu)
alphanumeric/symbolic? (e.g., written words for the menu)

Should it be a visual or auditory display? (see Table 11-7) (e.g., message will be referred to later
therefore visual display)

What will the client's response have to be to achieve this activity?

Will the primary output be motor or speech?
Must the information transmitted be continuous or discrete (e.g., continuous until understood)
What will the machine output be?

Refer to input needed for next action in the sequence (e.g., none)

Define each task using a verb/noun format (e.g., translate display)

---

that need consideration during the mock-up. This evaluation continues for all configurations that have been presented as potential options, enabling comparisons to be made on the basis of performance and cost-effectiveness. The interface analysis is concluded with a summary report.

Field Evaluation

When the organization is satisfied with the recommended system and is confident that it will meet their goals, the decision to purchase or build the system is made. Upon completion, training to use the system is required. Field evaluations are conducted periodically to assess the degree to which the system continues to meet performance requirements and user satisfaction. Modifications to the system are made as necessary. Follow-up evaluations are recommended every three months for a period of one year.

Table 11-7. When To Use The Auditory or Visual Form of Presentation

Use auditory presentation if:	Use visual presentation if:
1. The message is simple.	1. The message is complex.
2. The message is short.	2. The message is long.
3. The message will not be referred to later.	3. The message will be referred to later.
4. The message deals with events in time.	4. The message deals with location in space.
5. The message calls for immediate action.	5. The message does not call for immediate action.
6. The visual system of the person is overburdened.	6. The auditory system of the person is overburdened.
7. The receiving location is too bright or dark—adaptation integrity is necessary.	7. The receiving location is too noisy.
8. The person's job requires him or her to move about continually.	8. The person's job allows him or her to remain in one position.

From Deatherage, B. H. (1972) Auditory and other sensory forms of information presentation. In H. P. Van Cott & R. G. Kinkade (Eds.), *Human engineering guide to equipment design* (rev. ed.) (p. 124). Washington, DC: U.S. Government Printing Office. Reprinted with permission.

Systems for Individuals

Recent development in the area of minicomputer and microcomputers offer viable alternatives for handicapped individuals to live and perform more independently. Unfortunately, the available technology is not always affordable, expecially when individual needs are extremely specific and cannot be met by utilizing "shelf available" equipment. Nevertheless, it may not be necessary to wait for added demands or a significant drop in the cost of new developments to make the technology affordable if a systematic effort is made to match the user's abilities and goals to the available technology. The systems development approach utilized in the HUMAN-SD has great potential for individual users as well as for organizations. The systems development approach is the same, but slightly different questions are asked during the process.

Requirements Analysis

The requirements analysis level of the HUMAN-SD delineates the general features of a system that are necessary to meet an individual's stated needs. The ultimate goal of this first phase is to understand the client's goals and to gain a general sense of his or her abilities. Client information is gathered in any of three ways: a mailed questionnaire (Table

Table 11–8. 3.0   Task Analysis

3.2 *Determine Appropriate Controls and Displays*
Compare classification of each task behavior with appropriate equipment for each
  behavior. Select a tentative list of possible control-display devices to be used in
  performing these tasks
  Do they meet performance requirements?
  Do they optimize the input and output characteristics of the equipment?

3.3 *Analyze the Task Demands*
Analyze each task with reference to specific controls and displays
  What needs to be accomplished? (e.g., menu display)
      How must it be accomplished? (e.g., visual representation, clear,
        uncluttered)
  What are the task time requirements? (e.g., automatic advance to the next item
    after data are entered)
  How frequently must the task be performed?
  What category of behavior does it fall into? (e.g., transmission/receipt/storage of
    information, delay, decision, control operation, display monitoring)
  Diagram the task
Develop a flow diagram to show sequence of all tasks
List the tasks in order of performance
What interrelationships exist between tasks? (e.g., completion of one task initiates
  beginning of another)
Do these interrelationships match the client's abilities?
      Can the client perform the task? (e.g., sensory, motor, decision-making, and
        communication requirement)
      Are excessive demands imposed on the client? (e.g., frequency, duration,
        accuracy, etc.)
      Do the following events affect client performance?
          Speed of occurrence?
          Number of responses required?
          Length of event presentation?
          Amount of movement required?
          Level of intensity or stress of event?
          Predictability of events?
      Does the physical environment affect performance? (e.g., temperature, noise,
        vibration, lighting, safety, etc.)
      Is stress created by the task mission, potential emergencies, accuracy and speed
        requirements for responses, or task importance to the client?
      Are the displays too complex? (e.g., requires complex perception, memory tasks,
        etc.)
      Are the controls too complex? (e.g., motor requirements sequence)
Can the client meet performance requirements with this control or display?
      If no:
          Is the input to the client clear?
          Can the display be modified?
          Can the controls be modified?
          Is the process too complex?
          Does the client lack the skill or training?
          Does the client lack the motivation?
Reanalyze the new task demands by repeating Section 3.3.

Table 11–9. 4.0 Interface Analysis

4.1 *Select Appropriate Interfaces*
Determine the appropriate size
How many controls and displays are needed?
Is the display/control consistent with the purpose of the system?
Does the display/control limit system portability?
Can the number of controls/displays be reduced?
Determine the appropriate spacing of controls/displays
Does compatibility with expectations affect the spacing?
Spatial compatibility (e.g., physical similarities between controls and
displays)
Compatibility of movement relationships (e.g., turn the dial to the left to
move the display lever to the left)
Conceptual compatibility (e.g., use visual symbols that represent concrete
objects)
General population response tendencies (e.g., sequencing the controls left
to right)
How do client abilities affect the spacing requirements? (e.g., motor, visual,
hearing)
Create a mock-up of the system
Train the client
Analyze each task as the client performs it
Evaluate the client's ability to perform each task in sequence
Can the client perform the task?
Are excessive demands imposed on the client? (e.g., motor, memory, etc.)
Do the following events affect client performance?
Does the physical environment affect performance?
Is stress created?
Are the displays too complex?
Are the controls too complex?
Does the client meet the performance criterion?
Can the client perform all tasks in the required sequence within a specified
amount of time?
If not:
Determine error classification
Complete the Error Analysis Matrix (Table 11–16)
Can the error be prevented by:
Automating the error-likely operation? (e.g., automatically returning
to the menu instead of pressing a switch)
Modifying equipment or environment? (e.g., add more
microphones)
Modifying the sequence or procedure? (e.g., select multiple
appliances before activation)
Additional training?
Improving monitoring to eliminate some error?
Improving feedback (e.g., increase sensitivity to habits)
Modify the arrangement
Repeat questions in Section 4.1 beginning with "Determine the
appropriate size."
Are other alternatives available?
Is another sequence possible?

Table 11–9. Interface Analysis (Continued)

Are other equipment functions possible?
Can the tasks be reprioritized?
Can the frequency of task performance be changed?
Modify the arrangement
Create a new mock-up and try with the client.
    Repeat the questions in Section 4.1. starting with "Create a mock-up."

11–10), a phone interview, or a face-to-face interview. It is helpful to mail clients a questionnaire to allow them to begin thinking about their needs, and follow this up later with a face-to-face or phone interview to clarify and record the information. If insufficient information is available, the client should be referred for additional evaluation (e.g., psychological, physical, or occupational therapy).

Individual user goals generally fall into four categories: communication assistance, home control, adaptive living assistance, and instructional assistance. A description of each of these applications is contained in Table 11–11. Ideally, each of the targeted applications would be available to the user in the entire range of settings in which he or she functions. Home control, for instance, is critical in the home setting, but may also be necessary to perform independently in a work or recreation setting. In practice, however, portability may be the single most limiting factor to be considered for any system. Therefore, it becomes necessary to ask the client to prioritize the settings in which the system will be used. Table 11–3 summarizes the key questions that must be answered before moving to the next step in the requirement analysis process.

Based on the information gathered regarding client goals, abilities and limitations, basic system requirements are outlined and equipment categories are identified. This may include such general categories as a computer, voice synthesizer, switch, and so forth. In order to avoid the hazard of analyzing needs based on available equipment rather than client needs, no specific pieces of equipment are named at this point.

The first written proposal is then prepared, summarizing the information of the requirements analysis process. The feasibility of building a system that will meet the specific goals of the client is addressed in this report. If a system is indicated, it is described in very general terms with at least one alternative provided. To achieve a goal of verbal communication, for example, a system composed of a monitor, computer, disc drive, switch, switch interface, voice synthesizer, and software might be described. Estimates of range of cost and time are included to enable the client to make a decision regarding the continuation of the project.

Table 11-10. Initial Information Questionnaire

In each of the following questions "you" refers to the person who will ultimately use the computer system. When possible, the user should be the primary informant in answering the questions.

Client Goals

Briefly state your goals or reasons for considering a computer system.

Are there any special places or situations in which you would particularly want a computer system to assist you with your goals?

Rank these areas 1 to 4 according to what you are most interested in (with 1 being first interest area and 4 being last)
   Communication (system for talking or writing, or both)
   Instruction (system for teaching skills)
   Home control (system for controlling objects in your environment—lights, phone, kitchen appliances, etc.)
   Adaptive living skills (system for assisting in daily living—self-feeding)
   Other (please specify):

Rank the following to indicate which environments you would like to perform these goals? (Number them 1 to 5, 1 being first choice and 5 being last)
   Classroom or program site
   Home
   Job or work site
   Community facilities
   Other

How will you transport the system from place to place?
   It doesn't need transporting
   On a wheelchair
   Carried by yourself
   Carried by someone else
   Other (please describe):
   I haven't thought of that yet

How will you feel about carrying extra equipment around and needing it to assist you in your daily routine?
   It won't bother me
   I'll tolerate anything if it gets the job done
   I'll want it to be as unnoticeable as possible
   I don't want others to know I need help

Which range of total costs have you considered acceptable?
   $1000–2000 $2000–3500 $3500–5000

   Other (please specify): Unlimited (within reason)
   I have no idea what to expect

Table 11-10. Initial Information Questionnaire (Continued)

Client Abilities

> Verbal
> Gestural (e.g., signing)
> Assistive device (e.g., communication board)
> No functional mode

Please rank your abilities to voluntarily use/control the following:

	No Ability	Minimum Use	Some Limitations	Normal Use
Fingers	☐	☐	☐	☐
Hands	☐	☐	☐	☐
Elbows	☐	☐	☐	☐
Arms	☐	☐	☐	☐
Toes	☐	☐	☐	☐
Feet	☐	☐	☐	☐
Ankles	☐	☐	☐	☐
Knees	☐	☐	☐	☐
Legs	☐	☐	☐	☐
Neck	☐	☐	☐	☐
Head	☐	☐	☐	☐
Eyes	☐	☐	☐	☐
Eyebrows	☐	☐	☐	☐
Eyelashes	☐	☐	☐	☐
Mouth	☐	☐	☐	☐
Tongue	☐	☐	☐	☐

If voluntary motor movement is minimal, please describe what movement you feel is most consistent and easiest to use

Answering the following questions to the best of you knowledge, what is your:

> Receptive language level?
> Expressive language level?
> Reading level?
> Spelling level?
> Math level?

Do you have any sensory limitations? (e.g., vision, hearing)
If yes, please describe

When learning new things, do you prefer:

> Seeing them?
> Hearing them?
> Touching/handling them?
> No preference?

Is there anything else you would like to add that was missed in the above questions that is important for a full understanding of your abilities? (Continue on the back if more space is needed.)

Table 11-11. Potential Individual Uses of a System

Categories	Description
Communication assistance	Auditory: voice synthesizer or telephone line signals
	Visual: printer or video screen
	Tactile: Braille
Home control	Enables the user to control electrical objects, such as lights, kitchen appliances, etc.
Adaptive living assistance	Enables the user to move objects through space using robotics
Instructional and recreational assistance	Enables the user to access learning and recreational materials in a format that makes independent responses possible

Functions Analysis

If the client decides to proceed with the process, the system goals are further analyzed to determine both the human and machine functions that are required to achieve the goals. As described earlier, functions are the general means or actions that contribute to the system's ability to meet its requirements. In relation to educational terminology, functions are similar to performance objectives. The functions involved in the example of the written communication goal would include turning the system on and off, displaying the software options on a monitor, reading and interpreting the screen, making a decision from options offered, manipulating the input device to make the appropriate selection, detecting and decoding the selection that has been made, and executing that decision. These functions are then arranged according to a performance sequence and assessed in relation to client abilities, environmental factors, and performance requirements (Meister, 1971). As in all phases on the HUMAN-SD, potential alternatives and new functions that are required by those alternatives are identified, and the sequence is reexamined. This cycle continues until all functions have been identified and analyzed. Table 11-12 illustrates the possible results of the functions analysis for the goal of verbal communication assistance. The questions addressed were presented in Table 11-4.

Table 11-12. Describe Each System Function

Functions	User Information Required	User Response Required	Information Process Required	Additional Functions
Voice output	How to turn on Volume appropriate Direct sense– menu Static information	Switch activation Discrete– on/off toggle	Choice to use Position of cursor right Timing of switch activation Appropriateness of message for environment	
Monitor output	System on/off Direct sense– visual Static information	Control activation -discrete Get help to turn on	Status of monitor or system How to get help	Getting help
Detect/decode switch signal	Feedback from computer	Edit response if wrong (switch activation)	Choice correct?	Feedback on monitor Know edit procedures
Store information: short-term and permanent	View what's in short- term memory (status display) View long- term memory (via menu)	None	Read/interpret display or menu	
Activation of switch	Switch position	Motor response	Force necessary Timing ok?	
Decision making (mental process)	Choices available Environmental factors/ consequences	Mental process Decisiveness	Weigh environmental factors for appropriate ness	
Selection (action on decision)	Cursor position Position of switch	Activation of switch Estimate cursor movement	Judge timing of cursor movement	
Read/interpret display	Display format Symbols/words –meanings Cursor position	Mental process	Mental process Interpret meanings	

Table 11–13. Possible Alternatives for Verbal Communication Assistance

Sequence	Who/What	Alternatives
Monitor output	Computer	Voice output
Read/interpret display	User	Spoken display
Decision making	User	
Selection	Computer scan	User
Activate switch	User	
Detect/decode switch	Computer	
Store information	Computer	
Monitor output	Computer	Voice output
Edit inputs	User	
Decode switch	Computer	
Selection Options		
Disk output	Computer/drive	
Voice output	Computer/voice synthesizer	
Monitor output	Computer/monitor	
Adjust speed	Other person	User
Adjust volume	Other person	User
Expand vocabulary	Other person	User
Access stored information	Computer	

The capabilities of the handicapped user and those of machines are then compared to delegate functions to each. All systems under consideration should be included in the comparison process. Using, once again, written communication as the goal, a machine might be required to perform all the functions involved in this task with the exception of decision making. At the other extreme, the human might be responsible for all the functions, eliminating the necessity of a machine for that system requirement. Thus, each function must be evaluated in terms of the client's ability to perform that function and the degree to which the performance will meet the system requirements.

Since functions typically are not performed in isolation in real-life applications of a system, the sequence of functions as well as the person-machine interactions are important considerations in this analysis process. In addition, the feasibility and cost-effectiveness of each alternative system must be assesed. The evaluation questions for this phase of the analysis are those in Table 11–5. Two possible alternatives for our goal of verbal communication assistance might be as described in Table 11–13.

Task Analysis

Task analysis, the third phase of HUMAN-SD, continues to define and describe each function by breaking it down into its component parts

Table 11–14. Determine Tasks

Activity	Display Type	Client Response	Machine Output
Read and interpret the screen	Visual alphanumeric	Cognitive process	Display of menu
Decide option	N/A	Cognitive process	N/A
Locate cursor and know which column it is on	Visual qualitative	Cognitive and perceptual processes	Cursor location highlighted
Activate switch to change from column to row mode	N/A	Motor and perceptual processes	N/A
Know when cursor is in right place	Visual qualitative	Cognitive and perceptual processes	Cursor location highlighted
Activate the switch to make selection	N/A	Motor process	N/A
Locate cursor and verify choice	Visual qualitative and alphanumeric	Cognitive and perceptual processes	Cursor location highlighted
If wrong, activate switch to initiate cursor movement	Visual qualitative	Cognitive and perceptual processes	Cursor location highlighted
Locate "erase" function on menu	Visual alphanumeric	Cognitive and perceptual processes	Menu display
Repeat steps to select "erase"			

or tasks. For example, the human function of decision making can be subdivided into the following steps: look at the monitor, determine the available options, determine which option is appropriate, and select the correct option. The data in Table 11-14 list detailed task descriptions for our example and the equipment required to perform those tasks.

The next stage of the task analysis involves a determination of which controls and displays are appropriate for the performance of each task. To guide this planning, information regarding client abilities and performance specifications, gathered during the requirements analysis, is reviewed. Each task is then analyzed in terms of what control or display might be used, how the task will be accomplished, the time required and the frequency of task performance. For example, the "translate display" function of a written communication goal might be described as follows:

Display	Monitor
How accomplished	Cognitive process of understanding the symbols on the display
Time requirements	Reasonable and functional
Frequency	Very frequent
Behavior category	Receipt of information

This information is then considered in terms of the client's abilities. A complete listing of evaluative questions appropriate for this stage of analysis was presented in Table 11-8. For the handicapped user in our example, a visual display or monitor is the only control or display necessary for the task of translating or read the menu of options. An alternative might be an auditory display or voice synthesizer that would read the menu to the individual. The summary report for this phase of the HUMAN-SD yields a tentative list of control and display devices that match these specifications along with the revised estimates of the system's design and costs.

Interface Analysis

The interface analysis is the final planning activity prior to the construction or assembly of a system. At this stage, controls and displays are carefully considered in terms of their size, spacing, and placement on a panel or piece of equipment. This process is designed to ensure that the handicapped user can efficiently use the equipment. Table 11-15 contains a check list of items to consider in this evaluation process. When an acceptable option is found for each point of consideration, a mock-up or

Table 11-15. Mock-up Observation Chart

	Translate Display	Choose Option	Locate Cursor	Move Cursor	Detect Choice
I. Performance Alone					
II. Performance in Sequence	(Check all that affect performance)				
Task Performance:					
Sensory/perception					
Motor					
Decision making					
Communication					
Excessive Demands:					
Duration					
Frequency					
Information feedback					
Accuracy					
Error probability					
Errors cause stress					
Concurrent multitask					
Events:					
Speed of occurrence					
Number of responses					
Length-presentation					
Amount of movement					
Level of intensity					
Predictability					

Table 11-15. Mock-up Observation Chart (Continued)

	Translate Display	Choose Option	Locate Cursor	Move Cursor	Detect Choice
Physical Environment:					
Temperature					
Humidity					
Noise					
Vibration					
Lighting					
Safety					
Stress Created:					
Potential emergencies					
Accuracy requirements					
Speed requirements					
Importance of task					
Display Complexity:					
Too much on display					
Difficult to discriminate					
Response required too high					
Too many tasks in sequence					

III. *Performance in Required Time and in Sequence*

Table 11-16. Error Analysis Matrix

	Situational Examples	Idiosyncratic Examples
Incorrect performance	Switch too far to reach	Lack control—miss switch
Failure to perform	Visual cue too short	Vision limited—missed cue
Out of sequence	Switches in random order	Short memory—forgot sequence
Nonrequired action	Press two keys at once	Lack control—bump switch
Not within time limit or criterion	Knob hard to adjust— takes too long	Lack fine motor ability to adjust knob

Table 11-17. Comparison of Alternative Approaches

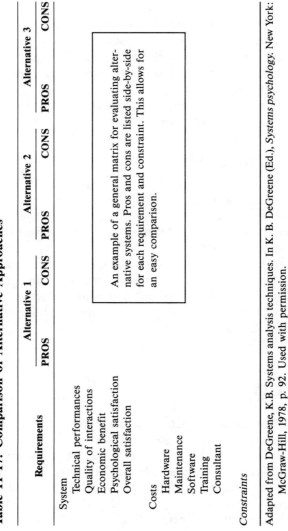

Requirements	Alternative 1		Alternative 2		Alternative 3	
	PROS	CONS	PROS	CONS	PROS	CONS
System						
Technical performances						
Quality of interactions						
Economic benefit						
Psychological satisfaction						
Overall satisfaction						
Costs						
Hardware						
Maintenance						
Software						
Training						
Consultant						
Constraints						

An example of a general matrix for evaluating alternative systems. Pros and cons are listed side-by-side for each requirement and constraint. This allows for an easy comparison.

Adapted from DeGreene, K.B. Systems analysis techniques. In K. B. DeGreene (Ed.), *Systems psychology.* New York: McGraw-Hill, 1978, p. 92. Used with permission.

prototype of the system can be constructed. The client is then asked to perform targeted functions in order to evaluate the adequacy of the system. Critical concerns relate to performance time, performance errors, and the client's ability to perform all the tasks in their proper sequence. An error analysis matrix that may assist in the evaluation process is contained in Table 11-16.

Cost-effectiveness is the final issue to consider before a system is recommended to the client. Many alternative system components and, in some cases, total systems, exist. With cost in mind, each system is evaluated in terms of the established performance requirements and client limitations. Technical features of the system as well as consumer input are important sources of information. This evaluation process is outlined in matrix fashion in Table 11-17, facilitating a comprehensive comparison of potential systems.

Field Evaluation

The last phase of the HUMAN-SD involves the actual construction of the system and the subsequent field testing. The handicapped individual is trained to use the system and then asked to perform all functions in each environment in which these functions will ultimately be used. Evaluation at this stage includes a consideration of system requirements, task performance, and client satisfaction. Modifications are made as needed. If time and resources permit, follow-up evaluations conducted three, six, and twelve months later will ensure the proper system performance over time.

SUMMARY

The application of computer technology to habilitative efforts with handicapped individuals holds great promise for expanding educational opportunities and increasing independence. The state of flux that characterizes this rapidly changing field, however, makes a carefully planned approach to the integration of this technology into school and home environments essential. This chapter has described an instrument, based on a systems development perspective, which was designed to guide individuals involved in the acquisition of computer hardware for use by both individual clients, and in settings in which a variety of users will interact with the system. The intention of this instrument is to identify the most efficient hardware configuration that will meet the needs that are identified by those who will ultimately use the system. At each step in the systems development process, the idiosyncratic behaviors, characteristics, preferences, and skills of the user are considered. It is anticipated that this degree of scrutiny will maximize the chances of achieving a successful match between human and machine capabilities.

REFERENCES

Bork, A., & Franklin, S. D. (1979). The role of personal computer systems in education. *Association for Educational Data Systems Journal*, *13*(1), 17-30.

Braun, L. (1979). How do I choose a personal computer? *Association for Educational Data Systems Journal*, *13*(1), 81-88.

Chapanis, A. (1969). Human factors in systems engineering. In K.B. DeGreene (Ed.), *Systems Psychology*, pp. 51-78. New York: McGraw-Hill.

Chapanis, A. (1965). *Man-machine engineering*. Monterey, CA: Brooks/Cole Publishing Co.

Deatherage, B. H. (1972). Auditory and other sensory forms of information presentation. In H.P. Van Cott & R.G. Kinkade (Eds.), *Human engineering guide to equipment design* (rev. ed). Washington, DC: U.S. Government Printing Office.

DeGreene, K. B. (1969a). Systems analysis techniques. In K. B. DeGreene (Ed.), *Systems Psychology*, pp. 79-130. New York: McGraw-Hill.

DeGreene, K. B. (1969b). Systems and psychology. In K.B. De Greene (Ed.), *Systems Psychology*, pp. 3-50. New York: McGraw-Hill.

Gagne, R. M. (1962). Human functions in systems. In R. M. Gagne (Ed.), *Psychological principles in system development*, pp. 35-73. New York: Holt, Rinehart and Winston.

Hanley, T., & Yin, R. K. (1984). *Microcomputers in special education: Findings and recommendations from a current study*. Presentation at the Technology in Special Education Conference, The Council for Exceptional Children, Reno, NV.

Ingersoll, G. M., Smith, C. B., & Elliot, P. (1983). Microcomputers in American public schools: A national survey. *Educational Computer*, *3*(6), 28-31.

Joiner, L. M., Sedlak, R.A., Silverstein, B. J., & Vensal, G. (1980). Microcomputers: An available technology for special education. *Journal of Special Education Technology*, *3*(2), 37-42.

Jongejan, T., & Johnson, J. (1978). The selection of a computer system: A dilemma for educators. *Oregon Computing Teacher*, *6*(2), 31-40.

Kennedy, J. L. (1962). Psychology and system development. In R. M. Gagne (Ed.), *Psychological principles in system development*, pp. 13-33. New York: Holt, Rinehart, and Winston.

Kidd, J. S. (1962). Human tasks and equipment design. In R. M. Gagne (Ed.), *Psychological principles in system development*, pp. 159-185. New York: Holt, Rinehart and Winston.

Matthews, J. I. (1979). Problems in selecting a microcomputer for educational applications. *Association for Educational Data Systems Journal*, *13*(1), 69-79.

McCormick, E. J., & Saunders, M. S. (1982). *Human factors in engineering and design* (5th ed.). New York: McGraw-Hill.

Meister, D. (1971). *Human factors: Theory and practice*. New York: Wiley-Interscience.

Naiman, A. (1982). *Microcomputers in education: An introduction*. Chelmsford, MA: Northeast Regional Exchange.

Ricketts, D., & Seay, J. A. (1979). Assessing inexpensive microcomputers for classroom use: A product-oriented course to promote instructional literacy. *Association for Educational Data Systems Journal*, *13*(1), 89-99.

Schiffman, G., Tobin, D., & Cassidy-Bronson, S. (1982). Personal computers for the learning disabled. *Journal of Learning Disabilities*, *15*(7), 422–425.

Taber, F. (1981). The microcomputer: Its applicability to special education. *Focus on Exceptional Children*, *14*(2), 1–14.

Thomas, D. B., & McClain, D. H. (1979). Selecting microcomputers for the classroom. *Association for Educational Data Systems Journal*, *13*(1), 55–68.

Tinker, R. F. (1982). *A decision model for microcomputer purchasing*. Cambridge, MA: Technical Education Research Centers.

Zinn, K. L. (1978). Considerations in buying a personal computer: What, which, when, how much? *Creative Computing*, *4*(5), 102.

CHAPTER 12

Future of Computers in Special Education

In a report on technology, Konosuke Matsushita stated, "Of all human inventions since the beginning of mankind, the microprocessor is unique. It is destined to play a part in all areas of life, without exception—to increase our capacities, to facilitate or eliminate tasks, to replace physical effort, to increase the possibilities and areas of mental effort" (Shanahan, 1982). The development of the microprocessor has propelled us into what has been described as "the information age." A common misconception of this phrase is viewing the microprocessor only as a communication and data management device. This is true in that the microprocessor at present can only manipulate information in the binary, on-off code and, therefore, its most basic function is information management. However, in order to realize the real and potential effects of the microprocessor, it is necessary to envision the multiplicity of applications and the inevitability that virtually all aspects of our lives will be touched by its power.

Widespread application of high technology often lags behind the cutting edge of research and development. This is particularly true in education, although the instructional technology may commonly exist in other fields, such as business and industry, defense, and medicine. The major factors influencing the application of technology in education appear to be financial (funding limitations), ideological (resistance to change), and experiential (resistance to learning about technology).

Traditionally, once technologic innovations penetrated education, the last population to benefit was the handicapped. However, as the result of P.L. 94-142 and court decisions such as Mills vs. the Board of Education (District of Columbia), handicapped children have been provided the rights of equal access to instructional methodologies and assistive devices to facilitate free and appropriate public education. The preceding chapters in this book have described how the microprocessor is revolutionizing special education. The purpose of this chapter is to describe some of the developing technologies not yet commonly found in educational settings.

This chapter will not delve into the realm of basic research for which viable application concepts have not yet been developed, such as "biochips"

This chapter was authored by Michael M. Behrmann, Scott Stevens, and Sheryl Asen Levy.

(Lemonick, 1984) in which living organisms are incorporated into computers as sensory input devices. Instead, it will concentrate on discussing the ways in which microprocessor technology can benefit the handicapped in the areas of integrated software, video disc technology, networking, artificial intelligence, and prosthetics.

INTEGRATED SOFTWARE

Software directs the computer to perform specific functions. There are over 150 computer languages, each of which was designed to serve a particular function. Computer languages are not true languages; they are systematized sets of instructions designed for the purpose of controlling the power and potential of the computer (Wold, 1983). The sole function of a computer language is to act as a buffer between the programmer and the binary language of the machine. New applications of software have the capability of integrated functioning—that is, the ability to perform several complicated tasks with a minimum of interaction with the computer. This primarily is a result of the development of low cost expanded memory in different forms, including internal memory, floppy and hard discs, optical storage systems, bubble memory, and so forth. This expanded memory can be partitioned and accessed by the new integrated software technology.

Integrated technology includes one or all of the following features: concurrency, shared technology, and functional integration (Chang, 1983). Each of these attributes permits utilization of various options, which lend diversity and power to the software.

Concurrency

The concept of concurrency allows a software programmer to partition memory, permitting the coexistence and interaction of independent programs. As the result of multiple programs residing in the computer's memory at the same time, the user can switch instantaneously from one to the other. For special education administrators, the ability already exists to combine word processing and spreadsheet programs. The time consuming and complicated process of loading and saving programs when moving from budget to word processing is transformed into a quick and simple process, such as a single keystroke or the positioning and click of a mouse (a handheld video pointing device). Not only can a multitude of programs be stored in memory, but *sections* of these programs can be accessed or stored as well. For example, some programs can assign code in memory that relates to specific tasks, and these tasks can be called up and used as needed.

Shared Technology

The idea of shared technology enables users to combine both "information management" in the form of words, numbers, and graphics with computer manipulation and control of other noncomputer technologies. This is a two level approach. The first allows the combination of different technologies available within the computer. That is, graphics capabilities can be easily incorporated into word processing, and both can utilize data management files to manipulate and present information. At the second level, which incorporates a higher level of integration, integrated software can provide a means for handicapped users to simultaneously access and control peripheral technology systems. An example of this "multiple function" capability, discussed in Chapter 10, described how a physically handicapped computer user should be able to leave the text being worked on with a word processing program to start an appliance, turn on the lights at dusk, or attend to other environmental demands that can be controlled by the computer without interrupting the word processing program.

Functional Integration

A powerful characteristic of integrated software is the capacity to utilize the outputs of one program in another and further manipulate both programs to weave together the results and produce a final product that reflects the individual traits of both. A currently available integrated software tool that is being used with mildly handicapped students is a combination of word processing and spelling correction programs. There also are integrated IEP packages which can generate separate reports for parents, teachers, and administrators that are tailored to the information needs of each.

The combinations of these features ensure that the users can concentrate on how they work instead of how the computer works (Warfield, 1983). In terms of the handicapped, special education teachers, and administrators, integrated software technology promises to shift the focus of computers toward accommodating learning styles, supporting data-based instructional decisions and accountability, and providing tools for individual use in learning and social interaction. Future applications will focus on user characteristics and needs rather than limitations or restrictions of the technology.

Future Directions: Integrated Software

Potential application programs that will benefit handicapped users and those who provide services for the handicapped may first appear as software that facilitates data collection and subsequent decision making. One of the major difficulties in interpreting results of data collection is that very often the original data is not organized or is collapsed, thus losing the original perspective from which the decision was made. Truly integrated software will allow the collection and analysis of individual student progress toward achieving IEP goals and objectives by allowing performance data to be integrated into CMI and CAM programs. In addition, other individualized data for audit trails can be incorporated, such as time in related services, transportation, testing, reporting, parent contacts, and so forth. This provides the data base for instructional and administrative decisions. Integrated software programs can be designed to meet different user needs, from student to highest level administrators, and can be adapted to provide confidentiality where necessary.

This approach describes a pyramid structure that parallels the current applications of integrated software in business and industry. It is reasonable to expect initial use to be by special education managers, and it is logical to anticipate a two-step sequence of further implementation for meeting user needs. The first encompasses entry of data by the teacher into classroom management programs (CMI), which later can be accessed at or uploaded to the administrative level. The second step involves direct collection of student performance data through computer assisted instruction (CAI), the results of which can be functionally integrated into other software. The reason that this sequence might be expected is twofold. First, the number of software programs that need to be developed for administrative use only is relatively limited. Instructional programs, particularly those with the dual capability of individualization and integration of data into other systems, can be limitless in number. Additionally, software programs that are flexible, meet the requirements of individualizing according to student needs and an instructional hierarchy, and are capable of integration with other existing programs constitute more complex design and programming problems for software developers.

Direct student applications of integrated software will take advantage of icons (graphic representations of program functions and menu options), input devices (such as the mouse, touch tablets, touch screen monitors, and light pens), and windowing (monitor output in which the screen is divided into spaces representing different programs or program components). These student applications fall into two categories: instructional uses and tool uses.

Instructional uses will provide students with levels of help or remediation, or both, which currently cannot be presented *simultaneously* on the monitor. An example of this would be the ability to call up a glossary or other reference material to assist in understanding a concept. Additionally, if further assistance were necessary, the student could call up a remediation program or illustration (diagrams, tables, pictures, outlines, and so forth). If desired, all the requested information or any part thereof can remain on the screen, subject to user control of what is to be presented. Programs will accept multiple input modes, e.g., the mouse, keyboard, or touch screen, depending on the student capabilities and preferences. Icons as menu selection choices can convey pictorially what may not be easily communicated in written word or within space confines. Using this type of an approach, mildly handicapped children can utilize iconic representations to access a thesaurus or dictionary to assist in expressing written communication more precisely and accurately. Ongoing evaluation and immediate student feedback could be incorporated through windowing by visually displaying measures of student performance. The presence of the display of the visual feedback could be determined for each student and could be continuous, intermittent, or summative and available to either or both student and teacher.

Tool applications to assist the handicapped in accommodating to restraints imposed by their disability will become more flexible, which will help the handicapped user to manipulate information and environments in a much more efficient and normal manner. Integrated software allows multiplicity of functions to be easily accessed through one system. For example, children with severe written communication handicaps could utilize an iconic language to assist them in translating thoughts into written communication. Integrated software is most often viewed as allowing integration for nonrelated tasks, as discussed earlier in reference to environmental control by the physically handicapped. Another example of a future tool application of integrated software is envisioned as follows. A hearing impaired individual may be interrupted while using the computer by a signal indicating an incoming phone call and, without jeopardizing current work or applications, be able to answer the phone with a voice synthesizer. The software will translate the caller's spoken words to text on the computer screen or printer and typed in responses will be translated to voice-synthesized speech, thereby providing spoken communication, the most common communication mode, to individuals to whom such capability otherwise may not be available.

For individual disabled users, functional applications of integrated software are already beginning to appear. As noted earlier, in public education the initial uses of integrated software will be at the administrative level. The first direct use of integrated software most likely will appear at the student level as a result of management utilization of built-in accountability systems for computer assisted instruction. Truly integrated software will allow the collection and analysis of individual student progress toward achieving IEP goals and objectives while providing the data base for higher level teaching and administrative decision making. This use illustrates the potential impact of integrated software, through its features of concurrency, shared technology, and functional integration, to augment the abilities of those serving the handicapped and to increase the capabilities of the disabled users.

INTERACTIVE VIDEO DISCS

Interactive video discs are potentially one of the most important new educational technologies. Video discs have enormous information storage capacity combined with rapid access to that information. Optical video disc systems offer the ability to store up to 54,000 individual pictures (or frames per disc side). Thus, one disc could store up to 10,000 books with any frame (or page of a book) displayed on a television monitor within a matter of a few seconds. Alternately, up to 30 minutes of motion may be played. One second of motion uses 30 still frames. Any combination of frames and motion may be used in a video disc lesson. For instance, a video disc could be designed with 29 minutes of motion and still leave room for 1800 still pictures.

During motion sequences, two separate audio tracks are available. This allows for two different verbal descriptions of a scene to be stored at the same time. These verbal accounts could be in two languages or different ways of describing the same event.

A user can access all of this information directly through a video disc player or, for expanded capabilities, through a computer. The computer interface allows lessons to be designed that request answers from the user in more flexible ways, such as in the form of words or by touching a certain point on the monitor. The capacity of combining the realistic presentation of video and the rapid access of any point on the disc with the interactive instructional capability of the computer makes the interactive video disc system a truly powerful educational tool.

Levels of Interaction

There are several ways a user can interact with a video disc system. The forms of interaction have been categorized into three levels (Currier, 1983; Daynes, 1982; Zollman and Fuller, 1982). A Level One video disc program may simply have a user passively watch the lesson. In addition, it may stop at special points and instruct the user to use such features as "step to" the next frame or "jump to" a particular frame. With these techniques the user may exercise a limited amount of control over the video disc, and the lesson can direct the learner to a small degree.

A Level Two video disc lesson has the capabilities to branch to a particular frame depending on the response of the user. As an example, a multiple choice question displayed on a single frame may offer a student up to nine options for the student's answer. The Level Two video disc will then respond with an appropriate video frame for the student's selection. This level requires the video disc player to have a small microprocessor to store the program for the lesson and to control the video disc player. "The Puzzle of the Tacoma Narrows Bridge Collapse" was originally designed as a Level Two video disc (Zollman and Fuller, 1982). Thus a Level Two video disc lesson can be designed to ask a question and then to display a particular message, depending on the response. This format is essentially limited to multiple choice questions. While the Level Two video disc may respond with a single frame or a motion sequence, this format is rather limiting.

In the highest level of interactivity, Level Three, the video disc is connected to and controlled by a computer. The computer is programmed to present the entire lesson by operating the video disc, asking the learner questions, presenting problems, and responding to answers or commands. This system was originally called an intelligent video disc. In the intelligent video disc (Level Three) system, the learner interacts with the lesson. The lesson can be programmed to respond to the user's particular needs. Intelligent video discs bring the features of computer assisted instruction and high quality video together in a combined system whose promise seems to be vastly superior to the sum of the individual parts.

Current Applications

Some of the first video disc applications made use of its large storage capabilities. Sears, Roebuck, and Company put one of their retail catalogs on a video disc. The U.S. Army uses a video disc system to deliver maintenance data for troubleshooting the M60A1 tank turret (Bernd, 1983).

Recently, video discs have even been designed for arcade games (Currier, 1983). Unfortunately, the great majority of video disc projects to date have been for government, military, or industrial training. Because of their high cost, few video discs have been designed for public education. At the Fifth Annual Conference on Interactive Video Discs in Education and Training (1983) only one of the nine sessions describing current applications of video discs was in education. The other eight were training projects sponsored by the Army or private industry. Bunderson (1983) surveys video disc projects at WICAT. Of the 15 video discs he describes, three were used in education, five in the military, and seven in industry. All three of the education projects were related to one another. Truly educational interactive video discs is an emerging field.

As noted, the U.S. Army is a prime investor in interactive video discs. Examples of the Army's video disc lessons include lessons developed for training technicians on troubleshooting practices for the I-HAWK Air Defense System and a Satellite System Repair Course (Bernd, 1983). These video disc systems allow for the simulated repair of equipment. While such a lesson may cost several hundred thousand dollars to develop, it is still significantly less expensive than practice on actual equipment costing several millions of dollars. The high price of real equipment translates to a cost of up to $4000 per student hour (Bunderson, 1983). In addition to the cost savings, students training on the video disc system solved 100% of a series of test problems, whereas students taught with conventional methods solved only 25% of the problems (Kimberlin, 1982). Furthermore, students trained with video discs took half the time to solve the problems than students taught traditionally. It appears that video discs may not only be cost-effective; they may also be a superior instructional system.

"The Puzzle of the Tacoma Narrows Bridge Collapse" (TNB) is a Level Two video disc designed for instruction in the physics of standing waves (Zollman and Fuller, 1982). The development of this video disc lesson was supported by the National Science Foundation as a demonstration project. The intent of the project was to develop a low-cost approach to video disc education. TNB cost approximately $50,000 to produce.

Winch (1981) evaluated student use of the TNB video disc. Approximately 100 students were administered a questionnaire after they used the TNB lesson. Winch found that

> [T]he students were quite enthusiastic in their response towards the video disc as an interactive learning device. It appeared as if this feeling was not due entirely to the novel nature of the system, but mostly due to the educational design of the contents of the disc. (p. 107)

In special education, there have been two major projects to develop and evaluate video disc technology. The University of Nebraska had a project called the Media Development Project for the Hearing Impaired. This project devised seven discs for stand-alone players to develop skills in fingerspelling, thinking, language, and social studies (Propp, Nugent, & Stone, 1980; Nugent & Stone, 1982). At Utah State University, the Interactive Video Disc for Special Education project has developed six instructional discs for mentally handicapped children. These discs address such topics as matching, telling time, identification of coins, functional words, sight reading, and directional prepositions (Thorkildsen, Allard,

& Reid, 1983). Evaluation of these video discs found that the value of the instructional design and content for different populations had varying levels of effectiveness. Thorkildsen and Friedman (1984) suggest that as a result of these evaluations, further investigation of the match between technology, instructional goals and objectives, and learner populations is necessary.

Future Directions: Video Discs

Educational applications of video disc technology have enormous potential. The effects of this technology are likely to be felt in the areas of instruction and assessment.

In the instructional realm, future applications in education will need to incorporate the desirable instructional traits discussed in Chapters 3 and 10. The same thing should hold true for incorporating CMI with video disc applications. However, there is much research to be done in ascertaining the effectiveness of such instructional procedures. Video discs are expensive to produce, mostly because of film production costs, and they will probably first be common in areas where they have broad application or areas in which training is expensive or dangerous. Video discs with the capability of computer interfacing can download computer programs that can manipulate the video disc. Generic curriculum video discs may be developed along the lines of curriculum materials, such as the Peabody Picture Vocabulary Cards. Teachers could select from literally hundreds of programs to manipulate that information. Additionally, course authoring programs could allow teachers to develop their own simple courseware.

Video discs also enable individuals to have realistic experiences that they might not otherwise have due to physical limitations, instructional costs, or danger. A video disc of a trip through a store where items for purchase might be selected could be developed for physically handicapped or cognitively low functioning individuals. Such reality-based training might facilitate generalization (a difficult task for retarded individuals) and the transition into the community, as well as reduce the cost related to community-based instruction. Finally, this technology has application in meeting the needs of bilingual handicapped individuals, since there are two audio tracks on the disc. The development of compressed audio, allowing up to 30 seconds of audio in a few frames, is reducing the current limitations of incorporating audio on a video disc (audio requirements now necessitate using 30 frames for one second of audio, even when a still frame is desired).

Assessment is an area in which intelligent video discs have much potential. Standardized tests could easily be developed utilizing a video disc. The human-machine interface provides a standard environment. By utilizing this technology a test could always be administered in a more standardized format. The input flexibility of the computer could allow adaptations for different handicapping conditions, and the computer could collect, analyze, and report results almost immediately. Criterion-referenced testing could also be done easily with the information obtained from instructional courseware.

Video disc technology also has the capability of being combined with other technologies discussed in this chapter. It is possible to generate computer overlays on the video projection. It is not unlikely, then, that the concepts of integrated software could be incorporated with the video disc. Students could work on an instructional program from a video disc, pause and call another program to aid them with the video disc lesson, and then return to the video disc lesson. An example of this would be performing simulations in which the child "weighs" apples in a grocery during a video disc lesson. This lesson might ask the student for the cost of the apples. The child could pause the lesson, call up a mathematics lesson, or consult a calculator built into the computer. When these were done, the student could return to the video disc lesson.

Video discs can also conceivably be combined with artificial intelligence-based systems in assessment, with the computer deciding what areas of evaluation to pursue, analyzing data, and making instructional recommendations. Finally, the storage capacity of video disc is sure to be involved in networking and information management. If a single disc can store up to 54,000 pages, libraries could easily increase collections. Besides written words, video disc "books" could contain motion and sound. A few video discs could contain a complete encyclopedia. Instead of still pictures, this encyclopedia could have motion and sound for "pictures" of places, animals, people, and things. Textual and pictorial information could even be transmitted from the library to the home, office, or school, and this material could even be directly incorporated into word processing or data bases for user manipulation.

NETWORKING

Until recently, data processing (information management) and telecommunication (via telephone, radio, television) have been independent entities. With the development of computer-based manipulation of information, data processing and telecommunications have converged. The union of these two common and sophisticated technologies is consistent with the combination of the Greek word "tele" ("far off") with "communication" to mean "communication over great distances."

The technology responsible for this convergence, called networking, is a computer-controlled system for managing information across locations. Ideally, any point on the network should be able to connect to any other point. The geographic areas covered range from local clusters of computers housed within a single classroom or building, multiple buildings (e.g., college campus facilities), or sets of buildings separated by distances up to approximately 70 miles (e.g., school districts) to national and international systems, such as the Telenet system (SpecialNet).

Historically, networking evolved from multiple terminals connected to a central mainframe or minicomputer (a centralized computing network), in which information was transmitted to and from the terminal by the central processor. Initially, microprocessors and desk-top minicomputers operated as "stand-alone" computers. However, the stand-alone capability and relatively lower cost of microcomputers has led to a distributive system in which the stand-alone computers can communicate through networks as separate entities.

There are two basic reasons to be involved in a networking system: to share peripheral devices and to access and share software programs and information. Networking methods include copper wire–twisted pair, base band, and broad band technologies. The various techniques of networking have inherent advantages and disadvantages. The copper wire system is much like the older telephone color-coded wiring system. The base band system uses an electronic signal directly implanted on a cable, usually coaxial. It sends messages in "packets" to destinations. These are similar to a postcard, with each packet containing a name and address. Messages can be broken up and sent on the most cost-effective route and then reassembled at the destination. Broad band uses a cable system like that currently used in cable television. Broad band systems can use frequency division multiplexing—i.e., can combine all information flow from multiple sources under one signal on a common carrier. This allows simultaneous transmission of multiple data at one time. Table 12–1 distinguishes capabilities, advantages, and disadvantages of each.

With the development of optical fiber systems (conversion of an electronic source to a light source and vice versa), the capacity potential of networking for transmitting information increases significantly. This increase in "carrying capability" is especially necessary for fast, large-scale multimedia transmissions. Cables made of optical fibers can now carry more channels than the purest copper wire. A single hair-thin strand of optical fiber has the potential to carry all of the telephone conversations and television channels in the world, all at the same time. Future refinements of fiberoptics will result in high speed and high capacity quality transmission of data, voice, and video into the home and school.

Current applications of networking in special education are primarily evidenced in information access and sharing. As discussed in Chapter 3,

SpecialNet and information retrieval systems are used by over 2000 special educators to communicate with a wide range of professionals over a wide geographic (i.e., worldwide) area. Specific special education–related data bases are available through computer-based retrieval services, such as ERIC and BRS. At the local level, school district networks are found primarily as administrative data bases. Although features of networking that permit classroom and home computer assisted instruction are available, they are not common.

Future Directions: Networking

In special education, the future of networking will expand beyond a radical increase in information access and sharing of textual and numerical data. Networking will incorporate video and voice capabilities with the flow of information. In addition to information access, networking technologies will be applied in special education through electronic publications, teleconferencing, instructional software, and interactive cable television.

The growth of electronic publishing is close at hand. Already there are floppy disc–based electronic magazines such as the education "diskazines" *Window* (Apple) and *PC Disk Magazine* (IBM PC). Curriculum can be supplemented by disc magazines much in the same way that children now use publications, such as "Weekly Reader." Although the present magazine discs are directed at software dissemination, there is great potential for using this technique for dissemination of professional literature, especially by organizations such as the Council for Exceptional Children. The advantages of this approach include user ability to screen journals to select issues relevant to the user's needs and interests; lower production and mailing costs (potentially resulting in lower consumer costs); more efficient editing and production; faster dissemination of information; ease of incorporation of information into user programs (e.g., incorporation into user word processing programs). Electronic publishing facilitates the storage and dissemination of information in a manner that maintains the efficiency of a personal library with the capacity of a major central library.

Permanent information access is essential to quality special education. Likewise, temporary information exchange facilitates meeting the needs of special education students. Such information exchange will be greatly enhanced by the application of teleconferencing and telecommunications to special education.

In combining the capabilities of telecommunications, voice, and video, teleconferencing provides professional educators, parents, and related services personnel with a communication technique that, regardless of physical distance, offers the highest level of direct interaction possible without being in the same room. The advantages are many: increased access to human resources and audiences; economy of time and financial resources; direct, face-to-face communication; ability to combine data transmission and human interaction; and removal of geographic barriers to sharing information.

Teleconferencing and telecommunications increase availability of and accessibility to specialist resource personnel essential to accurate and effective diagnosis and prescription. For example, medical expertise not possessed by local personnel can be obtained from a specialist in another city, state, or country. At a local level, parents and related services personnel may not have to travel from home or office to participate in IEP or progress conferences. Telecommunications may be used to maintain on-going communications with parents. In the Arlington, Virginia, Public Schools, for example, a computerized system automatically telephones parents or guardians of absent students. One resulting benefit has been the reduction of truancy. Through satellite-based teleconferencing, professional organization conferences can reach greater percentages of their membership. Presentations can be given at single or multiple sites and broadcast to regional centers. Audiences on both coasts would then be able to interact with a presenter in the Midwest. The ability to bring resources to regional or local centers may strengthen local organization chapters. Professional conferences are only one example of professional development. University courses are being offered through interactive telecommunications and teleconferencing. This ability to interact with instructors and video and computer-mediated software becomes particularly important in rural areas. These same advantages should be available to homebound or handicapped students in rural schools. Through teleconferencing, meeting the needs of handicapped students becomes more independent of limitations, such as distance, time, money, and training.

The concept of networking for information access and learning is just as important from the student's perspective as it is from the professional special educator's perspective. Students will increasingly use information access devices, particularly those that expand availability of instructional and supplemental materials. It is anticipated that they will primarily use local area networks and metropolitan cable networks.

In-house school interactive instructional networks would parallel the concept behind the language laboratory, in which students received instruction through self-paced, individualized modules in which teachers are able to monitor, interact with a student, and determine suitable instructional materials. A computerized instructional networking system overcomes disadvantages associated with language laboratories by its increased interactive capabilities with both student and teacher, data collection capabilities, and branching capabilities. One of the most important future characteristics of instructional networking should be the capability to integrate the products of student performance with teacher (CMI) and school division (CAM) data management software. (A detailed description of the advantages of computer assisted instruction is given in Chapters 2 and 3.) An example of an instructional networking system already in use is the PLATO system. A joint project by the State Department of Education of Minnesota and the Burnsville School District successfully used PLATO with highly distractible and other learning disabled students.

In a local "cluster" network, students download instructional programs from the teacher's desktop computer or from the school's minicomputer or mainframe computer. Additionally, networking permits peer interchanges through which students can help one another. One such activity that promotes peer interchanges is writing. Students can see what others are writing and add their own comments (Euchner, 1984).

A local cluster is not the only type of instructional network that will be effective in the direct teaching of students. Two additional types of networking systems should play an important role in the future of computer-based instruction for handicapped children. The first, which we will call a "national distribution network," will allow teachers or students, or both, to review software for suitability via a telecommunications network. If so desired, the software may be purchased and downloaded immediately for use. A parallel to this concept is being developed by Atari for distribution of computer games. One exciting development in this type of network is a system that utilizes FM audio transmission of data rather than telephone or cable systems. This system, being developed by National Information Utilities in Virginia, will, through a combination of satellite communications and local FM transmissions, be able to broadcast software and information over the air to individuals who have special receivers. The receivers will be rented, much as pay TV systems are. There will be no telephone charges or traditional time share costs since plans are to charge a royalty based on use (calculated by the receiver).

The second type of network utilizes broad band networks available through cable television systems. Broad band networks allow transmission of any combination of data, voice, and video in an interactive mode. The system can support approximately 70 channels of video and an enormous number of data channels. Some systems can support up to approximately 20,000 different devices (such as terminals, printers, and microprocessors) *at one time.*

By combining the high quality of representation offered by video with computer assisted instruction, a new interactive educational environment of a power and magnitude previously unobtainable is available. The same applications of broad band educational networking can just as easily be extended to the home environment. Some futurists project that schools will no longer be necessary as a result of this type of technology (The Futurist, 1983). However, the need for socialization and the trend toward dual income households and single parent families suggest that schools will remain as viable institutions.

Applications of this technology to supplement home-school interactions are likely. Cable networks, which are rapidly becoming pervasive, provide the mechanisms for extending instruction from school to home (e.g., homework, homebound instruction, access to extracurricular activities), and improving home-school communication (e.g., reporting to parents, providing schedules of events, fostering parental input). These features will enhance the desirability of cable systems, which already offer home shopping, banking, access to games, and other recreational or educational opportunities.

The concept of networking is a major step toward breaking down barriers to the education of handicapped children. Networking fosters professional development, professional communication, accessibility and integration of information and human resources, and direct individualized interactive student instruction regardless of possible geographic or physical limitations. Finally, it offers the opportunity to extend school services to the home environment and facilitate parent-school communication and interaction.

A recurring communication goal is augmented accessibility to and synthesis of information. Sophisticated communication networks that could one day give any individual on earth direct access to any computer bank on the planet by way of satellite communications systems are envisioned. With the exponential growth of knowledge, accessibility alone will not ensure effective use of that information. Currently, information must be synthesized by people through processes of "meta-analysis." A further step in the direction of optimal information management incorporates the development of artificial intelligence–based synthesizers of information. At present, our capability is limited to the identification of possibly useful information by key word searches. One day, using artificial intelligence–based systems, it may be possible to request from the computer a combination data search and synthesis that has been defined by one or more user questions, which will result in an analysis *by the computer* of information from various perspectives.

ARTIFICIAL INTELLIGENCE

Artificial intelligence (AI) has been defined as "the study of ideas which enable computers to do the things that make people seem intelligent" (Winston, 1979). As AI techniques expand the capability of computers into the realm of symbolic processing rather than just processing numbers, computers will be able to solve problems previously beyond their power (Manuel & Evanczuk, 1983). Several areas of artificial intelligence are of particular interest to the special educator: natural language analysis, vision, and expert systems.

Natural Language Analysis

Computers currently utilize and interpret specific syntax in a very narrowly defined "grammar." Examples include computer languages, such as BASIC, COBOL, LOGO, and Pascal. These languages force the user to conform to the rules of the computer. Even in games and educational software, the user has to understand the "grammatical syntax" expected by the computer program. More commonly, the program limits the user to simple numerical or multiple choice responses. Natural language analysis allows the computer to interpret either textual or spoken language. The computer is made to conform to the rules of the user's language rather than the user conforming to the computer's language. While this sounds simple, it is a formidable task, and adding the variable of discrimination between different speech patterns and dialects makes the task even more complex.

Human beings bring a storehouse of knowledge and previous experience to the interpretation of language. This permits people to "fill in gaps" and correctly interpret nuances of meaning. An example of how difficult this concept is can be understood from the following example: "The teacher returned to her room to find it very noisy." When reading this sentence, most people understand that children in the classroom are being noisy, not the room itself. As humans do, the computer must understand the grammar and contextual meaning of the language. However, for a computer to understand the meaning of this phrase, it must contain the knowledge that rooms generally are not noisy themselves, that teachers normally work in classrooms with children, and that these children might make noise if left unsupervised. Clearly this example is a simple one with a limited number of interpretations. As sentences and paragraphs become more complex or more ambiguous, they require a greater knowledge base to make accurate interpretations.

Current natural language interpreters function in a limited language domain and are found almost exclusively in mainframe computers or minicomputers. Today, typical natural language systems cost $25,000 to $70,000. A common use is for natural language analysis of queries to data-based management systems. "Intellect" by Artificial Intelligence Corporation, is a natural language analysis "front end" for interfacing with data bases and graphics systems. A front end program takes the user's command or query in plain English and translates it into the instructions of the data-based management system. The front end concept is generic, in that it enables users to use a natural language system tied to different applications programs in its domain.

Natural language analysis systems can easily be combined with speech recognition systems when these become more fully developed. Current speech recognition systems perform well when required to recognize words spoken distinctly and with pauses between words. Recognition of continuous speech poses a difficult task, since words tend to be run together. This is similar to trying to decipher "sentenceswrittentogetherwithno" spaces between the words. Some consider speech recognition outside the discipline of artificial intelligence, since it is much more algorithmic than other areas of AI. However, combining speech with natural language analysis can provide a powerful interface to the computer.

Vision

Other sensory perception systems are being designed to provide computers with vision. Human beings perform image analysis (vision) so easily it is hard to understand what a difficult task it is. To make a computer "see" one must first convert the light image into electrical signals. Typically, this is performed by an array of photodetectors. There are several types of photodetectors available, but basically they all convert the light signal into an array of numbers for the computer. These numbers represent the light intensities of individual picture elements (pixels). This is similar to a picture in a newspaper or magazine, in which the image is made of thousands of individual dots. The problem is for the computer to take these "numbers" (from the pixels) and discriminate and identify objects. Much current research is involved with identifying edges of objects and using that information to recognize the object (Poggio, 1984).

Current applications of vision by computer include using vision for robots in manufacturing and repair systems. An early robot for AI research was SHAKEY. SHAKEY incorporated vision and and an expert system (see next section) into a robot. SHAKEY was programmed with knowledge of ramps, tables, and simple objects. In one experiment SHAKEY was instructed to move an object from a table. The table was too high for the robot to reach; however. SHAKEY "looked" around the room and "saw" a ramp. SHAKEY then pushed the ramp to the table, went up the ramp, and pushed off the object, all without further instructions (Reggia, 1984; White, 1970).

An industrial application of computer vision was found on the SRI computer-based consultant. This system contained a "tool recognizer" from which it could build models to differentiate specific tool images from possible alternatives. In the consultant application (another expert system), the computer could visually scan a scene and using a laser beam point to an object requested by a user (Barr & Feigenbaum, 1982).

Expert Systems

The expert system allows computers to perform problem-solving tasks in limited domains in much the same way as experts in those areas. In fact, expert systems are used to develop the problem solving computer models. Expert systems have been devised in diverse areas, such as medical diagnosis, geologic exploration for mineral and oil deposits, locomotive repair, and education. There are a number of reasons for the development of such systems. In medicine, they provide expert diagnostic services to local general practitioners who may not have easy access to consultation with specialists. These systems have been reported to provide more reliable diagnoses than even specialists can achieve. An advantage the expert system has over the expert is the capability of unfailingly integrating large statistical data bases into its diagnosis. Other systems, such as the one for locomotive repair, have been developed as a hedge against the loss of experts in the field. The expert system trend is gaining impetus because it provides for perpetuation of human expertise in computerized form and replicates and multiplies the expert's value (Manuel & Evanczuk, 1983).

In education, a number of expert systems have been developed. One such system, WEST, was developed by Burton and Brown. WEST is an arithmetic game in which players are given three numbers and, using the basic operations of addition, subtraction, multiplication, and division, must combine these numbers in such a way as to achieve the most advantageous move. The computer constantly checks the players' moves and makes suggestions when it determines that a particular strategy is not working and the student is unable to correct this strategy. This process allows the player to explore arithmetic operations, with the computer providing "tutoring" when the player needs help. This is much more than giving a tutorial for wrong answers, because the computer must decide on when an intervention is appropriate and what that intervention should be based on the particular strategy the player is using (Barr & Feigenbaum, 1982).

Three common techniques utilized by expert systems are (1) forward chaining, (2) backward chaining, and (3) a cognitive model that utilizes both forward and backward chaining. These models proceed respectively forward from a series of known facts to a conclusion, backward from a hypothesized conclusion to the facts that would support it, or in a circular fashion, as a combination of these two processes, which continues until a conclusion is reached.

In the forward chaining model, the expert system works forward from a list of facts to a conclusion. For instance, the expert system might be given a list of attributes of an animal. The expert system would then attempt to use these facts to deduce the species. This process is achieved by utilizing what are called "productions." A production is a situation, action, pair, often in the form of "if, then" statements. For example, a simple production to help deduce the species of an animal would be "if it lays eggs and has feathers, then it is a bird." Knowing that it lays eggs is not enough, since a platypus lays eggs. Therefore, a conjunction is required in this production or additional productions are necessary. Further, this production does not provide enough information for the expert system to make a deduction of species, so additional productions are needed. The production, "if a bird is red, then it is a cardinal" may enable the expert system to deduce the species as a cardinal. It is not uncommon to have hundreds of productions in an expert system. An important advantage to production systems is that new information may be added by including new productions. The expert system's knowledge base and performance can be increased by the simple addition of new productions.

In the backward chaining model, the system starts with a hypothetical answer, usually supplied by the user, and works backward to find the facts necessary to support that hypothesis. The hypothesis might be "The child is learning disabled." The expert system would, through a question-answer format, begin to look for supportive facts. The system might first ask, "Does the child have a normal or above IQ?" If the child does not, then the child cannot be learning disabled. If the child does, then the computer continues to search backwards to determine what additional facts must be present if the basic definition of a learning disability is to be met.

The cognitive model combines a forward chaining model to establish initial hypotheses. It then utilizes the backward chaining model to test each of the initial hypotheses. This process is continued in a circular manner until a conclusion is reached or the knowledge base is exhausted. Often, conclusions may be given as probabilities with the user responsible for the final deduction. This allows for a synergistic relationship between the user and the expert system.

Future Directions: Artificial Intelligence in Special Education

There are four major areas in which AI will probably have a significant impact in special education. They are in the areas of management, evaluation and diagnosis, and instruction, and finally as a prosthetic "tool" for handicapped users.

In management, the application of natural language analysis to data-based management systems will open up their use to untrained computer users. For example, the administrator could ask, "Who are all the elementary school children in self-contained special education classrooms receiving Speech Therapy?" This is clearly much easier than requesting a set of fields such as "level = elementary and placement = self-contained and classification = special education and related service = speech therapy." Another potential use is in the area of forecasting staffing needs. Data bases such as previous staffing, information from IEPs, current incidence of children receiving services, and so forth, could be combined with information on demographic trends and other significant variables to suggest probabilities of future district-wide staffing needs for special education and related services. This information could be analyzed by an expert system. The expert system would incorporate the statistical information from past staffing needs as well as the decision models of expert special education administrators. One potential benefit from such a system is that it could provide a system that no longer requires children to be categorically labeled in order to receive appropriate special education and related services. If labels were still necessary for funding or other reasons, they could remain at the administrative rather than classroom level.

For direct services personnel, expert systems are likely to be developed to assist in diagnosis and placement of handicapped children. Expert systems, as in the medical diagnosis systems, could be developed to assist in the identification and referral for evaluation of handicapped children as well as in the evaluation process to determine specific disabilities. Using a forward chaining system, regular education teachers or even parents could provide the "expert" computer with information related to a suspected disability, and the computer could screen this information as well as probe for more information. The computer could then suggest whether to refer the child for further evaluation. In the diagnostic process, test scores and observational data could be fed into the computer, which could use its data bank and the expert model to provide suggestions for services, placement, and instructional goals and objectives.

In the learning process, the power of computers may be available to children as soon as they develop language. Natural language analysis systems will allow a direct interface to experiential learning and can even be used in assisting children in manipulating and experimenting with language concepts. AI programs could also be utilized with instructional software packages based on models such as the one suggested in Chapter 3. Using this hierarchical model, the system could test a child for prerequisite skills so that an appropriate entry level could be established. The system could then monitor the child's performance and determine strategies the child is using, when to provide remediation, what type of remediation to perform, and when to move on to higher levels. As each individual works more on the system, the computer can incorporate previous performance into the decision-making process, just as an expert teacher would do. Utilizing an expert model, it is conceivable that such a program would be able to determine that the child is best suited to learning through an experiential learning process rather than a tutorial and drill and practice process. The computer could also make decisions on whether to just provide some type of mnemonic cue or move to remedial training.

The prosthetic or tool uses of AI for handicapped learners provides the final area of future development. As noted earlier, utilizing natural language analysis, children may use computers as a tool to explore and manipulate their environment at very young ages. The concept of handicaps as we know them today may very well disappear during the next century, since AI, combined with robotics and other technologies, may remove dependence on primary caretakers. AI systems may be able to make the decisions necessary for daily living according to the physical and cognitive capabilities of an individual. That is, the system may determine that the child is hungry and a robotic device will prepare a meal and, if necessary, feed the child without the necessity of a human interaction. The human interactions can then be directed more toward improving the quality of life for those individuals. In the less distant future, we may expect AI-based programs to provide cognitive assistance in an analogous fashion to mechanical devices for the physically handicapped.

PROSTHETICS

Diffusion of technologic developments, according to a Coates' model (1983), occurs in three waves. At the first level, efficient and effective new technology is substituted for old systems. At the second level, accommodation is made to make application of the new technology yet more efficient. At the highest level, innovation occurs—new uses are discovered for the technology. A good example of this progression is seen in the evolution of prostheses.

Prosthetic devices provide the handicapped with sensory compensation, communication compensation, and compensation for control (Hannaford, 1983). The design and use of prosthetic devices already has been influenced by microprocessor technology. The microprocessor enhances independence by adding the power of programmable responses to stimuli; the prosthetic device reacts as well as acts.

Sensory Compensation

Microprocessors are being combined with artificial organs, such as eyes and ears, for sensory compensation. A bio-ear that provides rudimentary hearing to deaf individuals has been developed at Stanford University (Hannaford, 1983). A small microprocessor implanted behind the ear receives auditory stimuli and converts these stimuli to impulses, which are relayed to the brain by the auditory nerve. The impulses are then interpreted as sound. In a related area, research at Pennsylvania State University is addressing prebycusis, a tuning disorder resulting from damage to the inner surface of the cochlea (Science Digest, 1982). A newly developed device actually retunes sounds rather than only amplifying them. It offers a correction similiar to that of eyeglasses for myopia. In a similar vein, artificial vision research has had limited success in attaching a microprocessor and a video camera to electrodes implanted into the visual cortex (Hannaford, 1983). Applications such as these do not require the computer to discriminate or analyze information, as is essential in the development of artificial intelligence–based vision and aural prosthetics.

Communication Compensation

Technology for accommodating expressive communication already is relatively sophisticated. As noted in the chapter on sensory impairments, written and voice-synthesized vocal communications are available for wide use. The development of new memory technology, such as bubble memory, also has implications for speech prosthesis. The large memory capacity coupled with random access may enable digitized human voice or even phonemes taken from human speech to be easily accessible. This technology has the potential to produce human voice of exceptionally high quality coupled with extensive vocabulary and high-speed random access. This desirable combination of features currently is unavailable with digitized or text-to-speech voice synthesis. At present, Kurzweil (developer of the Kurzweil reader—see Chapter 7) is working on a marriage of speech recognition and artificial intelligence to produce a word processor that converts human speech to text with a vocabulary of 10,000 words spoken at a rate of up to 150 words per minute (Science Digest, 1984). Kurzweil predicts the availability of such a product commercially within two years.

Compensation for Control

Perhaps the most dramatic developments in assisting handicapped individuals through technology have been in the area of controlling and interacting with the environment. Within this area, the development of relatively low cost robotic devices has been the focus of much attention. The Robotics Institute of America defines a robot as a reprogrammable multifunctional manipulator designed to move material, parts, tools, or specialized devices through variable programmed motions for the performance of a variety of tasks.

Robots vary in complexity, from simple mechanical instruments that use limited computer memory and mechanical control to sophisticated intelligent devices with large on-board memory that allows the robot to change programs automatically, depending on task and environmental requirements. Most robots, primarily as a result of industrial application, are stationary or run on tracks. Examples are robotic arms that attach to a work surface and perform repetitive tasks, replicating movements performed by human shoulders, arms, and hands on assembly lines. The use of independently moveable robots, however, is rapidly growing, particularly in the area of robots used for educational purposes. Presently, robots such as Heathkit's HERO I (*Heath Educational RObot*) combine on-board memory with an impressive list of sensory capabilities. HERO can sense light, sound, movement, distance, and time. It is mobile (can move around its environment) and can grasp objects with an arm and gripper capable of moving in five degrees of freedom (directions, such as rotation). This robot can be controlled through on-board programming, through a microcomputer, or via a learning pendant (a handheld control device). Although robots like HERO offer extensions to the controller for environmental manipulation, ease of programming and sensory capabilities are limited and result in environmental inflexibility (they must be operated under the exact conditions for which they were programmed or operated by a human being, thus using human senses).

Previously use of robots in special education and rehabilitation had focused on the role of robots as tools for learning and environmental control and manipulation. Many handicapping conditions reduce the ability of the individual and maintain control of the environment, thus limiting learning through interaction. The LOGO turtle and robotic toys, such as Big Trak, are being used by handicapped students to explore and experiment with their environment and to develop problem-solving strategies through investigation of directionality, cause and effect, prediction, spatial relationships, geometric relationships, estimation, decision making, and so forth (Keller & Shanahan, 1983). Stanford University researchers have developed the palatal splint, an oral device that parallels a joystick to control manipulations through tongue movements. Simone of Johns Hopkins University has created a robot system that couples a mechanical arm with a table surface equipped with a computer, telephone, reading device, and eating utensils. Manipulations are chin controlled.

Future Directions: Prosthetics

The rapid growth in knowledge of human physiology combined with the microminiaturization of technology and the development of robotics with sensory and intelligence capabilities is rapidly affecting the development of prosthetic devices. This is emphasized by Kluger's (1982) statement, "The parallels between biology and machinery are so remarkable that human inventions and human beings may have passed the point of simple similarity. Rather, the two are slowly integrating, weaving into a single, inseparable unit, a human machine." The future points to a symbiotic relationship between robot and man.

The integration of robotics into the lives of handicapped individuals depends on several factors. These include increased capacity to sense, incorporation of artificial intelligence, physical integration of the prosthesis with the human body under control by the human, and physical integration of computer and human to restore physical function. Such integration takes advantage of developing computer intelligence and mechanical durability.

Most contemporary robots have limited sensory capability as the result of primitive tactile, optic, and auditory sensors. Sophisticated sensory capacity relies on artificial intelligence as AI systems enable data-driven rather than program-driven sensing systems. Data-driven systems free the robot from environmental constraints; the robot is able to operate in more than one set environment as it "memorizes" new facts about immediate surroundings as sensors feed them into its computer memory. The combination of increased sensory capacity and decision-making capabilities available through artificial intelligence allow robots to be "self-motivating"—that is, to plan its own motion as humans plan motion—by sensation. This will enable the robot to operate with flexibility in changing environments, making necessary adjustments without human programming.

Physical integration of prostheses under human control is possible in two ways. The first is through advanced sensory input devices. As discussed previously, natural language analysis will permit verbal control over prosthetic devices. For individuals who are so severely impaired that they lack almost all motor and vocal control, an eye input device is being developed in the Westinghouse Defense and Electronic Systems Center that enables users to look at a position on a screen as the only required human input. The operational control is similar to that of touch sensitive monitors. A potential utilization of "eye pointing" with a prosthetic robot could incorporate robotic vision which would relay video images of the environment to a monitor. The user would then select the desirable robotic action by looking at a control function and an image on the screen of the object to be manipulated.

The second area of development in human-controlled prosthetics is control by the nervous system—that is, impulses are conducted from the human body to the prosthetic device through a mediating microprocessor. The "Utah arm," developed by Jacobson at the University of Utah, picks up signals from electrodes placed over existing muscles to control a prosthetic arm that can lift more than four pounds. A similar artificial leg is being tested by Moskowitz of Drexel University. The next logical step of prosthetic device control involves surgical implants. One type of implant, studied at Case Western Reserve University by Crago, uses radio waves to transmit signals to the prosthesis from insulated stainless steel wires implanted directly into the muscles (Veggeberg, 1984).

The concept of microprocessor implants into the human body leads to another alternative approach to rehabilitation. This approach focuses on finding ways of making biologic machines (the human robot) perform where there is no human function remaining. An example of this concept is demonstrated by the work of Petrofsky, in which a microcomputer is used to control electrical stimulation of selected muscles. The computer acts as a bypass around the damaged area of the spinal cord by utilizing a microprocessor as part of a biofeedback system that monitors and coordinates leg muscles, thus enabling an individual without nervous system control of the legs to walk. This system is still in experimental stages of development but holds great promise for the physically disabled. However, there are limitations to this process: it cannot help in situations in which the muscles cannot be built up again as a result of a prolonged handicapping condition. In the future, the human biologic machine may incorporate both machine and remaining human functions, and the severity of disabilities may be reduced as a result of early intervention and advancing technologic innovations.

CONCLUSION

The future of microprocessor technology, as discussed in this chapter, is based on current applications research and technologic advances already in the development phase. The promise of the future, with the advent of new technology generations every few years, is virtually unpredictable. What can be predicted is the changing perceptions of handicapping conditions as technology provides increased learning and independence. It is the responsibility of educators to ensure that the technology is *applied* to the living and learning needs of the handicapped. As Dewey stated, "The purpose of education is to enable a person to come into possession of all his powers."

REFERENCES

Barr, A., & Feigenbaum, E. (1982). *The handbook of artificial intelligence* (vol. 2). Los Altos, CA: Wm. Kaufmann, Inc.

Bernd, R. (1983, August). U.S. Army training applications of interactive videodiscs. Presented at the Fifth Annual Conference on Interactive Videodiscs in Education and Training, Arlington, VA.

Bunderson, C. V. (1983). A survey of videodisc projects at WICAT. *Performance & Instruction Journal*, *22*(9), 24–25.

Chang, W. (1983). An introduction to integrated software. *Byte*, *8*:12, 103–108.

Coates, V. (1983, February). The potential impact of robots. *The Futurist*, pp. 28–32.

Currier, R. (1983). Interactive videodisc learning systems. *High Technology*, 51–59.

Daynes, R. (1982). The videodisc interfacing primer. *Byte*, *7*(6), 48–59.

Euchner, C. (1984). Computer network will link West Virginia schools by 1986. *Education Week*, *3*(25), 1, 18.

Hannaford, A. (1983). Microcomputers in special education: Some new opportunities, some old problems. *The Computing Teacher*, *10*(6), 11–17.

Keller, J., & Shanahan, D. (1983, May). Robots in the kindergarten. *The Computing Teacher*, *11*(1) 66–67.

Kimberlin, D. (1982, August). *Videodisc for training and simulation*, Videodisc presented at the Fourth Annual Conference on Video Learning Systems Proceedings, Society for Applied Learning Technology.

Kluger, J. (1982). The Human Machine. *Science Digest*, *90*(6), 64–71.

Lemonick, M. (1984). Machines with living parts. *Science Digest*, *92*; 2.

Manuel, T., & Evanczuk, S. (1983, November). Artificial intelligence: Commercial products begin to emerge from decades of research. *Electronics*, pp. 139–142.

Nugent, G., & Stone, C. (1982). The videodisc meets the microcomputer. *American Annals of the Deaf*, *127*(5), 569–572.

Poggio, Tomaso. (1984). Vision by man and machine. *Scientific American*, *250*(4), 106–116.

Propp, G., Nugent, G., & Stone, C. (1980). Videodisc Update. *American Annals of the Deaf*, *125*(6), 679–684.

Reggia, J. (1984, April). *Expert systems*. Paper presented at Artificial Intelligence: Machines That Think Seminar, Washington, DC.

Science Digest. (1982). Electronic ear is hard of hearing. *90*, p. 89.

Science Digest. (1984). Newscience/Innovations. *92*(2), p. 73.

Shanahan, D. (1982, September). The computer—a technology that breaks the "sound" barrier. *American Annals of the Deaf*, *127*(6) pp. 476–482.

The Futurist. (1983). Computerized home education movement to take off. *17*(4), p. 69.

Thorkildsen, R., Allard, K., & Reid, B. (1983). The interactive videodisc for special education project: Providing CAI for the mentally retarded. *The Computing Teacher*, *11*(2) 73–76.

Thorkildsen, R., & Friedman, S. (1984, April). Videodisks in the classroom. *T.H.E. Journal*, *11*(7) 90–95.

Veggeberg, S. (1984, March). Microcomputers give the disabled a hand. *American Way*, pp. 62–66.

Warfield, R.W. (1983). The new interface technology. *Byte*, *8*(12), 218–230.

White, P. T. (1970). Behold the computer revolution. *National Geographic*, *138*(5).

Winch, D. (1981). An evaluation of the student use of the puzzle of the Tacoma Narrows Bridge videodisc. *AAPT Announcer*, *11*(2), 107.

Winston, P. (1979). *Artificial Intelligence*, Reading, MA: Addison Wesley.

Wold, A. (1983). What is a programming language? *Classroom Computer News*, *3*(5), 24.

Zollman, D., & Fuller, R. (1982). The Puzzle of the Tacoma Narrows Bridge Collapse: An interactive videodisc program for physics instruction. *Creative Computing*, pp. 100–109.

Appendix A
Software and Other Resources

Advanced Music System. Atari, Sunnyvale, CA.
Author I. Radio Shack, Tandy Center, Fort Worth, TX.
Bagels. Minnesota Educational Computing Consortium, St. Paul, MN.
Bibliographic Retrieval Services (BRS). Education Service Group, Latham, NY.
Chemistry of Living Things. Educational Activities, Freeport, NY.
Compuserve. Compuserve Information Service, Columbus, OH.
Creativity Life. Avant Garde, Eugene, OR.
Delta Drawing. Spinnaker Software, Cambridge, MA.
Dialog. Dialog Information Services, Palo Alto, CA.
Doodle Drawer. Dynacomp, Rochester, NY.
Magic Melody Box. Atari Program Exchange, Sunnyvale, CA.
National Scholarship Research Service, San Rafael, CA.
Rendezvous. A. W. Peller & Associates, Hawthorne, NJ.
The Source. Reader's Digest, Pleasantville, NY.
SpecialNet. National Association of State Directors of Special Education, Washington, DC.
Three Mile Island. A. W. Peller & Associates, Hawthorne, NJ.
The Wizard and the Princess. Sierra On-Line, Coarsegold, CA.
Zork. Infocom, Cambridge, MA.

Author Index

Subject Index

Page numbers in *italics* refer to illustrations; (t) indicates tables

Visual analysis computers, 259–260
Visual impairments, computer hardware
        and, 108–112, 116–119
  use of computers in, 112, *113*, 114–119
Vocational training, for mildly handi-
        capped individuals, 99–100
Voice based learning system (VBLS), 92
Voice synthesizer, 116–117

W

Word processing, by mildly handicapped
        individuals, 95–97
  in CAM, 171–172
  programs for, 73–74
Writing difficulties, in mildly handicapped
        children, 95–97

Y

Young children, use of computers by,
        146–155
  CAI in, 148–153
  input devices for, 146–147
  output devices for, 147–148